The W̱SÁNEĆ and their Neighbours

Diamond Jenness on the Coast Salish of Vancouver Island, 1935

edited by Barnett Richling

Rock's Mills Press

Published by

Rock's Mills Press

Copyright © 2016 by Barnett Richling.

Library and Archives Canada Cataloguing in Publication data is available on request. Contact us at customer.service@rocksmills-press.com.

Contents

Appendices

Illustrations and Credits

Preface

In October, 1935, New Zealand-born anthropologist Diamond Jenness (1886–1969) began five months of fieldwork in Coast Salish communities on Vancouver Island and adjacent portions of British Columbia's lower mainland. Sponsored by the National Museum of Canada (his employer since the early teens), this work formed part of an ongoing nation-wide research program whose aim, as described at its founding in 1910, was to make a "thorough and scientific investigation of the native races of Canada, their distribution, languages, cultures, etc., and to collect and preserve records of same."[1] Thanks largely to a smattering of U.S. and European institutions, a few groups in the country's Pacific northwest, the Kwakwaka'wakw (Kwakiutl) above all, had been studied in some depth over the preceding quarter-century. On his appointment to head up the new program, Edward Sapir took steps to fill in the gaps, identifying five "important tribes" in this region as research priorities; these were groups, he said, "about whom we are relatively uninformed, except in regard to particular points here and there."[2] By the early twenties, intensive research was underway on three of them: Marius Barbeau's with Tsimshian-speaking communities around Prince Rupert and inland on the Skeena and Nass rivers; Harlan Smith and Thomas McIlwraith's with Nuxalk (Bella Coola); and Sapir's with Nuu-chah-nulth (Nootka) at Port Alberni. In 1921, Sapir recruited Paul Radin to follow suit among the Coast Salish, but museum management—grown increasingly indifferent after the war to all things anthropological—balked at hiring him. Fourteen years were to pass before Jenness was able to take on that work, just one of many research projects postponed or, as happened with study of the Bella Bella, the fifth of Sapir's "important tribes," shelved altogether for want of sufficient staff and money.[3]

By the time he was ready to return home to Ottawa in March, 1936, Jenness had worked with members of six different Coast Salish groups: four of these were on Vancouver Island, and the others in the Fraser River valley, east of Vancouver. On reaching the field five months earlier, however, his only firm plan was to start investigations on the Saanich Peninsula. For some reason or other, the W̱SÁNEĆ—or Saanich, the more familiar rendering of their name—had yet to receive any but scant attention from ethnologists. Even Franz Boas, the discipline's most assiduous and experienced student of Northwest Coast indigenous society, all but ignored them, focusing instead, as did the ubiquitous chronicler of Salish traditions, Charles Hill-Tout, on

---

1   Reginal W. Brock to Edward Sapir, 6 March, 1910.
2   Sapir, "Anthropological Survey," 792. The lion's share of those details are scattered through the writings of Franz Boas, the doyen of North American anthropology, and of Charles Hill-Tout, British Columbia's leading avocational ethnologist.
3   Richling, *Twilight and Dawn*, 144–46, 268–69.

their geographic and linguistic near-neighbours, the Lekwungen (Songhees).[4]
And then, as if their very presence (on the outskirts of Victoria, no less) had
suddenly been discovered, the W̱SÁNEĆ captured the attentions of not one
but two researchers.

Homer Barnett, a doctoral candidate at Berkeley, was first on the scene,
dispatched to collect data on spatial distributions of culture elements here
and from eleven other island and mainland groups.[5] Unlike Barnett, whose
visit in the summer of 1935 was, in William Newcombe's words, "too hurried to be considered more than a survey (preliminary),"[6] Jenness stayed on
in W̱SÁNEĆ territory from early October through November, shuttling between his lodgings in Sidney and whichever of the group's reserves—Tsartlip (aka Brentwood Bay), Tsawout (East Reserve), and Tseycum (Patricia
Bay)—where work happened to take him on any given day. (Why he skipped
Pauquachen, their fourth reserve, isn't known.) Drawing on the knowledge
and recollections of six local elders, the youngest of whom was in her early sixties, the oldest in his late eighties, he gathered information bearing on
a wide range of topics, everything from architectural styles and subsistence
techniques to rites of passage and conceptions of the natural world. He also
recorded fifty-some myths and legends. Bolstered with comparative material obtained in neighbouring communities from Lekwungen, Cowichan, and
Snuneymuxw (Nanaimo) informants before the year was out, the product of
Jenness's three months on Vancouver Island was several hundred pages of
notes that contained the makings of what would have been the most compre-
hensive account of W̱SÁNEĆ life as it existed in the mid to late nineteenth
century, a period when aboriginal beliefs and practices were still strong despite the rapidly rising tide of Western influences. But as luck would have it,
the monograph he started writing in the late thirties, "The Saanich Indians of
Vancouver Island," was never finished; instead, it was permanently set aside,
as was the rest of his museum work, on his secondment to wartime duties in
the autumn of 1939.

Over the seven-plus decades that have since passed, surprisingly little has
appeared in print on the W̱SÁNEĆ, and certainly nothing equivalent to the
work that circumstances led Jenness to leave incomplete. Among available
titles, Barnett's *The Coast Salish of British Columbia*, published in 1955, is
perhaps the leading source.[7] Embedded in a general study examining a dozen

---

4   Boas, "Second General Report"; Hill-Tout, "Ethnology of South-eastern Tribes."
5   Barnett, *Coast Salish*, iii.
6   William Newcombe to Jenness, 21 August, 1935. For the record, Barnett returned to Coast
Salish territory for a second field season in summer, 1936.
7   By coincidence, 1955 also saw publication of Jenness's *The Faith of a Coast Salish Indian*,
the result of his collaboration with Katzie elder Peter Pierre in February and March, 1936. Fully
drafted before the war, the manuscript was finally shepherded into print at the urging of University of British Columbia anthropologists Wilson Duff, Harry Hawthorn, and Wayne Suttles;
Richling, *Twilight and Dawn*, 271–72; Suttles, *Katzie Notes*, 5.

groups, however, his portrayal of them is necessarily abbreviated. While the monograph Jenness began on the W̱SÁNEĆ covers much the same ground, it does so in more depth, particularly in giving prominence to the words and oftentimes conflicting perspectives and opinions of the elders with whom he worked on the Saanich Peninsula, and in neighbouring areas. By virtue of their age, a good deal of what these two women and ten men related to him of the "old ways" stemmed from first-hand experience, most of the rest from learning at the feet of parents and grandparents who knew no other life. Combined with its author's twin penchants for favouring description over analysis and plain language over jargon, the result is an account that deftly straddles the boundary between ethnography and oral history. Preserving as it does a valuable body of W̱SÁNEĆ traditional knowledge, while simultaneously contributing to the scholarly literature on an under-represented Coast Salish people, its rescue from archival obscurity seemed at once a worthwhile undertaking, and long overdue. With that in mind, I proposed finishing the manuscript and readying it for publication to the good folks at Rock's Mills Press, editor Jen Rubio, and publisher David Stover, with whom I had previously worked. They responded with enthusiasm, as did Stuart Jenness, Diamond's son, who gave the project his blessing. And with that, I turned to the business at hand.

...

Along with a thick stack of field notes, Jenness left behind 130 typescript pages of text. All but twenty of this total was arranged under sixteen chapter (or subject) headings—fishing, clothing, childhood, potlatches, etc. The remainder was contained in five appendices. Excepting occasional emendations of spelling and anachronistic (by today's standards) usage and the deletion (or insertion) of passages referring to certain illustrations,[8] the present version retains both the language and substance of those pages as Jenness himself wrote them. At the risk of retribution served up from beyond the grave, however, some editorial license was taken, primarily with a view to improving organizational clarity: first, in reducing the number of original chapters from sixteen to nine; and second, by moving all except tabular material from appendices (and footnotes) into corresponding portions of the main body. Finally, as testament to my inability to resist meddling altogether, all nine chapters are peppered here and there with clarifications (enclosed in square brackets), annotations (in editorial footnotes), and wherever corroboration was possible, with the names of informants who, for reasons known only to Jenness, he chose not to identify in the text.

The lone guide to Jenness's intentions for finishing his book, and it is barely

---

8   Although they are mentioned in the original text, several of the illustrations Jenness intended to use could not be identified. Wherever possible, appropriate alternates have been used.

that, is a handwritten list of the main topics he intended to include, a single sheet inconspicuously filed away amidst his papers. Three remained uncovered: guardian spirits, illness and medicine, and winter (or spirit) dances. Added to the nine chapters he authored, therefore, are three more, written by me. Actually, these are basically from his pen as well, my job being less one of writing than of assembling each chapter using unabridged (or lightly edited) passages in his notes. In the case of the first of these, on guardian spirits, the mode of presentation is modelled directly on the one he employed in treating the same subject matter in *The Faith of a Coast Salish Indian.* Together, these twelve chapters comprise The Saanich Indians of Vancouver Island, Part I of the present volume.

In keeping with the day's ethnographic practice, Jenness regularly wrote down myths and tales narrated by informants, as he did with the W̱SÁNEĆ, their Vancouver Island neighbours, and with the few groups he visited on the lower mainland. A selection of forty-five, the majority from Saanich Peninsula communities, are presented in Part II. Once again, an occasional emendation or modified title aside, they appear here as they do in Jenness's field notes.

One final matter warrants mention: the appearance, throughout the text, of words in SENĆOŦEN, the language of the W̱SÁNEĆ. Rather than strictly adhering to the standard method of phonetic transcription widely used in the profession for decades,[9] Jenness adopted a hybrid approach, one employing ordinary Latin orthography as much as possible to approximate the sounds of local speech. This was done for two main reasons. First, as a publically funded federal institution, the National Museum encouraged anthropologists on its payroll to make their work accessible to a general readership, readers who were unlikely to be familiar with phonetic transcription. Second, and arguably of greater importance to museum management, doing so saved the government printer the extra costs incurred in setting type for special characters.[10] While presently unprepared to give them my full endorsement, I (grudgingly) concede that computers do offer a reasonably good (if far from perfect) solution to the second of these complications. On that basis, and with high praise and admiration for the industry of linguist Timothy Montler, the book's footnoted annotations include "standardized" spellings—given in phonetic characters and in the SENĆOŦEN alphabet—for most of these words.[11]

...

---

9   Boas, "Phonetic Transcription." For information on SENĆOŦEN and Hul'qumi'num' (Cowichan and Snuneymuxw) orthography, see Appendix 5.

10   Richling, "Scaenae," 58–59.

11   Dave Elliott, a W̱SÁNEĆ elder from Tsartlip, developed this alphabet—one using all upper case characters—in the 1970s to overcome the limitations of its standard Latin counterpart in representing specific sounds; see http://wsanecschoolboard.ca/about-the-school/history-of-the-sencoten-language. For a thorough analysis of the language, also known as North Straits Salish, see Montler's *Outline of Morphology and Phonology.*

It goes without saying that the very existence of this book is owing to the twelve Vancouver Island elders who shared their knowledge and experiences with a notebook-toting, question-asking, fifty-year-old white man from Ottawa. In W̱SÁNEĆ territory, they were Johnny Claxton, of Tsawout; Edward Jim, Tseycum; David and Mrs Latasse, Tsartlip; Louis Pelkey, Tsawout; and Tom Paul, Tsartlip. Their counterparts in neighbouring areas were Annie and Kaypemulthw Bob, Halalt (Westholme); Jimmy Fraser, Esquimalt; Johnson, Quamichan; George Kwakaston, Koksilah; and Albert Westly, Nanaimo. And across the Strait, in the valley of the lower Fraser, two other elders did likewise: Peter Pierre, of Katzie, and William Sepass, Sardis. However belatedly expressed, all are due special thanks.

I am grateful to Jen Rubio and David Stover, of Rock's Mills Press, for their unwavering support of this project, and for agreeing to publish the finished product; to the Canadian Museum of History for making available the two documents on which it is based; to Brian Thom for his many comments and suggestions for improving the text; and to the University of Winnipeg for providing a grant to defray sundry expenses. Similar votes of thanks are owing to Stuart Jenness for his encouraging words, to Ken Dewar for listening whenever glitches demanded a sympathetic ear, and above all, to JoAnn Richling, ever a voice of reason.

Finally, it is only fitting that I acknowledge my singular debt to Diamond Jenness, an anthropologist whose life and career have engaged my scholarly interests since the late 1980s, and who, twenty years before I entered this world, inadvertently made possible the collaboration that brought his Vancouver Island researches to light at long last.

Barnett Richling
Bedford, Nova Scotia
June, 2016

Part I
The Saanich Indians of Vancouver Island

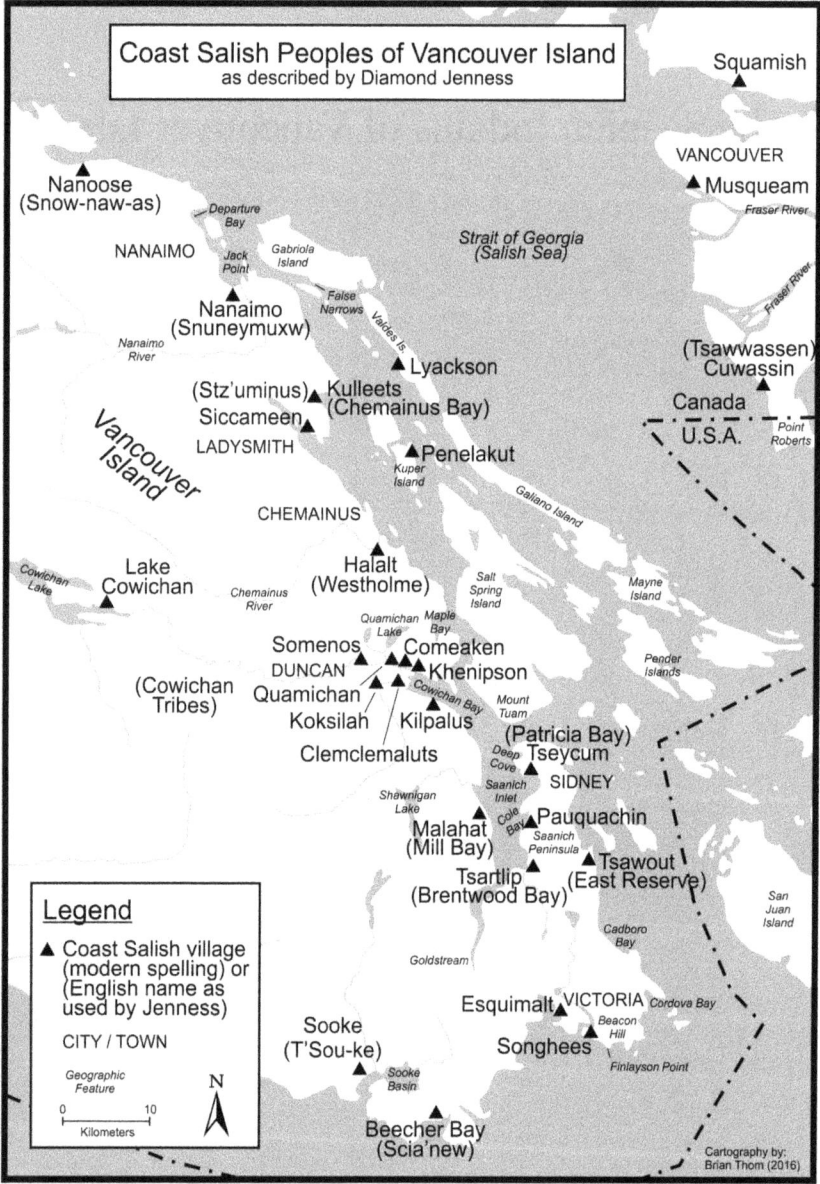

Coast Salish Peoples of Vancouver Island
as described by Diamond Jenness

Squamish

VANCOUVER
▲ Musqueam
Fraser River

Nanoose
(Snow-naw-as)

Departure Bay

NANAIMO

Jack Point

Gabriola Island

Strait of Georgia
(Salish Sea)

Nanaimo River

Nanaimo
(Snuneymuxw)

False Narrows

Valdes Is.

(Tsawwassen)
Cuwassin

Canada
U.S.A.

Point Roberts

Lyackson

(Stz'uminus) Kulleets
Siccameen (Chemainus Bay)

LADYSMITH

Penelakut

Kuper Island

CHEMAINUS

Galiano Island

Vancouver Island

Cowichan Lake

Lake Cowichan

Chemainus River

Halalt
(Westholme)

Salt Spring Island

Mayne Island

Quamichan Lake

Maple Bay

Somenos

Comeaken

DUNCAN

Khenipson

Quamichan

Cowichan Bay

Koksilah

Kilpalus

Pender Islands

Mount Tuam

(Cowichan Tribes)

Clemclemaluts

Deep Cove

(Patricia Bay)
Tseycum

Shawnigan Lake

Saanich Inlet

SIDNEY

Malahat
(Mill Bay)

Cole Bay

Pauquachin

Saanich Peninsula

Tsawout
(East Reserve)

Tsartlip
(Brentwood Bay)

San Juan Island

Cadboro Bay

Legend

▲ Coast Salish village
(modern spelling) or
(English name as
used by Jenness)

CITY / TOWN

Geographic Feature

Goldstream

Esquimalt VICTORIA Cordova Bay

Beacon Hill

Songhees

Sooke
(T'Sou-ke)

Sooke Basin

Finlayson Point

0   10
Kilometers

N

Beecher Bay
(Scia'new)

Cartography by:
Brian Thom (2016)

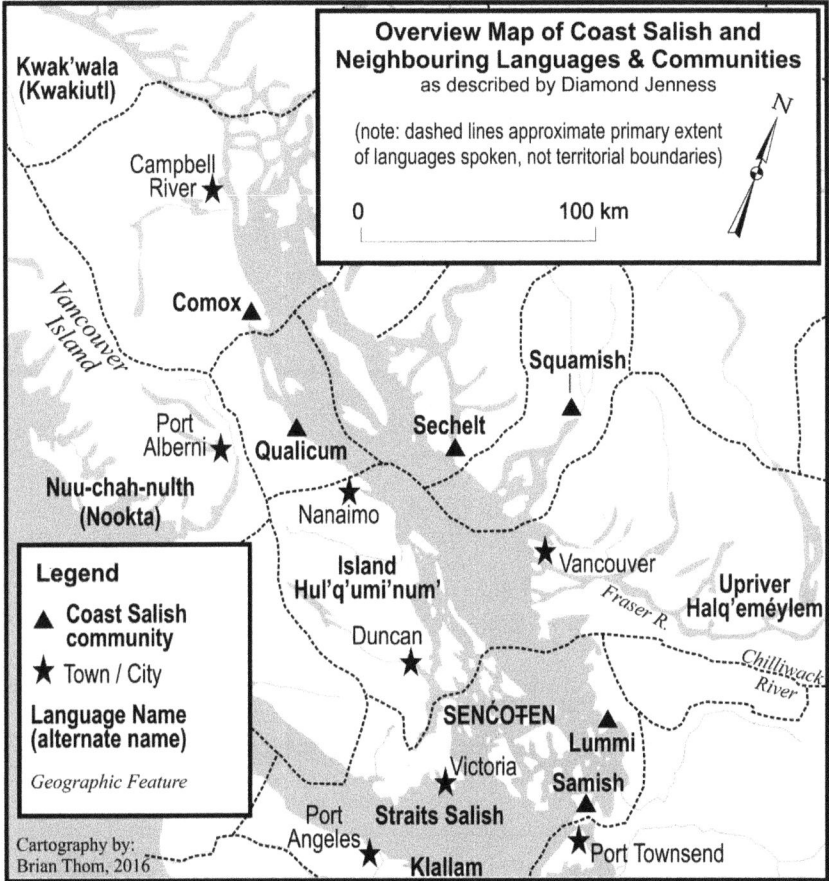

Overview Map of Coast Salish and Neighbouring Languages & Communities as described by Diamond Jenness

1

Introduction

At one time or another practically every sheltered bay and nook along the southeast coast of Vancouver Island, and on the small islands adjacent to it in the Strait of Georgia, carried a settlement of greater or lesser size; but at the coming of Europeans late in the eighteenth century the Coast Salish inhabitants of this area appear to have been divided into four main groups. Around Victoria were the Songish [or Songhees] whose main body wintered at Cadborough Bay and summered at a place called Xthapsam, just above The Gorge at Victoria,[1] while a lesser body occupied the territory around Sooke Basin.[2] The second—Saanich—inhabited the Saanich Peninsula, extending down its east side as far as Cordova Bay, and in the west, along the length of Saanich Inlet. From about Mill Bay to Qualicum lived the Cowichan-Nanaimo group, and from Qualicum northward the fourth group, the Comox, who abutted on the southernmost Kwakiutl, about Campbell River.

The division into four groups is somewhat arbitrary, based more on geographical considerations than on differences of dialect or culture.[3] There were such differences, it is true, but they were slight, in some cases hardly greater than the differences between individual settlements within the same group. Society was organized on a family, not on a tribal basis, and since each family intermarried both within and without its group, the customs and the dialects spoken, even in individual villages, were not always uniform, but reflected the marriage ties with other communities. For example, there could be two families in the same village which, though more or less closely related, practised slightly different rites for ushering their sons into manhood.

Neighbouring groups maintained friendly relations, only occasionally broken by personal feuds that did not involve whole villages. The principal enemies of the Vancouver Island Salish (and also of Coast Salish groups on the mainland) were the Kwakiutl Indians from more northerly parts of the island. The Comox group which, being nearest to the Kwakiutl, absorbed many of their customs, seems to have joined them occasionally in their raids on the Saanich, Songish, and Fraser River groups across the Strait of Georgia. At

---

1 The Gorge (or The Gorge Waterway) is a narrow passage connecting Victoria Harbour to Portage Inlet. –Ed.

2   Some Klallam Indians from Port Angeles, in Washington State, settled in Beecher Bay during the nineteenth century; Gunther, *Klallam Ethnography*, 179.

3   In fact, the people of this region spoke four different languages: North Straits Salish among the Saanich and Songhees (and T'Sou-ke); Klallam (*nəxʷsƛ̓ay̓əmúcən*) among Beecher Bay Klallam; Hul'qumi'num' (or Island Halkomelem) in the Cowichan-Nanaimo area; and Island Comox, or Salhutltxw, among the Comox. Nowadays, the Saanich call their language SENĆOŦEN (*Sənčaθən*), and themselves W̱SÁNEĆ (*x̌ʷsénəč*); Montler, "SENĆOŦEN Word List"; Suttles, "Central Coast Salish," 455–56. Montler is the source for all subsequent notes on SENĆOŦEN words; for Hul'qumi'num', the source is Gerdts et al., *Hul'qumi'num' Words*, and for Upriver Halkomelem (Sto:lo) it is Galloway, *Dictionary of Upriver Halkomelem*. –Ed.

1

all events, the latter today bracket their Comox kinsmen with the Kwakiutl, and the west Saanich natives attribute the destruction of their old village in Brentwood Bay about 1850 to either Comox or Kwakiutl Indians (they are uncertain which), who attacked the settlement at a time when nearly all its inhabitants were fishing on the opposite shore of Saanich Inlet, near Malahat, and burned its three long, shed-roofed houses, as well as several smaller ones. One old Saanich woman, Mrs Latasse,[4] stated that her grandfather, a Cowichan native, used to intercept the Comox war parties after they had raided the more southern Salish, ransom any persons of rank whom they had captured, and restore them to their people, collecting the ransom price with interest. Some natives of the Cowichan-Nanaimo group declared, on the other hand, that they were always friendly with the Comox, in whose territory they rested during their periodic raids against the Kwakiutl. Since a few Saanich Indians accompanied them occasionally on these raids, it seems probable that the Comox did not actively make war on their southern kinsmen, but attached a few volunteers to Kwakiutl raiding parties.

It was through fear of both the Comox and the Kwakiutl that the Songish retreated in summer above The Gorge at Victoria, and the Saanich sent their women and children to secluded spots during May and June, the usual season for raids, while the men maintained a nightly watch on the housetops. During the nineteenth century, indeed, the Saanich abandoned one of their villages near Sidney, on the east side of the peninsula, and moved to Patricia Bay, on the west side, where they were less exposed to attack.[5] The last fight between the Kwakiutl and the Salish took place in Maple Bay, near Cowichan, about 1860, when the Cowichan natives, assisted by the Saanich and Songish, annihilated a Kwakiutl war party and, travelling north in their enemies' canoes, destroyed the village from which it had set out and took both women and children as captives. After this the Kwakiutl made peace with the Cowichan and Saanich by giving two girls as wives to two leading Cowichan warriors. The Cowichan returned their prisoners and peace reigned thereafter.[6]

The present-day Salish seem to remember no conflicts with the Nootka Indians of the island's west coast until the middle of the nineteenth century, when the penetration of the Nootka to Cowichan Lake occasioned some skirmishes. However, about 1860, with the consent of the Cowichan natives, the Nootka erected two houses beside the falls on Cowichan River, and from that

---

4 Nowhere does Jenness record this informant's first name, referring to her instead as Mrs Old David, after the European given name of her husband. They lived on the Tsartlip reserve. The other of his female informants, Mrs Old Bob, of Halalt (Westholme), received similar treatment. According to a handwritten note (dated 3 May, 2000) left with Jenness's papers by their great-granddaughter, Jillian Harris, of Duncan, BC, Mrs Old Bob (née Louie) was Annie, or Snumethiya, her husband Old Bob, or Kaypemulth. Bob is the family surname. –Ed.

5 The Sidney village was known as Sai'klam, "Clay," and Patricia Bay was called Klangan, "Salty Place"; but when the Sidney inhabitants moved over to Patricia Bay they transferred the name "Clay" to their new home.

6 This battle, and its political context, are examined in Angelbeck and McLay, "Battle of Maple Bay." – Ed.

date the two peoples mingled in harmony. Lummi and Samish Indians from what is now the State of Washington occasionally raided the Saanich Peninsula, and perhaps northward, but that occurred so long ago that the details of their raids have practically faded from memory.

To determine either the population or the number of houses in an average Coast Salish village of pre-European times is no longer possible.[7] The old kitchen middens that accumulated in and around them vary in length from a few yards to many hundreds. One at Sidney, on the Saanich Peninsula, stretches for more than a mile, and varies in depth from six to nine feet. There may have been a score of houses on this site, but they are not necessarily contemporaneous. Moreover, the houses themselves varied greatly in size, so that even if one knew their number at any given time, it would give us little clue to the total population. In all cases they formed one, two, or three lines facing the water of the bay; canoes were drawn up on the sandy or gravelly beach. Behind them stretched the forest to which the inhabitants could flee for refuge in case of attack, and within a few hundred yards was a stream of fresh water.

The sheltered position of the settlements within bays afforded many advantages that offset their exposure to sudden attack. In any case raiders always came in canoes, giving the villagers ample time to organise resistance or flight, unless, as sometimes happened, the attack occurred at night. Not always did they flee to the forests behind the houses. Occasionally they took refuge on rocky headlands impregnable on three sides, and protected on the fourth by a ditch and an artificial rampart of earth. Traces of such ramparts, originally surmounted by wooden palisades, are still visible in certain places, even on Beacon Hill, within the city limits of Victoria. Most of them date from prehistoric times, but one, at Khenipson, near Duncan, was constructed as late as the middle of the nineteenth century.

Archibald Menzies, who sailed with Captain George Vancouver in 1792, described a fortified

Aboriginal Village and Defensive Site on Finlayson Point, Victoria, 904 A.D. to 1689 A.D

7   The Coast Salish on Vancouver Island are now thought to have numbered about 12,250 before the era of European contact began, in 1774. Over the next century, however, introduced infectious diseases caused heavy population losses. From a pre-contact estimate of 2,600, the WSÁNEĆ and Lekwungen had been reduced to no more than 500 souls by the early 1860s, a decline of 80 percent. Around 1910, the two peoples were said to number 249 and 182, respectively; Boyd, "Demographic History," 136, 144; Anon., "Sanetch," 432; Swanton, "Songish," 617. –Ed.

Coast Salish village near Homfray Channel, on the mainland side of the Strait of Georgia:

> At the farther end of these Islands we came to a small Cove in the bottom of which the picturesque ruins of a deserted Village placed on the summit of an elevated projecting Rock excited our curiosity and induced us to land close to it to view its structure.
>
> This Rock was inaccessible on every side except a narrow pass from the Land by means of steps that admitted only one person to ascend at a time and which seemed to be well guarded in case of an attack, for right over it a large Maple Tree diffused its spreading branches in such an advantageous manner as to afford an easy and ready access from the summit of the Rock to a concealed place amongst its branches, where a small party could watch unobserved and defend the Pass with great ease. We found the top of the Rock nearly level and wholly occupied with the skeletons of Houses—irregularly arranged and very crowded; in some places the space was enlarged by strong scaffolds projecting over the Rock and supporting Houses apparently well secured—These also acted as a defence by increasing the natural strength of the place and rendering it still more secure and inaccessible.[8]

By the end of the nineteenth century, the huge, shed-like dwellings in which the Vancouver Island Salish were living at the time of their discovery had been abandoned or destroyed, and the Indians had built houses of more modern form, though not always on the same sites as the old ones. It had been necessary, indeed, in the interests of white settlement, to move one or two of their villages; thus one, inhabited by the Songish, which hindered the development of Victoria, was moved a few miles west of the city.[9] Early in the twentieth century the Canadian government appointed a Royal Commission to delimit the lands to which the Indians should be given legal rights, taking into consideration the villages they were occupying at the time, the places in which they buried their dead, and the streams on which they had plied their nets and built their fishing weirs.[10] Thus were created the present-day reserves on which the Indians live, reserves that correspond in the main with the sites of some of their settlements of earlier years. In 1929 the entire Coast Salish population of Vancouver Island, to the number of 1,892, was distributed among twenty-six reserves, arranged from north to south as follows, with their populations in brackets:

Comox (35); Qualicum (2); Nanoose Bay (25); Nanaimo (222); two

---

8   Menzies, *Vancouver's Voyage*, 66–67.

9   Governor James Douglas initiated a series of land conveyance agreements beginning in 1850, eleven of them affecting indigenous communities in the Victoria-Saanich Peninsula area; Horne, "WSANEC," 10; Lutz, *Makúk*, 79–80. –Ed.

10   Organized in 1912, the McKenna-McBride Royal Commission, as it was known, issued its highly contentious final report four years later; LaViolette, *Struggle for Survival*, 130–32. The complete text of the Commission's report can be found at http://www.ubcic.bc.ca/Resources/final_report.htm#axzz4HEGCcBjC –Ed.

reserves near Ladysmith: Kulleets (79) and Siccameen (44); Halalt [Westholme] reserve near Chemainus (23);[11] Cowichan Lake (8); seven reserves around Duncan: Khenipson, (45), Quamichan (245), Clemclemaluts (135), Koksilah (16), Comeaken (60), Somenos (170), and Kilpaulus (10); Malahat, in Mill Bay (24); four reserves on Saanich Peninsula: Pauquachen (53), Tseycum (25), Tsartlip (102), Tsawout (106);[12] Songhees reserve between Victoria and Esquimalt (90); Esquimalt (18); Beecher Bay (37); Sooke (28); and off the east coast of Vancouver Island, Lyacksun reserve on Valdes Island (50), and Penelakut reserve on Kuper [now Penelakut] Island (240).

The map below shows the position of the four Saanich Peninsula reserves whose inhabitants are the main topic of this paper.

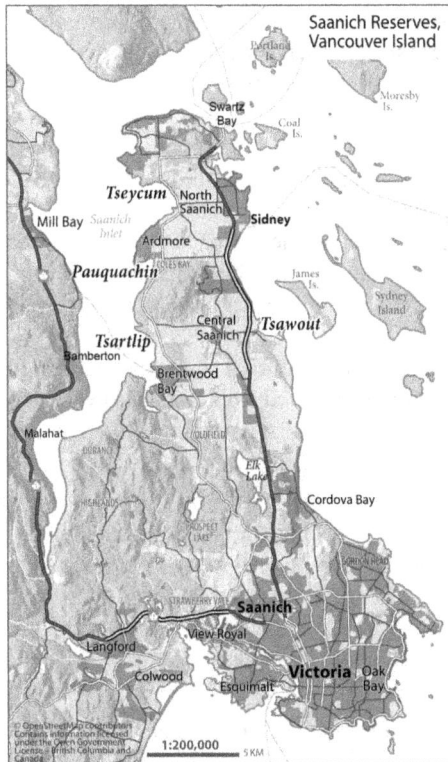

---

11 In his original manuscript, Jenness refers to this community as Westholme. The people of this place, also known as Halalt Reserve No 2, relocated there in the 1920s from an older reserve—Halalt Island No. 1—situated at the mouth of the Chamainus River; http://www.hulquminum.bc.ca/hulquminum_people/halalt In view of its history, the name Halalt, rather than Westholme, is used throughout the book. –Ed.

12 Jenness refers to the two west Saanich Peninsula reserves on which he worked, Tseycum and Tsartlip, as Patricia Bay and Brentwood Bay, respectively; Tsawout, on the peninsula's east side, is referred to as East Reserve. –Ed.

2

Economic Cycle

Throughout the Coast Salish area, the Indians counted the passage of time by winters, the year being the period from one winter to the next. It was divided into four seasons: winter, spring, summer, and autumn. Spring was the shortest of them, marked by disappearance of snow from the land and ice from the rivers. It corresponded roughly to the month of March; hence, that season and month commonly bore the same name.

The year was not only divided into seasons but into months, or moons, although the number of days in each month was indefinite. Apparently, each community roughly equated its social and economic activities with a lunar period, and as these activities varied from district to district, and even in the same district, so also did the names of the months. Furthermore, certain activities did not extend over a full lunar month, while others exceeded the period; therefore, one group might readily count thirteen months against another's twelve; and the name given to a month in one village might be the name for the succeeding month elsewhere. That is to say, the actual lunar count was subordinated to a count of the major activities, and thus varied from place to place throughout the region. This is made clearer in the table comprising Appendix A where the English months, of course, correlate only roughly with the Indian counts.

In the early nineteenth century, life in the Saanich communities followed a seasonal rhythm which varied from village to village owing to slight variations in the economic and social environments. In the west Saanich village of Tsartlip, on Brentwood Bay, for instance, the cycle ran thus:

December–February: This was the season of the winter dances [see Chapter 12], when the population remained in the village. On fine days the men fished off shore for cod and grilse, or caught a few ducks, and the women gathered clams and a variety of seaweed, green with brown edges; but for the most part the people subsisted on the dried fish and berries they had gathered during the summer.

March: In this month seals and spring salmon supplemented cod, grilse and ducks. The regular winter dances ended, but the members of the secret Black Dance held their ceremonies.[1]

---

1   The secret society known as Black Dance— *han'hán'iti (x̣ənx̣aníti)*, "growling at one another," in Northern Straits Salish—spread into southernmost Vancouver Island from the Klallam. It reached the W̱SÁNEĆ by way of their Lekwungen neighbours, but appears to have diffused no farther north. What details Jenness's informants supplied on the topic are both sketchy and contradictory, agreeing only that membership required a secretive initiation, dancers painted their faces black, and only members were allowed to witness and participate in dances held in March,

April: On land the men hunted deer and elk; at sea they fished for cod, grilse, spring salmon, halibut and particularly herring, which spawned in this month.

May: While the men pursued the same activities as in March the women gathered camas roots [wild hyacinth], wild carrots, and rushes for making mats.[2] The camas season lasted only about three weeks, but an energetic family could fill ten or twelve bags with the roots during that period. If the weather was warm many of the people left the village and camped near their camas grounds on San Juan Island [east of Victoria], using for shelter either a few boards taken from their houses, or rush huts.

June: Many of the villagers went out to the islands to fish for halibut in deep water. Others contented themselves with capturing cod, spring salmon, and grilse near the village. They paid many visits to neighbouring villages, and occasionally held a potlatch, though the usual season for potlatches was later.

July: From the beginning of this month until the end of August the village was deserted. Its inhabitants crossed to Point Roberts, on the mainland, to net the sockeye salmon which was their staple winter food, and the humpback salmon that succeeded it. In the intervals of salmon fishing the men killed a few elk and deer, which were now in their prime. Throughout July and August, the women gathered berries, and also dried large quantities of seeds of the consumption plant [*Lomatium nudicaules*] that they used for flavouring their meat and fish, and as an antidote against supernatural contagion.

August: Over and above the activities of the previous month, the men repaired their boats or made new ones, and one or two small parties, leaving their women behind, sometimes wandered away into the mountains to hunt goats. The women gathered and dried many Saskatoon, salal, and other berries that ripened in this month.

September–November: Early in September the people returned to their village, where they set their houses and graveyards in order and laid in a stock of wood for the winter. Often three or four canoes manned by men only went

---

following close of communal winter (or spirit) dancing. One elder remarked that in the past, dancers wore wooden masks representing the thunderbird, the wolf, and Skwanelets, the fish spirit, another that society paraphernalia also included cedar head bands and bird rattles. Tom Paul, of Tsartlip, recalled his father owning a large wolf mask whose mouth could be opened and closed, and which had a representation of *shopship* (šapšəp, "night-bird") affixed to its top. This mask, he said, was lost in a house fire; Jenness, "Saanich Notes," 224–25; see also Barnett, *Coast Salish*, 285–86; Suttles, "Central Coast Salish," 468. –Ed.

2   Only the round variety of rush was gathered in May, when it was easily pulled out of the water; the bulrush, which required cutting, was usually gathered about July. After being thoroughly dried in the sun, the rushes were rolled into bundles and stored away until needed. Subsequently, the women steeped them in water, stripped off the outer edges for thread, and, spreading them in rows, stitched them together with a 24 or 30-inch needle of hardwood, usually *Spiraea discolor* [ocean spray]. Then she bound their edges with a grass [reed] (*Phagmites sp.*) that flourishes in the Fraser River valley, and flattened the seams with a curiously grooved wooden presser. In the nineteenth century the Vancouver Island Salish purchased halibut from the Nootka Indians with rush mats.

out among the islands to hunt seals, sea lions, and sea otters. Other men fished near the village, or hunted deer, while the women gathered clams, made blankets and rush mats, and attended to other duties around their homes. Late in September dog salmon [chum] appeared, which the Tsartlip Indians caught as they approached the river at Goldstream. Both September and October were favourite months for potlatches, so that there was much going and coming between one village and another. November, with its frosts and high winds, checked this travelling. In that month the villagers settled down for the winter, and the women left their homes only to gather clams and fern roots while the men made canoes and hunted and fished in the immediate neighbourhood.

The east Saanich natives, the Songish, and those near Chemainus followed practically the same routine as the west Saanich; they too abandoned their villages in the middle of summer and netted sockeye and humpback salmon on the mainland, off the mouth of the Fraser River. The Cowichan Indians, however, had no fishing rights on the mainland, but only over the waters immediately adjacent to their shore and around Mayne and Saltspring Islands;[3] so while many of them fished for herring, cod, and halibut off these two islands during the mid-summer months, living in rush huts on their shores, others preferred to remain year round in their villages, where they were far less exposed to enemy raiders coming down from the north. Food was always plentiful, even without the sockeye and humpback salmon, which did not enter the Cowichan river; for the steelhead [pink] salmon began to ascend this stream in January, increased in numbers during March, and continued until June, when blue-backs [young cohoe salmon] made their appearance in the weirs.

The blue-backs lasted until August, and were followed by the cohoe; and when the cohoe run ended in October the dog salmon entered the river and ran until Christmas. Both in Cowichan Bay and near Saltspring Island, herring spawned in great numbers during April; seals, too, frequented the waters near shore, and sea lions a little farther out. Deer, elk, bear and grouse abounded in the Cowichan woods and could be captured at every season of the year. There was no lack, too, of vegetable foods, since camas and ferns of every kind grew all about. Even rushes for mat making were procurable in Quamichan Lake.

The Nanaimo Indians followed the Saanich custom of visiting the mainland in midsummer. There were five communities in the district: Solachwan ("swampy ground"), Tewahchin ("village to the north"), Anuweenis ("village in the centre"), Kwalsiawahl[4] (meaning unknown), and Ishihan ("end

---

3   Jenness's assertion here, and again on a later page, that the Cowichan lacked fishing rights on the mainland, appears to conflict with Barnett's findings. The latter noted that in July, "able-bodied Cowichan" crossed the strait and camped on Lulu Island, in the Fraser delta, where they fished for sockeye and sturgeon, or else bartered for same; Barnett, *Coast Salish*, 22, 122. Though not explicit on the point, this evidence suggests that the Cowichan may well have had fishing rights on the mainland.
4   Although it has been corrected here, Jenness erred in his spelling of Kwalsiawahl since Hul'qumi'num' language lacks the phoneme /r/. In fact, his notes correctly record the name qwaʹlsiʹáwaɬ; Thom, per. comm. 10 August, 2016; Jenness, "Saanich Notes," 268. Review-

village"). The first was within the present city of Nanaimo, the other four strung out along the Nanaimo River two or three miles away. These river villages were occupied only from about September until Christmas when their inhabitants moved to Departure Bay to celebrate their winter dances, carrying with them the walls and roofs of their houses so that only the bare frames remained on the bank of the river. The Solachwan natives, however, occupied their village until about April, when they joined the others in moving out to False Narrows and Gabriola Island to fish for cod, grilse and other species, to hunt seals and sea lions, and to gather clams and camas; for every family had its own bed of camas on Gabriola Island. In August, all the Indians moved again to the mouth of the Fraser River for the sockeye and humpback salmon season, returning to Nanaimo in time for the dog salmon.

...

In addition to special regulations governing the pursuit of such animals as the whale and sea lion (see below), the Saanich had one general rule: that a man should never hunt (or fish) on a full stomach, because the taint he acquired from eating would offend the game and keep it beyond his reach. The hunter or the fisherman therefore started out before daylight, and did not break his fast until he returned home. Even his wife and children in the village fasted and moved about quietly, lest some action on their part should militate against his success. Only if he had gone far away and would be absent for several days did they eat and behave as usual.

Deer and elk were caught in three ways: in pits, in nets, and by individual hunters with bows and arrows. In many places the natives dug pits about ten feet deep along the animals' trails, placing in the bottom of some pits sharpened stakes and notched poles for ascending and descending. The pits trapped far more deer than elk, the latter being, of course, less numerous. A Duncan native stated that his father commonly trapped two deer in a week.

The deer net, made of plaited sinew, or, on the Fraser River, from a grass called *sakwats*, varied in length according to the number of hunters, each of whom brought his own section to join to those of others along the line of stakes.[5] While some of them drove the deer towards the net, others concealed themselves behind it to kill the trapped animals. They then divided up the meat more or less evenly, but the man in whose section a deer was caught could claim its hide and sinew. A Saanich Indian said that his people never used dogs for driving animals, having only the woolly-haired variety that was unsuitable for hunting;[6]

---

ing this same material in his study of Vancouver Island Hul'qumi'num' place names, David Rozen revised the names of the five villages accordingly: sólexwem, t'iwelhxen, enwínes, kw'elsíw'elh, and éy'th'exen; "Place Names," 48–50. Appendix 4 contains a list of place names Jenness collected in W̱SÁNEĆ territory. –Ed.

5   Simon Fraser speaks of "a net ... made of thread of the size of cod lines; the meshes were 16″ wide and the net 8 fathoms long;" Fraser, "Journal of a Voyage," 192.

6   On Salish wool dogs, see, for example, Keddy, "Prehistoric Dogs of B.C." –Ed.

but a Halalt native, Kaypemulthw Bob [aka Old Bob], said that in his district they did use the woolly-haired dog in deer drives. The mainland natives along the Fraser River, in whose territory elk were unusually numerous, drove them, in historical times at least, with a larger breed of dog. Hunters who went out singly in pursuit of deer and elk often painted their faces with red ochre, or wore red caps; and they carried a pair of horns to plant on their heads in close stalking. To attract a buck elk, they whistled with their mouths, to attract a female deer they whistled through a blade of grass.

The rituals connected with deer hunting varied slightly in the different family groups. All agreed that a man should never mention by name the animal he intended to hunt, lest it hear him and keep out of his way.[7] All agreed, likewise, that he should purify himself beforehand and keep away from his wife for at least one night. A Tsawout (east Saanich) medicine man said that he should keep away from his wife for four nights, and pray night and morning to the shades [ghosts] of his dead relatives and ancestors. A Tsartlip (west Saanich) native denied this, asserting that only a priest (*thitha*), or a medicine man,[8] would dare to pray to the shades, and then only that he might spoil a hunter's luck by making the shades frighten the animals away. In his own family group, he added, the hunter hired a priest to paint his face with red ochre and teach him the incantation he should say in the woods the night before, and again in the early morning before he started out for the chase, an incantation that would check the deer from fleeing. Then, when he shot an animal, he opened it up (taking care not to inhale any of the warm steam, which would cause his early death), sprinkled around a few handfuls of blood for any shades that might be near, both human and animal, and held up the heart to the sun as a thank-offering. Finally, on returning home, he scrupulously removed all blood from his clothes lest it prevent him from finding any more deer tracks.

---

7   While I was talking to an old Tsartlip Indian one afternoon, a youth came up to borrow two cartridges, saying that he intended to hunt for deer on the morrow. After he had gone the old man said to me, "He will not get any deer. He has let them know that he is going to hunt them and they will flee far away."

8   Homer Barnett prefers the term "ritualist" to Jenness's "priest," describing a person whose command of a sacred body of magical knowledge and practice, *siwín*, passed down within families from ancient times, made him (or her) "indispensable on occasions of crisis," individual and communal alike. However, "In the sense that he was an intermediary between the layman and certain supernatural forces over which the layman had no control, he might be termed a priest holding office for the public benefit"; Barnett, *Coast Salish*, 129, 147. Unlike the priest, a medicine man (or shaman) acquires the knowledge to heal by seeking the help of certain powerful spirits. In SENĆOŦEN, ŚNÁ,EM (*šné?əm*) is "Indian Doctor," or "shaman." In the present text, Jenness renders the term *cnem*. His use of *thitha* (*θiθə*) for "priest" appears to have no modern-day lexical equivalent; however, the Hul'qumi'num' word *θiθə* (or *xwθiθə*) denotes a "native spiritual practitioner"; Donna Gerdts, per. comm. 18 April, 2016. In SENĆOŦEN, LEP-LIT (*ləplít*), "priest," is derived from the French *le prêtre*, by way of Chinook Jargon (*le plet*); Gibbs, *Dictionary of Chinook*, 6. –Ed.

Edward Jim, an old Tsekum (west Saanich) Indian, observed the following rules. For three or four days in succession he wandered into the woods about sunrise, bathed, scrubbed himself with branches, and prayed to the sun "Bring what I wish into my path." The night before he actually went hunting, his soul (*smastimauch*)[9] left his body and discovered the location of the deer, and learned also whether he would be successful. He set off from his house before daylight, fasting, since if he ate any food the deer or elk would see steam issuing from his mouth and flee; and he carried with him a deer knucklebone to attract the game by its smell. As he walked along, he prayed that his feet and the ground would cause no earth movement that might warn the deer; and after he had shot an animal, he cupped up some of its blood in his two hands, raised it toward the sun as a thank-offering, and poured it on the ground.

Among Cowichan, Quamichan natives observed similar rules: they bathed and separated from their wives one or more days before going out to hunt, avoided mentioning the name of the animal, and poured out a little of the blood for the shades of dead relatives. At Halalt, however, Old Bob and Mrs [Annie] Bob, told me that their people never prayed to the sun or to the shades for aid in hunting, and never made any blood offerings.

Another old Tsartlip Indian used to pray to Haylse [or Xe.ls] in the solitude of the woods early in the morning, and again at evening, on the eve of the day before he went hunting.[10] Then, during the night, he would dream where to find the deer, and how many he would kill; he would dream, perhaps that he met two women and a man, who would ask him what he was seeking; and he knew by this that he would kill two does and a buck. Long before daylight he would leave the house to search for them; his family, finding him gone, would remain very quiet throughout the day lest the deer, which learns through dreams as man does, should hear their noise and flee far away. This man sprinkled on the ground some drops of blood from the first deer he shot after the close of winter, as a thank-offering for Xe.ls.

The Vancouver Island Salish only killed those bears that they encountered accidentally, and in most cases hunters paid no special respect to the dead animal. However, Edward Jim, the Tseycum Indian mentioned above, following a custom which he claimed was restricted to his family, shouted "*he*" when the bear fell mortally wounded, then chanted a song to please its soul and check it from crying out in agony.

Hunters kept their bows and arrows in deerskin cases to protect them from the rain. Most bows were made of yew, curved at each end by steaming inside

---

9   Jenness recorded the term *smastímaux* in his notes; in his work on Katzie, it appears as *smastíax*ʷ, which he defined as "vitality"; *Faith of a Coast Salish*, 46. These forms equate with the Halkomelem (*Sto:lo*) word for "soul," *smestiyexw*. In contemporary SENĆOŦEN usage, *SELI* (*shəli*) means "soul," or "life spirit." The nature of the soul is examined in Chapter 9. –Ed.
10   Haylse is the Coast Salish Transformer. Jenness transcribed the name (as he did many Saanich words) inconsistently, sometimes giving it as Haylse, other times as Xe.ls, or Xe.ls. In SENĆOŦEN, XA,EL,S (*xeʔəl's*) denotes "supreme being," as it does "Transformer." For purposes of consistency, hereafter the name appears as Xe.ls. –Ed.

a length of kelp; their strings were of elk hide or sea lion gut. These bows are said to have lacked backing, but from the mainland some of the Saanich Indians obtained bows of yellow cedar that were backed with twisted deer sinew set in a groove and then covered with sturgeon glue. One measurement for the weapon was the distance between the elbows when the finger knuckles were joined on the chest; but this excluded the horns, which were extra. Arrows were made of cedar, or, more rarely, of Saskatoon wood; and one measure for them was the distance from the tip of the middle finger to the middle of the chest. The Tsartlip native who gave these measurements said that arrows were winged, preferably, with two golden eagle feathers lashed on with cherry bark, and that they carried any one of three kinds of points: a stone or mussel shell point that disengaged when it struck, used for deer and for war; a bone point, round and knobbed to skip over the water, for ducks; and a bone point with two barbs, for other birds. This man used the primary release, and held the shaft of the arrow between the middle and third fingers on his left hand. A Tsawout native said that in his village, the points were fastened with sturgeon glue as well as with cherry bark, and that while two feathers were usual for small game, three were preferred for large animals. The golden eagle feathers were purchased from mainland natives, since the bird does not frequent the south of Vancouver Island.[11] Toy arrows of the present day carry duck feathers.

On the mainland, usually at the close of the salmon season, the Saanich killed a few mountain goats with their bows and arrows, but perhaps not before the nineteenth century. They may have trapped, too, a few beaver and muskrats which were present in the lower Fraser valley, though absent on Vancouver Island; in any case, they were of little importance.

Two men often paddled out at night to where waterfowl, principally ducks, were resting on the water, kindled a small fire in an earth-filled box to attract the birds, and speared or clubbed them when they drifted within reach. Johnson, a Duncan native,[12] said that his people used a spear with two points, which seems to have been the usual type, but Johnny Claxton, of Tsawout, stated that the spears of his family group had four points, three blackened, the fourth painted white for aiming. He described the procedure for hunting waterfowl as follows:

> Two men paddled out to a place where two currents met, for that was where the ducks slept. The man in front had a four-pointed spear that rested on a cross-beam and on some noiseless material set on the bow. The steersman sat a little forward of the stern; behind him a small fire burned in a wooden box filled with earth. When they drew near the ducks the steersman muffled himself under a cape to resemble a stump and sat motionless, merely steering the canoe

---

11   The price of one golden eagle feather in the second half of the nineteenth century was said to be one dollar.

12   Jenness recorded no other name for this informant, a man he judged to be about seventy years old in 1935; Jenness, "Saanich Notes," 261. –Ed.

without raising his paddle. Then the man in front, paddling with as little noise as possible, speared the ducks one after another and drew them into the boat.

The Saanich disclaimed any use on Vancouver Island of the square net which their neighbours, the Lummi Indians to the south [in Washington State], sometimes threw over flocks of ducks that were resting on the water. Nevertheless, they did use two kinds of nets for waterfowl. Over the spawning grounds of herring they occasionally stretched a net horizontally, about three feet from the bottom of the sea, to enmesh and drown the ducks that dived down to eat the spawn.[13] Again, in favourable localities, they erected two or more high poles at distances up to one hundred feet apart, stretched between them a long net to intercept the ducks as they flew to their feeding grounds at dawn, and returned from them at evening. In certain places this net was stretched over water, in others (e.g. on the Tsawout reserve), over dry land; and some natives changed its height morning and evening. Old Bob said that the Cowichan of Halalt strung the net on a rope between two trees on opposite sides of a stream in such a way that it could be drawn from one side to the other. One man drove the ducks, one man was stationed in each tree, and the net owner supervised the operations. Most ducks were caught by the neck, but now and then one fell to the ground, stunned. If only two or three birds were trapped, one of the men stationed in the trees pulled the net over and disengaged them; but if a number struck the net, the men in the trees released its ends simultaneously so that it

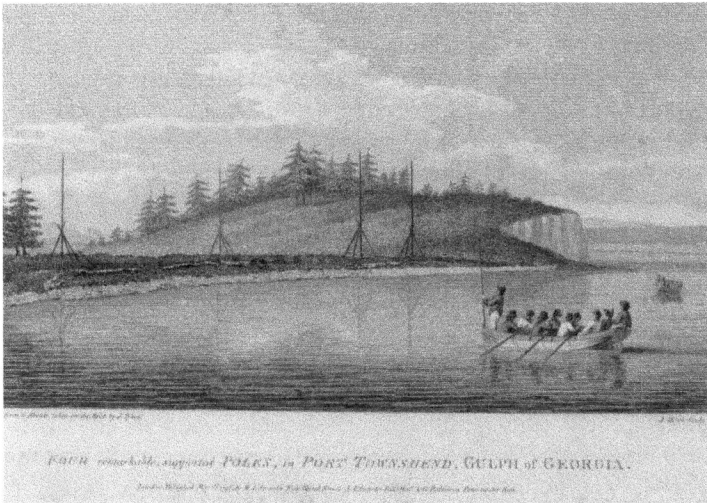

Four Remarkable, Supported Poles, Port Townsend, Gulph of Georgia

---

13 In shallow Sumas Lake, up the Fraser River [between Chilliwack and Abbotsford], the Indians stretched out the nets on the surface and floated a dead salmon below it; ducks and geese that were attracted by the bait became caught in the meshes as they pushed their heads up to breathe.

dropped to the water, whereupon they paddled or waded out and wrung the birds' necks. The accompanying figure illustrates poles erected for this type of hunting by the Klallam at Port Townsend [see above], in Washington State, in the late eighteenth century.

Grouse and other birds were caught in nooses, while swans and eagles were shot with the bow and arrows. None of them, however, played an important role in the Saanich economy except the swan, and that not for its flesh but for its down, which the natives strewed over their heads in many of their ceremonies and dances. Hunters sometimes filled the skin of a swan with its down and sold it.

Harbour seals were hunted all along the coast, most commonly on moonlit nights. The harpoon, of yew wood, had two heads fitted with stone or shell points set in bone or antler sockets; the line was of twisted cedar twigs and bark, or, very rarely, of nettle. According to Old Bob, the hunter did not attach the end of his line to a cedar bark buoy, as for sea lions, but retained it in his hand. Seal hunting, like the porpoise hunting conducted with the same weapons, was not regarded as an occupation requiring hereditary power or knowledge and so was open to any native. Two men generally went out in a boat together. The oil obtained from seals and porpoises was stored in the bladders of seals to eat with dried fish.

The Saanich killed very few sea lions, which the present-day natives say were not plentiful off their shores, though common a little farther north. Harpooners of these animals inherited their profession, together with the songs that accompanied it; for the natives believed that while other men might succeed in harpooning the animal, they could never bring it to shore unless a professional tamed it by his chants. Each canoe generally carried three weapons: a double-pointed harpoon for any seals that might be encountered; a single-pointed harpoon attached to a cedar buoy for sea lions; and a stout wooden spear whose tip had been hardened in the fire for dispatching the wounded animal. While the crew of laymen paddled, the harpooner kept watch in the bow.

Every harpooner had to dissociate himself from women for three or four days before the sea lion season, and while the boats were away the women of the village had to refrain from washing their hair. If either regulation were violated, a sea lion would bite one of the harpooners and probably drown him. The captured mammal was dragged ashore, cut into cross-sections, and divided among all the hunters. The flippers and the intestine were the special perquisites of the harpooner, the intestine because, when slightly twisted and dried, it made a very stout cord suitable for a bow string or a halibut troll.

Whaling was similarly an inherited profession, practised mainly by the Songish group, and occasionally by the Saanich. Usually, several canoes went out together, each of them carrying ten men. In the bow of the leading canoe sat its owner, the harpooner, a man of high rank in his community; besides the heavy yew harpoon with shell or stone point, he carried a bone club which had come to him, supposedly, from his guardian spirit (*saila*),[14] and without which he dared not whale.[15] The second man bore a long spear pointed with elk bone, used for stabbing the exhausted whale behind the forearm. The third took care of the bulky harpoon line, made from twisted cedar twigs; and the fourth had charge of the three (one native said four) seal skin floats. The next five men merely paddled, and the tenth was the steersman.

Before the whaling season opened, the harpooner spent from ten days to a month in the woods, half-fasting, bathing, and praying to his guardian spirit.[16] A Tsartlip native stated that when the wounded whale towed the canoe along, harpooner and crew chanted the following incantation in order that the animal might drag them towards some creek near the village where they could conveniently cut up its carcass:

> "Turn to that mountain. Go quietly to the creek. There I shall meet you."

As the canoe approached the shore they chanted again, and the villagers on the beach joined in, some of them beating drums:

> "Whale spirit, do not desert me. Give me your protection for the future."

The men drummed and danced and repeated the second chant, under the harpooner's leadership, after the whale had been cut up. The crews then divided the meat and oil according to certain rules, the harpooner, of course, receiving the largest share, and they invited the people of neighbouring villages to join them in the feast.

...

Custom demanded that the bones of all fish, whatever their species, should be thrown into the water, since it was believed they re-clothed themselves with flesh and became fish again. A popular belief among the Saanich was that the moment the bones of a sockeye salmon touched the water they changed into a fish that leaped from the surface. If a bone were missing it leaped only a little, whereupon the Indians searched for the missing part and threw it in. The salmon then leaped high out of the water. Animal bones also were generally thrown into the water, not to restore them to life, however, but to preserve them from molestation by dogs, which would annoy the animals' shades. It was forbidden to roast fish and meat at the same fire, under penalty of failure in fishing and in hunting.

---

14   The list of contemporary SENĆOŦEN words contains no entry for "guardian spirit." In Jenness's *The Faith of a Coast Salish Indian* (p. 41), the term appears as *sʔályə*. This corresponds with the Sto:lo word *s'éliyá*, denoting a "spirit dream" or "vision." Tutelary spirits reveal themselves to people through dreams or visionary experiences. –Ed.

15   A Tsawout man hunted whales in Saanich Arm during the nineteenth century. So heavy was his harpoon, it was said, that he alone had the strength to wield it.

16   Certain restrictions were laid on the villagers while he was at sea, but I failed to discover them.

The Tsartlip natives threw back into the water every fish that was disfigured and begged the forgiveness of the fish spirit, Skwanelɛts, for catching it. They state that towards the end of the nineteenth century a young girl made fun of a disfigured fish and laughed when her mother reproved her; a few days later her own face became contorted like that of the fish, and she died. Other Coast Salish groups on Vancouver Island held similar beliefs.

The Saanich, and probably other groups, speared many cod by night (and not only cod, but salmon, perch, flounder, and sole). The fishermen generally went out alone, lit a fire in a box of sand at the bow of the canoe to illuminate the water, and impaled the fish from the stern with a two-pointed spear. Some cod were speared also by day, close to shore, during the spawning season; for the Indians claimed, rightly or wrongly, that a few one or two-year-old fish always guarded the spawn from the depredations of other species, and that these guardian cod were so savage that they even attacked the spears of the fishermen. The latter, not wishing to deplete their stocks, speared two or three only and left the rest to keep watch. It was common Coast Salish practice to use a peculiar two or three-vane spinner of light cedar to attract cod to the surface. They thrust down the spinner almost out of sight with the shaft of the spear, or else with a long pole, and, when it came spinning upward again, stabbed the fish that darted after it. More successful than the spear, perhaps, was the hook and line, the latter made from kelp.

For halibut, the Saanich used a wooden hook bent into the shape of a horse-shoe and fitted with a bone barb. The wood was either a hemlock knot or a piece of straight-grained balsam bent into shape by steaming, then lashed until it dried. The favourite bait was octopus, and the line commonly used was made of spruce root. Dog fish sharks were caught with the same tackle as halibut. The skin, peeled off when the fish was half-dry, served as sandpaper. The meat was generally squeezed into a pulp before it was eaten.

Sturgeon were common only in the [lower] Fraser River and in the lakes that drained into it, so that the Saanich rarely saw this fish. The Fraser River Indians captured it at different seasons, but mainly in spring during the eula-chon run, when it seemed most plentiful. They caught it in three ways: with a bone hook baited with eulachon or salmon roe attached to a line; with a bag net woven of nettles that was dragged between two canoes; and with a long, two-pointed spear whose detachable bone points were fastened by a long line to a float of light cedar. Often a man would drift downstream in his canoe and probe the bottom of the river with his spear, stabbing whenever it touched a fish. On Sumas Lake, the Indians walked down a long weir and raked the bottom of the water with a detachable hook set on the end of a long pole and fastened to a line.

There is a story that long ago, when the Indians at the head of the Fraser Delta were suddenly attacked by enemies during the celebration of a ten-day festival, some of them jumped into the river and changed to sturgeon; hence, the sturgeon still gather at this place every year for ten days.

Eulachon shoaled in the Fraser River in May, when the local Indians raked them in with long poles studded with spikes made from Saskatoon wood, and also caught them in dip nets made from twisted nettle fibre. The Saanich employed exactly the same methods for herring, which shoaled round the coasts in April for about three weeks, on two high tides, the Indians say, after which they retreated into deep water.

While the herring were spawning, the fishermen suspended cedar branches three or four feet above the mud bottom by means of wooden floats and stone sinkers, then drew them up with the spawn after the herring had departed and shook them out in their canoes. Unlike eulachon, herring do not consistently return each year to the same places to spawn, but change from one locality to another. The Saanich have frequently tried to establish them in convenient bays by transporting the roe, but without success. Many years ago Mrs Latasse, of Tsartlip, carried some roe from Cole Bay to Brentwood Bay, hoping that the fish which hatched from them would return the following season. When they failed to return she blamed, not the wandering habits of the herring, but a fellow villager whom she accused of offending the fish by capturing some with his rake just after his wife had been initiated as a winter dancer. This same woman stated that in earlier times the Indians sometimes squeezed the sperm of the male salmon over the roe of the female, packed it in a special kind of moss inside a cedar chest, and deposited the box under some cliff on a mountain face where the sun would shine on it all day, but no rain could penetrate. Before departing they chanted certain prayers to the spirit ruler of all fish, Skwanelɛts. Years later, if for some reason the salmon failed to revisit their usual haunts, they retrieved this roe and placed it in the sea. Then not only salmon, but fish of other species appeared there in large shoals.

Both herring and eulachon were dried in the sun for about ten days, either strung on sticks or laid out on racks; but the largest herring were often smoke-dried, which in the eyes of some Indians improved their flavour.

Salmon of one kind or another was the main food of the Saanich, as it was of all other Coast Salish Indians. Wherever weirs could be built across rivers they set basket traps to capture them; at other places on the rivers they used dip-nets of nettle fibre, or else willow bark purse-nets drawn between two canoes. Many salmon were also impaled on two-barbed bone points, detachable from a long wooden handle while still remaining lashed to it. On the Cowichan and Chilliwack rivers three men in one canoe, and two in another, sometimes blocked the river with a long gill net made from willow bark and drove the spring salmon into it. The Saanich also employed gill nets for spring salmon, nets that averaged perhaps ten fathoms [60 feet] long by one-and-a-half feet deep; but for the sockeye and humpback species they used a larger purse net called *agwala*.[17] The top and bottom ropes of this net were generally made from twisted cedar boughs, and the meshes from willow, gathered in

---

17   In the tale "Origin of the Willow Fishnet" (see Part II, no. 30), the word *agwala* is used in reference to the willow bark from which the net is made, not to the net itself. –Ed.

May or June, peeled, and split into thin strands that were then twisted together to form a long rope. The Halalt natives fashioned their purse-nets from a flax-like plant that grew on the mainland. Stones made convenient sinkers, and blocks of light cedar served as floats.

A weir belonged to the five or six men who built it, each of whom common-ly set against it three or four traps. It was understood, however, that other men in the same community might set their own traps at the weir as soon as the owners had satisfied their needs.

Most of the natives regarded the sockeye as the choicest of all fish, but not all of them possessed fishing rights over waters where the sockeye ran; for, like the humpback, it does not enter the streams on [southeastern] Vancouver Island. The Saanich had an immemorial claim to the fishing off Point Roberts, near the mouth of the Fraser River; there, during July and August, they caught and stored for the winter large quantities of both sockeye and humpback. Sim-ilarly, the Westholme natives owned the fishing rights at Cuwassin [Tsawwas-sen], as did the Songhees at San Juan Island. The Cowichan around Duncan, however, lacked any corresponding rights on the mainland, and for the most part disregarded the sockeye fishery, although they did catch a certain number of these salmon off Pender Island.

Because one man alone could never make a purse net long enough for sock-eye and humpback, several Saanich families cooperated by making sections that could be joined together at the fishing grounds. The leader of the group then supervised the fishing, appointed one man to watch, with painted face and feathered head, which way the shoals were running, and apportioned the catch equally among several families, without regards to their social rank. Each family then dried its share on its own rack. Not until all other require-ments were satisfied did the leader provide for himself.

At Point Roberts, each family dried its fish in the same spot year after year, and left there its stone net sinkers. The same custom prevailed, probably, at all other Coast Salish fishing grounds. In distributing the salmon, the leader, or the man he assigned to the task, counted the fish in twos up to ten until he had made the requisite number of heaps of ten pairs, when he started the count over again while two old men sat near to check his figures; from one good haul each family might obtain as many as four lots of ten pair plus five, i.e. eighty-five fish. Most of the Vancouver Island communities used the ev-eryday numeral system for the count, but the Tsartlip natives of West Saanich employed a special vocabulary derived, they claimed, from the fish spirit that taught them to make the net.[18] This count ran, in pairs, thus:

---

18   David Latasse (aka Old David), who supplied this vocabulary, claimed that he was the last man to remember it; he died in 1937, at the age of about 90. When the two met in 1935, Jenness said the elder claimed to be 105; Jenness to Ethel Kenney, 15 October, 1935; Lutz, *Makúk*, 79. –Ed.

tsez (one pair); *cez* (two pair); *t'lǝkwe'*; *ŋǝse'ł*;
skǝtce'z; *tkǝŋe'z*; *slokwe'z*; *tese'z*; *tǝkwe'uҳ*; *apen.*

The same strange tongue provided the vocabulary they employed when handling the net:

> *nilǝ'sit* (prepare to pull on the net); *sele'u'kum* (lean back and pull hard); *kuntohwétcum* (pull); *lámat te'heu,* (throw stones far out beyond the fish, to frighten them into the net); *klestáutsił* (throw stones to the side of the net.)[19]

The Saanich, in common with other Coast Salish groups, deeply revered the salmon, believing that they were human beings from some far-away land that transformed themselves into fish during the migration season. At this season, therefore, they never referred to any species by its common name, but called it *selewa* (elder brother), or *ceas* (rich man), [20] and they allowed no dogs at their fishing grounds. Furthermore, they honoured the dead bodies of the fish by cutting them up on ferns, which they afterwards threw into the water; and when they dried the fish in a hut, they burned in it, day and night, the seeds of the consumption plant, which was their specific against supernatural contagion.

Every Salish group on Vancouver Island celebrated the first catch of the season with a special rite, the First Salmon Ceremony. But whereas the Songhees, Saanich, and Halalt natives celebrated it over the sockeye or humpback, those around Duncan and Nanaimo celebrated it over the dog salmon.

The Tsartlip, and, I believe, other Saanich natives, related their ceremony only to the humpback, because it was the one variety that young and old might eat at all times, fresh or dried; for even the sockeye, which ran and was captured with it, was forbidden to sick people lest it cause haemorrhages. When the men discovered the first humpback in their nets, therefore, all the children in the camp, from the age of five or six to puberty, bathed in the sea, painted their cheeks with red ochre, sprinkled bird down on their heads, and lined up in a row on the beach. The priest, whose face was painted also, chanted a prayer over the fish,[21] then laid one in each child's arms as if it were a baby, with the head pointing toward the water. The children gripped the dorsal fins between their teeth, and marching in line, carried them to the fire pit, where they laid them on a pile of ferns, very gently, so that they would call on other salmon to follow them. After the priest had daubed each fish with ochre, the old women cleaned them, sprinkled them with the seeds of the consumption plant, and roasted them on the hot coals. The children lined up again as soon as they were ready and received each one a whole fish (if there were enough to

---

19 A Tsawout native said that one man in each of the two canoes that worked the net streaked his face with red ochre and wore a hat trimmed with goat wool, while a priest on shore chanted "*tcala skwansilawa*" (look back and go into the net).

20 In SENĆOŦEN, ŚÍEȽ (*šǝyǝł*) refers to "elder brother" or "elder sister"; SI,ÁM (*siʔém*) denotes "rich," as well as a "person of high class" (i.e. a noble). –Ed.

21 A Tsawout man said the prayer ran "*tsam skwatsilawa*" (come up out of the canoe).

go around), while the priest prayed to Skwanelɛts, the spirit-lord of all edible fish, in words to the following effect:

> O Skwanelɛts, our children this day eat the first of the fish that you have sent us. We thank you. We shall treat the fish carefully as we have always done.

He then ordered the children to eat, and, marching behind them with a stick, forced them to swallow as much as they were able. When they could eat no more the old women gathered up all the fragments and bones into baskets and made the children empty them in the sea. A Tsawout native said (without being able to give the reason) that the children were supposed to limp as they carried the fragments down.

The Songhees celebrated over the sockeye, which they netted at San Juan Island. They considered their net to represent a human being with head, body, arms and legs, and they believed that unless it was set in a certain definite way, the leading sockeye would turn back disapprovingly and warn those behind. Since only a few priests knew how to set it, one always superintended the fishing, apportioned the catch, and directed the ceremonies. In their ceremony over the first salmon that were brought in women and girls, not boys and girls, carried up the fish, men and women as well as children ate them, and the boys and girls gathered up the bones, then lined up along the beach before marching into the water at a given signal and dropping them. They dried their second haul of fish on logs, the third and all subsequent ones on stagings [drying flakes]. There was a ceremony at the first utilization of the stagings. All the people lined up, with painted faces and feathered heads, and, after the priest had chanted a prayer, made three feints at hanging up their fish before completing the operation. Again, at the ceremony that closed the season's fishing, the priest chanted a prayer and threw consumption plant seeds into the flames while the people piled all the refuse into the bonfire, after which the older natives chatted and sang while the children played nearby. Thus in numerous small details the Songhese rituals seem to have differed from the Saanich; but I suspect that these differences were more apparent than real, since probably no two priests ever directed the ceremonies in exactly the same way.

The Cowichan around Duncan, unlike the Saanich, allowed salmon bones to be thrown anywhere, even to the dogs. Only one species they excepted, the spring salmon, which they caught with a net; they caught other species with spears or long hooks. Yet it was not the spring salmon that they honoured with religious rites, but the dog salmon. When the season arrived for this species to ascend the Cowichan River, a man who claimed it as his guardian spirit painted two male and two female dog salmon on a board and carried it down to the mouth of the river. There, in the presence of his fellow villagers, he dipped it into the water, and prayed that the shoals would be large and numerous. Then they split the first dog salmon they caught so that the heads remained attached to the backbones and tails, and they cooked the heads on the fire while the meat was hung overhead to dry. A few consumption plant seeds thrown into the flames fed the shades of the fish. As soon as the heads were cooked the people gathered and ate them, while three or four old men chanted a song nearby and drummed on a board with a stick.

It was the run of the dog salmon that the Nanaimo Indians celebrated also. At Jack Point, close to the city of Nanaimo, is a petroglyph, carved so long ago that no one remembers the artist. It represents a dog salmon, a cohoe, a spring salmon, a humpback salmon, and a flounder. Each year before the dog salmon season opened a priest covered the designs with red ochre, lit a fire in front of them, and threw various kinds of food into the flames to feed the souls of the dog salmon. Present-day natives claim that the custom originated with a priest whose daughter, in ages long past, married a dog salmon; and that it was probably this priest who carved the petroglyph. The legend, told by Albert Westly, is as follows:

> An old priest who lived in Solachwan village, near Nanaimo, with his wife and daughter, went up where the highway bridge now crosses the river and caught there a fish that he had never seen before, a dog salmon. He placed it in his canoe, paddled home, and asked his wife if she would cook it for him; and when she undertook to cook it he sent his daughter down to the canoe to bring the fish into the house. The girl lit a bundle of cedar sticks to light her path, and, when she reached the canoe, put her hand down to take up the salmon; but it changed at her touch into a young man, who seized her wrist and said "You cannot go back. You must come home with me and be my wife."
>
> Her father and mother wondered why she did not return and the old man went down to the canoe to look for her. He found the canoe where he had left it, but no trace either of the girl or the fish. The next morning, he called in several seers (*siowa*)[22] to discover what had happened but not one could find out. Finally, one of them announced that the salmon had carried her away. At first the old man refused to believe the seer, but he was finally convinced when his daughter sent word to him in some way that she was safe in the home of the dog salmon and would visit him at a certain time of the year.
>
> At the appointed time the dog salmon brought the girl back to Nanaimo and waited for her in the water while she went up to the house and visited her parents. She stayed with them only a little while, then went down to the river again, leaped in, and returned with her husband to their home.
>
> When spring came, her father paddled away in his canoe to search

---

22   A *siowa* was a person endowed with a special power: clairvoyance, or second sight. Jenness described the power as an unsolicited gift, not as something a person deliberately sought, or underwent training to acquire; *Faith of a Coast Salish*, 37; see also Barnett, *Coast Salish*, 150. In SENĆOŦEN, the word is SYEU,E (*syáwә*), "seer." –Ed.

for her. After travelling a long distance, he reached the home of the humpback salmon, who told him that his daughter lived farther on. From the humpback salmon he continued to the home of the coho salmon, who told him that his daughter lived in the next village. There he found her, and remained with her for some time. When he was on the point of returning she said to him, "My husband and I with many of his people will visit you in the fall. Tell my aunts and uncles not to harm either my husband or myself. We will leap out of the water side by side so that they may know us.

In the fall many dog salmon entered the Nanaimo River, among them two that leaped side by side. These two the Indians did not touch, but of the others they caught great numbers.

The Saanich celebrated also the close of the sockeye-humpback season, but with a purely secular entertainment. The women and children, under the supervision of the priest, gathered up all the loose sticks and refuse on the beach and piled them in a heap. Then, towards midnight, everyone rose, lit the bonfire, and threw into the air little balls of mixed deer fat, camas, and bird's down, one ball for each place in which they and their kinsmen were accustomed to net the sockeye and the humpback. As they threw away their balls they shouted the names of these places: "Point Roberts, I feed you this; Sooke, I feed you this," etc. Then they scattered their fire, threw the burning brands in play at one another, and yelled and danced until daylight when they packed up their belongings and returned to the Saanich Peninsula.

...

The eggs of salmon, like its flesh, were dried in the smoke of fires, unless their envelopes were broken, in which case they were thrown into baskets and warmed over a fire. The heat then congealed the outside of the mass, leaving the eggs in the middle still raw, but so tightly enclosed that they kept fresh all winter. Before cooking them the women washed them in cold water, when all dead eggs floated to the surface. Oil from salmon eggs was a regular ingredient in paints.

The Saanich sometimes buried their fresh salmon in the ground for ten days or more before boiling them in wooden boxes. The Indians around Sardis [near Chilliwack] often boiled salmon (and also sturgeon) in a canoe, and with a wooden spoon skimmed off the fat into bags of sturgeon or bear bladders.

The enormous quantities of clam shells in the kitchen middens along the coast indicate the importance of clams in the diet. The women dug them out on the beaches with sharpened stakes and carried them home in baskets of cedar bark or spruce roots. Sea urchin eggs were gathered with light cedar bark nets, about the size and shape of a large bucket, fastened to long wooden handles; a few octopus were captured with the two-pointed spears, and some crabs in wicker traps. These and other sea foods gave variety to the diet, but did not play an important role in Saanich economy.

3

Dwellings

Only the oldest Saanich Indians today recall the long shed-roofed dwellings which seem to have been the characteristic homes of all the Coast Salish at the beginning of the nineteenth century. The houses in the Songish village at Victoria, built after the establishment there of a Hudson's Bay Company fort and dismantled about 1880, were shed-roofed, and one persisted near Duncan until about the same time.[1] On the Saanich Peninsula itself, however, dwellings of this type seem to have been replaced about the middle of the century by gabled-roofed ones that combined both native and European characteristics.

Judging from the houses still standing on the Saanich Peninsula and near Duncan, this gable-roofed dwelling averaged from sixty to eighty feet long by thirty-five to forty feet wide, with wallboards outside the posts running perpendicular, not horizontal as in the shed-roofed type, and with a roof of overlapping boards or shingles. There were usually two doors, one in a corner of the long side, the other at the opposite end of the house near the middle of the short side. The interior had no flooring and was not divided into compartments except by temporary mats, but around the four walls ran a low wide platform on and under which the inmates stored some of their possessions, depositing the remainder, especially cedar bark sacks filled with dried fish, on racks suspended from the rafters. They slept on the platform, lying feet to feet and head to head, on mattresses of rush mats and blankets made from [mountain] goat wool, or, before goat wool became plentiful, on blankets made from nettle fibres spun with bird down, or on cedar bark mats interwoven with the same down.[2] These nettle-and-down mattresses were very strong and warm, but because they rapidly spoiled with dampness, the Saanich, at least, never used them in their summer camps where they slept on the bare ground, but substituted seal or sea lion skins. Three or four families generally occupied a single house, and the women took turns in cooking for the entire household over one of the fireplaces in the middle of the floor.

---

1   James Douglas, HBC chief factor and later colonial governor of Vancouver Island, founded the post (Fort Victoria), in 1843; Ormsby, "Douglas," 240. –Ed.
2   Peter Pierre [aka Old Pierre], a Katzie native, said that on the lower Fraser, some mattresses were woven from dog's hair (see Chapter 4).

Fig. 2.—Section of Lku'ñgɛn House.

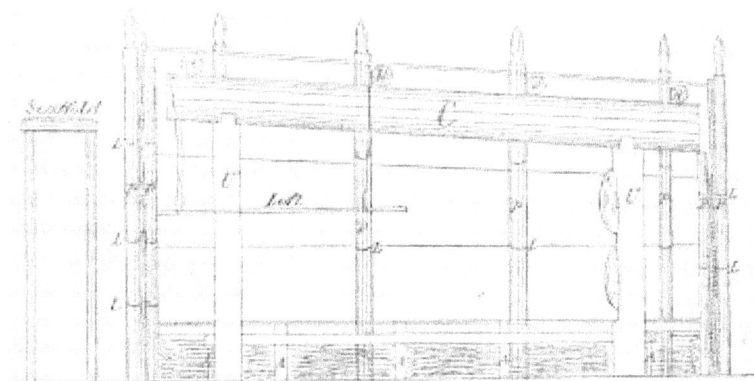

Plan of Lkū'men [Lekwungen/Songish] House

Franz Boas has published a plan of the older, shed-roofed type of house [see illustration above], and several of the early explorers have left us rather indefinite verbal descriptions. Some of these houses attained enormous lengths. One, visited by Simon Fraser on the river that bears his name, was

> Six hundred and forty feet long by sixty broad, under one roof; the front is eighteen feet high and the covering is slanting; all the apartments, which are separated by petitions, are square, except the chief's which is ninety feet long. In this room, the posts or pillars are nearly three feet diameter at the base and diminish gradually to the top. In one of these posts is an oval opening answering the purpose of a door through which one man may crawl in or out. Above, on the outside, are carved a human figure as large as life, with other figures in imitation of beasts and birds. These buildings have no flooring the fires are in the center and the smoke goes out an opening at the top.[3]

Fraser mentions no door except the oval opening in the carved post of the chief's room, which may have been a corner post, but is more likely to have been a centre post, thus corresponding to the doorway in the northern type of house seen by [British explorer John] Meares at Nootka, and common in the Queen Charlotte Islands down to the second half of the nineteenth century.[4] In Fraser's house there must have been other doors along the front leading

---

3   Fraser, "Journal of a Voyage," 196–97.
4   Among the W̱SÁNEĆ and other Coast Salish peoples, the term "chief" does not denote a position of political authority. Although it may be translated as "chief," the SENĆOŦEN word SIYI,ÁM (siyi?ém) properly refers to an individual, female or male, of high social status. Suttles notes that as a term of address, "it was the equivalent of 'Sir' or 'Madam,' or perhaps 'My Lord' or 'My Lady' …"; Salish Essays, 177. –Ed.

into the different partitions or rooms, perhaps, too, one at the end opposite the chief's room, and one at the back; but there were apparently no corridors or lane-ways from front to back separating the different rooms, as in the shed-roofed houses that Captain James Cook visited at Nootka:

The houses are disposed in three ranges or rows, rising gradually behind each other; the largest being that in front, and the others less; besides a few straggling, or single ones, at each end. These ranges are interrupted or disjoined at irregular distances, by narrow paths, or lanes, that pass upward; but those which run in the direction of the houses, between the rows, are much broader. Though there be some appearance of regularity in this disposition, there is none in the single houses; for each of the divisions, made by the paths, may be considered either as one house, or as many; there being no regular or complete separation, either without or within, to distinguish them by. They are built of very long and broad planks, resting upon the edges of each other, fastened or tied by withes of pine bark, here and there; and have only slender posts, or rather poles, at considerable distances, on the outside, to which they are also tied; but within are some larger poles placed aslant. The height of the sides and ends of these habitations, is seven or eight feet; but the back part is a little higher, by which means the planks, that compose the roof, slant forward, and are laid on loose, so as to be moved about; either to be put close, to exclude the rain; or in fair weather, to be separated, to let in the light, and carry out the smoke. They are, however, upon the whole, miserable dwellings, and constructed with little care or ingenuity. For, though the side-planks be made to fit pretty closely in some places, in others they are quite open, and there are no regular doors into them; the only way of entrance being either by a hole, where the unequal length of the planks has accidentally left an opening; or, in some cases, the planks are made to pass a little beyond each other, or overlap, about two feet asunder; and the entrance is in this space. There are also holes, or windows, in the sides of the houses to look out at; but without any regularity of shape or disposition; and these have bits of mat hung before them, to prevent the rain getting in.

On the inside, one may frequently see from one end to the other of these ranges of building without interruption. For though, in general, there be the rudiments, or rather vestiges, of separation on each side, for the accommodation of different families, they are such as do not intercept the sight; and often consist of no more than pieces of plank running from the side toward the middle of the house; so that, if they were complete, the whole might be compared to a long stable, with double range of stalls, and a broad passage in the middle. Close to the sides, in each of these parts, is a little bench of boards, raised five or six inches higher than the rest of the floor, and covered with mats, on which the family sit and sleep. These benches are commonly seven or eight feet long, and four or five broad. In the middle of the floor, between them, is the fire-place, which has neither hearth nor chimney. In one house, which was in the end of a middle range, almost quite separated from the rest by a high close partition, and the most regular, as to design, of any that I saw, there were four of these benches; each of which held a single family, at a corner, by without any separation by boards; and the middle part of the house appeared common to them all.[5]

It appears from Cook's description that the Nootka built rows of small, shed-roofed dwellings that might be called either compartments (or rooms), because all in each row were joined together by a common roof, or houses, because although joined by this common roof, each was separated from its neighbours by a narrow corridor. Seeing that there were no fixed walls between them, but, in some cases at least, mere pieces of wood, easily removable, that ran out towards the middle, the term compartment might seem more applicable.

Potlatch at Nanaimo, BC [showing shed-roof house], c. 1880

---

5   Cook, *Voyage to the Pacific*, 314–15.

An exactly similar building plan appears in a photograph taken at Nanaimo in 1880 [see illustration above] which shows the back of a row of shed-roofed compartments or dwellings with lanes or corridors separating most or all of them, and on the extreme left, two single, shed-roof houses corresponding to the straggling ones present in Nootka. In one respect these Nanaimo dwellings differ from the Nootka ones; their roofs slope downward toward the back, not upward, so that the highest portions are the fronts. Higher in front also is the Songish house at Victoria, depicted in a painting by Paul Kane in the 1850s [see illustration below].[6] There appear to be no lanes or corridors separating the compartments, though the painting shows a low door near the junction. They correspond in this respect to two houses near Duncan described to me by two old Indians, George Kwakaston of Koksilah, and Johnson of Quamichan, who were familiar with them in childhood.

Interior of a Lodge, Vancouver Island

The first of these houses stood about 1870 at Quamichan, where it sheltered all the families of that community. It was from 700 to 800 feet long, very similar, apparently, to the house seen by Simon Fraser except that it lacked the special compartment for the chief. There were three entrances, all rectangular, one in each of the two short ends, and one in the middle of the long side, facing the Cowichan River. The interior was divided into rooms on each side by fixed wooden partitions, leaving a wide aisle down the middle, the entire length of the building, in which the villagers celebrated their dances; and ev-

---

6   This illustration, with a caption reading "Interior of a Coast Salish Lodge at Esquimalt, B.C.," appears in Jenness's *Indians of Canada* (p. 140). On the National Gallery of Canada website, however, the painting is called "Interior of a Clallam Winter Lodge, Vancouver Island, c 1851–56"; http://gallery.ca/en/see/collections/artwork.php?mkey=4410. –Ed

ery room had two rows of benches, the lower for seats, the upper for sleeping. Each family had its own fireplace, but quite often one cooked for all the rest, in which case the men ate together, and the women and children afterwards. There was no palisade around this house, because its distance from the sea sheltered it from sudden attack.

The other house also stood near Duncan, but its exact locality I did not ascertain. Although only about one hundred feet long, much smaller than the Quamichan house, twelve families occupied it, six married brothers and their six married sisters. Each family had its own compartment or room, separated from one another, however, not by fixed partitions, but by rush mats that were removed at potlatches, leaving the whole house open. As usual, the walls were lined with rush mats, but the position of the doors, and whether there were two rows of benches or only one, I failed to enquire.

We find still a third pattern of settlement near the mouth of the Fraser River (possibly Musqueam), where, in a row facing the water, the natives seem to have built a number of small, single-roomed dwellings so far apart that it was impossible to unite them under a single roof [see illustration below]. It was a village of this type, apparently, but of rather larger houses, that Menzies inspected at Boundary Bay; it was a

> ... large deserted Village capable of containing at least 4 or 500 Inhabitants, though it was now in perfect ruins—nothing but the skeletons of the houses remained, these however were sufficient to show their general form structure & position. Each house appeared distinct & capacious of the form of an oblong square, & they were arranged in three separate rows of considerable length; the Beams consisted of huge long pieces of Timber placed in Notches on the top of supporters 14 feet from the ground, but by what mechanical power the Natives had raised these bulky beams to that height they could not conjecture. Three supporters stood at each end for the longitudinal beams & an equal number were arranged on each side for the support of smaller cross beams in each house.[7]

These varying descriptions leave little doubt that the Coast Salish did not build their houses to a single pattern, but modified them as circumstances required. Such is the opinion of Mr. W.A. Newcombe, to whom I am indebted for the photograph of a shed-roof dwelling at Nanaimo (see above). He writes:

> As you [Jenness] are aware from your visits to many of the "old middens" in the Coast Salish area, few of the localities permitted the continuous structures for many hundreds of feet as stated by some of the early writers; the rising or falling of the ground level, local streams, points, etc. caused a break in the structural line ... As far

---

7   Menzies, *Vancouver's Voyage*, p. 60.

Fraser River Dwellings

as interior arrangement is concerned the area occupied by the family was governed by its size. This practice was retained until quite recent times in the barn-like (gabled) houses of which you saw a number of examples. The individual groups were arranged along both walls. There were one or two doors, sometimes at the ends, in other cases on the sides, depending on which was the most convenient to the canoe landing. What I remember of my earlier visits to these [gabled] houses is an apparent jumble. It was hard to distinguish a dividing line in the interior of the house between two families other than the matting partitions in the sleeping quarters. The belongings hanging from the house beams and those on the ground towards the centre of the house did not appear in any particular section to have any relation to the sleeping quarters. Some sort of order was made of this jumble, no doubt, when the house was to be used for ceremonial purposes, but otherwise the Indian was similar to many whites today, leaving things scattered about ready for the next meal or for whatever the items were used for.[8]

It would have been impossible for the Indians to build houses of this character without metal tools had they not been surrounded with magnificent stands of soft red cedar trees, which tower to a height of fifty or one hundred feet without a single branch. To fell them the Saanich hacked all around the trunk with a stone chisel set in bone or antler, using a heavy hand hammer, also fashioned from stone. A number of these stone chisels and hammers have been found in cedar swamps. Two old men stated that instead of a chisel of

---

8 W.A. Newcombe to D. Jenness, 17 June 1939. –Ed.

stone they sometimes used one made from the sharpened leg bone or antler of the elk, but they disagreed as to whether or not it was necessary to char the trunk in such cases.[9] After the tree had fallen they split the straight-grained log with wooden wedges, and dressed the rough planks with small hand adzes. Thus they obtained posts and rafters for the frames of their houses, and planks for the walls and roofs as well as for the boxes and chests that held their food and household possessions; the house planks required no further dressing, but those used for chests and boxes were smoothed with dogfish skin. Incidentally, it was with the same four tools—chisel, hammer, wedge, and adze—that they hollowed out the trunk of the cedar to make their canoe. Some of them opened out the hollowed log by heating water inside it and spreading it with cross-bars; but an east Saanich native said that his people did not soften the wood with water, but warmed it by building fires along the outside. After finishing the inside of the canoe, the maker turned it over and charred and trimmed the outside, giving it a final smoothing with hemlock and other branches, since dogfish was too scarce to use on so large a surface.

George Kwakaston described how the people in his district, near Duncan, handled the heavy pillars and rafters of their houses in the middle of the nineteenth century; his description probably holds true of other Salish natives. At that period, a notable warrior named Tzuhaylem decided to settle on the then-uninhabited Khenipsen reserve, at the mouth of the Cowichan River, and to build for himself and his retainers one of the later type, low-gabled houses.[10] Higher up the river, for its ridgepole, they felled a cedar tree with a trunk about four feet in diameter, cut holes at regular intervals along its length, and inserted stout poles in the holes. Three or four men then lifted each pole and carried the log to the river, where they dropped it into the water and let it float down to the sea.

At the chosen site in Khenipsen they dug a deep hole for each of the two pillars on which the ridgepole would rest, and laid a broad plank against the back of the hole so that the bottom of the pillar would slide downward. Then, with poles beneath, they lifted the top end of the pillar until it was high enough to be caught in a V formed by two struts that were notched into each other and lashed in such a way that they opened and closed like shears. By using a number of such struts and gradually closing them at the bottoms, they succeeded in raising each pillar high enough to slide into its hole and stand vertical. Then they tamped it in place, and braced it with posts and anchor ropes until it was firm enough to receive the ridgepole.

Men from villages all around Duncan gathered to help with the ridgepole. First they lifted one end by means of the poles in the holes, resting it on

---

9　William Sepass, a Sardis [lower Fraser] native, said that when using the elk horn chisel alone it was necessary to char the tree, but that an elk horn chisel was often used in conjunction with the stone chisel to knock off the loosened chips, in which case charring was unnecessary.

10　Elsewhere, the famed warrior's name is spelled Tzouhalem. A mountain, said to be named for him, is situated a short distance north-east of Duncan; Rozen, "Place Names," 142–43.

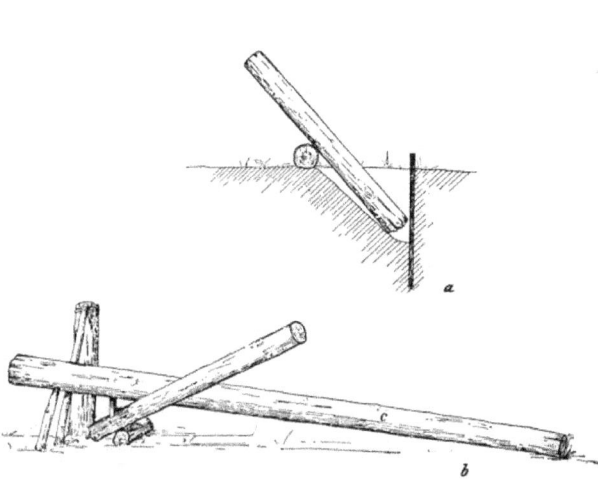

Kwakiutl Engineering
(top) method of raising house post;
(bottom) method of raising roof beam

posts of various lengths until it was high enough to receive the struts, which also were of different lengths. Then with their struts they raised it a trifle higher than its pillar, but its weight was so tremendous that to lower it again, even a very little, they had to dig under the struts before they would open. Raising the other end of the ridge-pole from the ground was even more difficult, though they finally accomplished that also in the same way. Tzuhaylem made only one door into this house, in the middle of one of the shorter sides; and, for still greater protection, he surrounded it with a mound and a palisade pierced by a single gate that was guarded by a sentry. He did not subdivide the interior into rooms, though at one time he is said to have kept in it ten women, besides numerous retainers and slaves.

It was the custom of the Saanich, along with other Coast Salish Indians, to remove the wall boards of their houses in summer and use them for temporary shelters at fishing and other camps where they intended to stay for several weeks. That explains why in many places early navigators saw only the frames of houses, and imagined the settlements had been abandoned—as indeed, they were, though only for two or three months. On brief journeys, when it was not convenient to freight heavy house planks, the Indians contented themselves with a few rush mats thrown over some cross-poles. Slaves commonly lived in the same houses as their masters, sleeping wherever they were assigned places, since each family arranged its space to suit its needs; but if their masters died and left them without homes they too made dwellings for themselves of poles and rush mats, in which they lived winter and summer alike.

Neither the Saanich nor the Cowichan Indians gave names to their houses. The carvings on their house posts did not represent crests, as in the gabled dwellings of northern British Columbia, but dream spirits of their owners, or, in one case at least, of the man who was hired to carve them. This was a house on the Quamichan reserve, near Duncan, whose pillars were carved by a Vancouver (Musqueam) native.[11] Actually, it is not the pillars themselves that were carved, but the heavy false boards nailed to their fronts. The four boards on one side depict fisher, those on the other a fanciful creature believed to fly through the air and to prey on two-headed snakes. They were initially carved for a house on the neighbouring Somenos reserve; when that fell, the nephew of the original owner removed them to the newer house at Quamichan, which later passed to another nephew, the present owner. On the Fraser River,

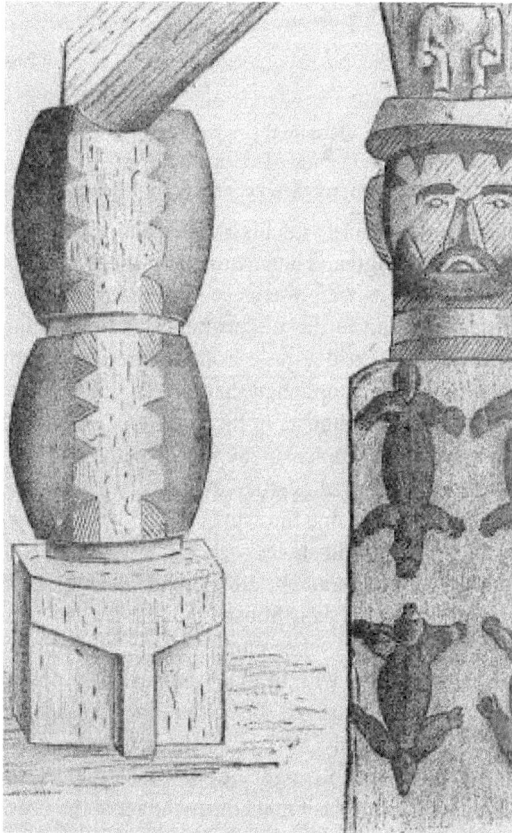

Lkū´men [Lekwungen/Songhees] Carved House Posts

11   The same Musqueam artist carved four fishers and a two-headed snake on his own coffin, which was later transferred from the Musqueam reserve to the National Museum, in Ottawa; see photo in Jenness, *Indians of Canada*, 349.

a house post carved with human and animal figures served also as a door, like the posts in the gabled form of house described by Fraser (see above); but the Songish, Saanich, Cowichan, and Nanaimo natives seemed to have no recollection of this feature in their dwellings. The carving was invariably naturalistic, not conventionalized, though in recent times some conventional-ized carvings of northern type have appeared at Chemainus and other places farther south in Coast Salish territory.

The furniture in the houses, apart from the bedding and the rush mats, con-sisted mainly of rectangular boxes and chests of various sizes, all made from cedar. Some, fitted with lids, held spare clothing, paraphernalia used in cere-monies, fishing tackle, or miscellaneous tools and weapons; others, without lids, were cooking vessels, water buckets, or trays for serving up meat and fish. Few if any of these boxes bore animal carvings such as were common farther north. Food was generally stored in cedar bark bags and baskets, but some also found its way into these wooden chests.

...

Every village appointed some old man to go from house to house at dawn, greet the inmates, see that the boys had gone down to the sea for their morning plunge, and that the slave-women were tending to their cooking. There were no regular meal hours when the men were at home, but the Saanich usually ate twice, once in the morning and again towards night. The morning meal commonly consisted of dried fish dipped in some kind of oil, generally seal or porpoise oil, and fern roots baked in the ashes of the fire. Most families served up their oil in large horse clam shells, but nobles sometimes used the highly prized haliotis [abalone] shells. The main dish of the evening meal was roasted or boiled fish, but supplementing it were dried berries, wild carrots, or some other vegetable food. After Europeans introduced potatoes into British Columbia, the Saanich often bought them from mainland natives, paying as much as one goat wool blanket for a small basketful.[12]

When camping alone, all the members of the family ate together, but in the big village houses, as we have seen, it was quite common for the women to cook in turn for the whole household, and the men then ate first, the women and children afterwards. Occasionally a man invited some friends from anoth-er house to dine with him, or was himself invited out, in which case, again, the men ate alone and each guest received some extra food to carry home with him. Polygamists had to provide each wife with a separate compartment, or room in which she kept her own stock of dried fish and berries. Slaves usually

---

12 The earliest European accounts of the Coast Salish, dating to the 1790s, describe them as hunters and fishers. But as Wayne Suttles has written, half a century later "Indian women of nearly every tribe... [were] cultivating patches of potatoes with digging sticks." The practice was probably encouraged by the region's pioneer generation of fur trading outfits; Suttles, *Salish Essays*, 137–39. –Ed.

ate after the women and children, but occasionally with them. Under ordinary circumstances food was so plentiful that no one ever went hungry.[13]

To light a fire, the Saanich struck together two lumps of pyrite and caught the resultant spark in crushed, dry cedar bark; or else, more commonly perhaps, they drilled a stick of cedar into a log of cedar;[14] the friction then ignited the powder at the base of the drill. Both methods were troublesome, especially in rainy weather, so in their settlements the natives lit a cedar bark torch in another house if their own fire went out, and when they were travelling they enclosed some live coals in large shells.

They prepared their fish and meat in one of three ways. When cooking for a few people only they generally roasted it before a fire on sticks; but when cooking for many, they boiled it by dropping hot stones into a wooden box half-filled with water. The ordinary cooking box required six stones, but the exact number naturally varied with the size of the box. The third method was to bake the meat or fish on a bed of stones that had been brought to a moderate heat by a fire kindled on top of it. The charcoal and ashes were swept away with branches, the meat laid directly on the bare stone, surrounded with moss, and covered with old rush mats that were then buried under clean sand or gravel.

Camas roots were cooked by the third method, on hot stones, which were covered with kelp, and the kelp first with bark that had been pierced in numerous places, then with salal and blackberry bushes.[15] The roots were piled on the bushes, and water poured through a hole in the centre of the pile, creating a column of steam. Everything was then buried under a layer of fern and other leaves and covered with about three inches of sand. Finally, a great fire was built over the heap, and the camas left to steam for from twenty-four to thirty-six hours. A favourite dish was camas whipped up with soapberries.

Fern roots (*Pteris aquilina*) were roasted over a fire, stripped of their outer integuments and pounded with a stick to release the fibres. Dipped in seal or porpoise oil that had been previously warmed in a horse clam shell, they were a popular after-meat course.

The usual beverage was cold water, but the Indians enjoyed the broth from boiled fish or meat; with the broth made from meat they sometimes mixed the animal's blood. They made, too, infusions from various plants, but these were primarily medicinal.

---

13 Slavery is discussed in Chapter 5. For a more detailed account of the practice in the Pacific northwest, see Donald, Aboriginal Slavery. –Ed.

14 William Sepass, of Sardis, said that his people used a hearth and drill of very dry cottonwood root, placing shredded cedar bark under the hearth to catch the spark.

15 Mrs Latasse, of Tsartlip, said arbutus bark was used, but whether this bark was large and thick enough for the task seems doubtful.

4

Clothing and Personal Adornment

So mild is the climate in the south of British Columbia that among the Saanich Indians, as in other Coast Salish groups, men often wore no clothing at all in summer, and women only a diaper (*st'kwaelak*) [loincloth] woven from cedar bark or dog hair. The women, however, generally covered their diaper with a short cedar bark skirt (*sqallitch*) that was tied around the waist, reached to about the knees, and, sometimes at least, was laced down the thigh.[1] Old [Peter] Pierre said that on the lower Fraser River men always wore loincloths of either cedar bark or tanned deerskin; but on the Saanich Peninsula these loincloths, together with deerskin shirts (*smeluk*), sleeved or sleeveless, that both sexes put on in cold weather, came into use, apparently, only in the first half of the nineteenth century. At that period a few men also wore moccasins and even leggings, whereas in earlier times both sexes went barefoot, or else covered their feet with strips of deer or elk skin tied around the ankles.

To protect themselves against flies the natives rubbed grease and ochre over their bodies. In rainy weather they wore a hat of woven cedar bark or spruce roots (*sqaas*), and also a mat of woven cedar bark (*lapus*) either square so that it could be thrown over the shoulders and tied at the neck with sinew, or rectangular, with a hole through the middle so it could be drawn over the head like a poncho. According to Mrs Latasse, similar ponchos or capes, occasionally fringed around the bottom with sea otter fur and with the down of water birds woven in with the cedar bark to make them warmer, were worn also in winter; but at that season most of the natives wrapped goat wool blankets (*sorqual*) around their shoulders, or, if they lacked wool blankets, robes of deer or elk hide (*spetsatsan*), seal, sea lion, or sea otter skins.[2] In cold weather, too, a few of them replaced the rain hat with a cap of racoon or other fur.

Such was the general costume of the Saanich Indians, in common with other south Vancouver Island natives and with those of the lower Fraser River; however, differences in rank occasioned differences in its details. Thus only poor or slave women wore diapers of cedar bark; women of high rank wove their diapers, and occasionally also their skirts, from dog hair, which the Saanich beat with diatomaceous earth and spun with fireweed fibre before working it up into garments. The dogs (see illustration below) that supplied this hair belonged to a small breed [Salish wool dog] now extinct, though very numerous before the introduction of trade blankets destroyed their utility.[3]

---

1   The Indians preferred the bark of the yellow cedar for clothing, the bark of the red cedar for mats and baskets.

2   When this blanket bore colored designs, the Katzie Indians, on the lower Fraser, called it *hoksalwit*.

3   This Paul Kane painting appears in Jenness's *Indians of Canada* (p. 68) with the following

Woman Weaving a Blanket

During the sockeye and humpback salmon season the Indians commonly abandoned these dogs on islands with whatever dried fish remained over from the winter; then they recovered them in the autumn and sheared them with mussel shell knives. In 1936 I noticed an old, creamy-white dog on the East Saanich [Tsawout] reserve which seemed to carry some of the old strain; its owner had sheared it every autumn and sold the hair to a relative on the mainland, who knitted it into mittens.[4]

In pre-European times, again, goat wool blankets were rather scarce, especially on Vancouver Island, because the natives killed comparatively few mountain goats prior to the introduction of firearms. Consequently, the majority of the Indians wore fur robes in winter; but while the leading men and women paraded in sea otter and other rich furs, the slaves, who were always scantily clad, were fortunate if they could secure a common deerskin. Rain capes of woven cedar bark, and rain hats of cedar bark or spruce roots, generally indicated prosperity and high standing; the poorer people and the slaves wore rush mats (*snowas*) woven along the top edge and either tied around the neck like capes, or worn as hoods so that they could cover the head and trail far down the back. Most hats were made of cedar bark, not of spruce root; occasionally a little goat wool was woven in with the bark. Some bore animal designs painted on their surfaces; whether any designs were also woven into the hats, as at Nootka, I did not discover. A west Saanich woman said that the

---

caption: "Coast Salish woman weaving a blanket of dog's hair and mountain-goat wool; in the foreground is a shorn dog." The Royal Ontario Museum notes the weaver is either Songhees or Saanich; http://images.rom.on.ca/ public/index. php?function=image&action=simpledetail&image_name=ROM2005_5163_1 –Ed.

4   See F.W. Howay, "Dog's Hair Blankets."

designs were heraldic, referring to some episode in the family history; but I obtained no confirmation of her statement.[5]

The Vancouver Island communities obtained practically all their goat wool and goat wool blankets from the mainland natives in exchange for rush mats, woven hats, and skins of deer, seal, and sea lion, and in the nineteenth century, potatoes.[6] Apparently they never mixed the wool with cedar bark, dog hair,[7] bird down, or any other material, though they sometimes dyed it brownish red with alder bark, brown or dark red with hemlock bark, and gray with willow bark.[8] Like dog hair, it was cleaned by pounding diatomaceous earth into it, then spun on a distaff and woven on a crude loom.[9] Most of the blankets were pure white, but during the nineteenth century the Indians often introduced into their wefts, at wide intervals, bands of brightly coloured stroud [imported coarse woolen fibre]. The designs on the decorated blankets that utilized coloured yarns were invariably geometric. The garment was sometimes thrown over the shoulders and pinned at the neck; more often, it passed over one shoulder (commonly the left) and under the other so that it left an arm free, and was fastened in front with a wooden or bone pin, or else held in by a belt.

The tanning of the deer and elk hides devolved on the hunter, not on his wife. If he wished to retain the fur he scraped away all the fat and flesh from the underside with a stone or bone scraper, rubbed it with the brains of the animal,[10] and, after letting the brains soak in for a few days, dried the hide in the sun. Skins for de-hairing he first soaked in water for from four to five days, when the hair could be readily scraped off with a bone or wooden knife. These hairless skins were not usually dried in the sun, but in the smoke of a fire.[11]

Since their clothing was not tailored, the Saanich had comparatively little use for thread. The back sinew of the deer supplied such as they did require, and a wooden or bone awl took the place of a needle.

---

5   Two Katzie natives, Peter Pierre and his son Simon, said that the woven hat characteristic of the Fraser River area, and also of south Vancouver Island, had no brim in front, but a very wide one behind to protect the shoulders. Moreover, it was pointed on top, or slightly knobbed, not rounded like some hats made in recent times by the North Vancouver (Capilano) [Squamish] natives, who had copied, they claimed, a more northern style.

6   See page 33, footnote 12. –Ed.

7   William Sepass asserted that on the lower Fraser River, the Indians added to the goat wool some dog hair, crushed cedar bark, and bird feathers, and beat them all together with two sticks before spinning and weaving. The warp was either nettle fibre, or, preferably, a certain species of grass.

8   Other dyes used by the Saanich, but for basketry rather than woolen blankets, were: a brown from balsam bark; a black from swamp water; a slate-blue from a certain mud; a pink by combining ochre and white balsam bark; and a yellow from the Oregon grape (*Berberis aquifolium*), or else from a moss (*Leucolepis acanthoneura*).

9   See Kissell, "New Type of Spinning"; "Salish Blanket Pattern."

10   At Sardis, and perhaps elsewhere on the lower Fraser, boiled salmon heads were substituted occasionally for animal brains.

11   Old Bob said that his people never used a stone scraper for removing the fat, but a tool made from the deer's leg bone, split and sharpened along one edge. Duncan natives (and probably others) commonly used the shoulder blade of a deer to scrape away the hair.

...

In pre-European times women commonly wore necklaces made from arbutus berries or from the dried fruits of the wild rose; occasionally, strings of small stone beads were also worn. Whether they had armlets and anklets, and of what kind, I could not discover. Haliotis and dentalium shells were extremely rare before the nineteenth century; the former served not only for ear and nose pendants, but to decorate the front of a nobleman's war hat or cedar chest. In the early years of that century shells of various kinds became quite common, together with metal ornaments and glass beads, although the Saanich have never regarded beads with much favour.

What they lacked in ornaments, the Saanich made up for in paint. On every important occasion they streaked their faces with ochre or with a black pigment obtained by mixing fat with the charcoal from burned devil's club [*Oplopanax horridus*]. They often laid on these paints in definite patterns to represent their guardian spirits or to convey some other religious meaning; and, to heighten the effect, sprinkled on a top layer of glistening mica. Very

FIG. 11.—Tattooing.

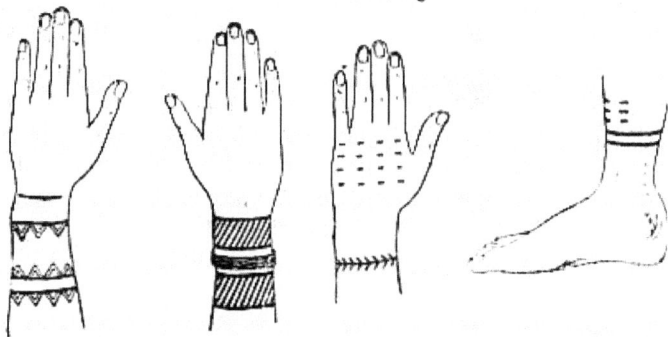

Lkū´men [Lekwungen/Songhees] Tattooing

rarely they used also a white paint from diatomaceous earth, but only for the purpose of banishing infection of supernatural origin.

Men seldom resorted to tattooing, and when they did they merely marked on their arms some design that commemorated an adventure, real or imaginary, of an ancestor.[12] About the age of puberty, however, all girls (except perhaps slaves) were tattooed by a skilful relative on the face and wrists, sometimes, too, on the backs of the hands, the legs, and the bosom. The usual marks, according to Mrs Latasse, were four parallel lines across each cheek and two or three short ones on the chin, parallel lines all or part-way round the

---

12   An old Tsartlip man bore on his left forearm a heart, tattooed with needle and thread by his mother when he was a small boy, for what purpose hid did not know.

wrists, and rows of W or V-shaped lines on the backs of the hands. The skin, she said, was first punctured with a sharp bone awl and the wound rubbed with a mixture of fat and charcoal obtained by burning devil's club, giving a bluish-black colouration. The same woman declared that they produced red tattoo marks through the use of a red powder obtained by burning together cedar, alder, and a fungus that grows on hemlock trees.[13]

Boas states that the Songish women tattooed themselves by introducing charcoal from bulrushes under the skin with a needle held horizontally.[14] Mrs Johson, an old Cowichan woman on the Quamichan reserve, near Duncan, bore on the back of one hand several parallel lines made by running a nettle fibre under the skin with a find needle of hardwood.

---

13   George Dawson has reported red tattooing among the Haida Indians of the Queen Charlotte Islands; "Queen Charlotte Islands," 108.
14   Boas, "Second General Report," 574–75.

5

Social Organization and Potlatch

Every Saanich (and indeed almost every Coast Salish) village (*auhwulmuk*)[1] was a unit by itself, linked by economic and cultural ties, and by intermarriage, with neighbouring villages, but politically quite distinct. During the first half of the nineteenth century the old village near Sidney that has since disappeared contained six and probably more big houses, each of which sheltered several families, while some single families occupied smaller huts; and there were at least two big houses in each of the other Saanich villages. Just as the villages lacked all political cohesion, so also did the big houses in the villages, even though they were separated from one another by only a few yards. Thus the enemies of one household could be the friends of another in the same village; and one household would send out a party to trade or raid without consulting or notifying the others. Faced with a common danger, as from war parties of Comox or Kwakiutl Indians, all the households in a village united in self-defence; and they collaborated at certain feasts and ceremonies; but as soon as the emergency or special occasion passed they immediately dissolved this temporary union and lapsed into their customary independence.

The real political unit was therefore not the village, but the big house occupied by a number of kinsfolk—an enlarged or genealogical "family" to which the Saanich applied the term *hunit´se´lakum*, and we, in speaking of the similar European nobility, the term "House."[2] Each Saanich House, as we may call it then, possessed its own long shed-roofed dwelling,[3] its own camas beds on Galiano and neighbouring islands, its own fishing place on the beach at Point Roberts, its own set of ancestral names or titles, and its own stock of legends, songs, and medicinal remedies.[4] Other Indians knew some of these songs and legends but might not recite them in public, or depict them on any carving or painting, any more than they might usurp one of the titles.[5] Whether the Saanich set up weirs in any place I did not discover; if

---

1   The contemporary SENĆOŦEN term for village is Á,LEN,ENEȻ (*ʔeʔəŋə́nəkʷ*) –Ed.

2   For a contemporary interpretation of the *hunit´se´lakum* (*hwunutsaluwum*, in Hul'qumi'num'), see Thom, "Senses of Place," 273–80. Thom describes this central unit of Coast Salish society as a bilateral cognatic descent group. –Ed.

3   The extremely long houses reported from two or three places in Coast Salish territory must have sheltered more than one House and its dependents.

4   Additionally, the patrimony of each house included *siwín*, the knowledge associated with the work of priests; See page 10, footnote 8. –Ed.

5   Almost any departure from established custom might become the privilege of a House, heritable by later generations, and by them alone, provided the public had ratified it; and the public ratified it when, during some potlatch, it heard the statement of claim without demur and accepted the gifts that followed the statement. All such privilege or rights, however, hinged upon proof of lineal descent, and the most obvious indication of such descent was the possession of an ancestral title.

so, they, too, were almost certainly the property of individual Houses, or of certain members of individual Houses, as they were around Duncan, where one stood in front of every large dwelling facing the Cowichan River, not blocking the stream completely, of course, but with gaps through which the salmon could ascend beyond.[6] On the other hand, the sea near the villages, the hunting grounds and berry patches round about, were common property; any villager, whatever his station in life, might fish and hunt wherever he wished within the village territory.

In one or two rare instances a House seems to have comprised merely a group of brothers with their married sons and grandchildren; but because mortality was high and many of the houses very large, the group commonly included first and second cousins and relatives even more remote. Each married family in this group occupied one segment, or room, in the dwelling; it owned the wall and roof boards of that segment, either through inheritance or through having cooperated in the building; and it might remove these boards whenever it wished, leaving that portion of the common home wide open.[7] Within its segment or room were its individual fireplace and racks for storing food and other possessions; but the families seldom confined themselves strictly to their own space or maintained any great semblance of orderliness.

Not all the residents of a House possessed equal standing. Those who had acquired ancestral names at potlatches were addressed by the honorific title *siem*,[8] whereas those who lacked such names because they could not afford the expense of potlatches ranked as "undistinguished people," or "commoners" (*sas musteemuch*).[9] Theoretically, not only did all Houses enjoy perfect equality, but so, too, did all the *siem*, or nobles, in each House, since they claimed a common ancestry and attached little or no importance to primogeniture. No village and no House, therefore, recognized any one officially as its chief. Nevertheless, nobles did differ from one another in prestige and influence, partly through their personal characters and achievements, and partly through the varying prestige attached to their titles, which depended to some extent to the prestige of previous incumbents. Generally, therefore, one noble exerted so much influence in his House that he became its leader (*salweans*) in fact, if not in theory; and if his House was numerically the strongest in the

---

6   Johnson, Jenness's Quamichan informant, said that the villages at Duncan formed a single unit, and that while each family might have its own weir on the river, all were free to hunt anywhere in the surrounding territory. George Kawkaston, of Koksilah, agreed with these points, adding that in the mid-nineteenth century, "west coast natives" began pushing into the hunting grounds around Cowichan Lake, giving rise to "several skirmishes" between the two peoples; Jenness, "Saanich Notes," 271–72. –Ed.

7   As a rule, a family only removed its wall and roof boards for temporary shelter in a spring or summer camp; but occasionally (e.g., in the event of a quarrel) it removed them permanently and used them for the construction of a new home.

8   Modern SENĆOŦEN uses the word *SI,ÁM* (*siʔém*) to refer to someone of "high class;" a "low class' person is *TSOS* (*tsas*); see also page 24, footnote 4. –Ed.

9   Another word, *sweeawilas*, was used sometimes, but meant strictly any person, even the young child of a *siem*, who had not received an ancestral name.

village, he was recognized as the principal man in the community. Less often, two or three men competed for the leadership.

Each House had its stock of names or titles that it handed down from one generation to another and guarded as jealously as the nobles of Europe guarded their titles. Some of them dated back, in theory, to a "golden age" when the world was very different; and they had descended in the same family line, century after century. In theory, too, the families had dwelt in the same localities from time immemorial, so that the names were inseparably linked with certain villages.[10] The Saanich villages, it is true, were so near to one another, and so closely related by intermarriage, that the titles current in any one of them received recognition in them all; but in other districts, even in Victoria and Duncan, they had no official standing. Inheritance of titles or of property, however, was not entirely restricted to the male line. A man acquired a title from his father's House, as a rule, because women commonly went to live with their husbands, and a child was raised in his father's community. If, for any reason, he was raised in this mother's village, or even if he visited it for any length of time, he received a title from her House that made him a full member of her community. The Saanich intermarried with so many of the surrounding Coast Salish groups that a man could find relatives nearly everywhere, and assume, or be given, a different name or title in each group. Yet there were two restrictions on multiplicity of titles: first, some, through their historic or legendary associations, carried greater significance than others, even in neighbouring groups, and a man naturally preferred to be known by an important title rather than by an insignificant one; and, second, every title required confirmation by the House and community that claimed it, and this confirmation was obtainable only at a potlatch, when the recipient or his sponsor had to disburse large amounts of food and property.

At the present day the Saanich, like other Coast Salish, have adopted European names by which they are known in ordinary life, and they use their old titles only on ceremonial occasions, mainly at the winter dances. Many, indeed, neither know nor trouble to acquire any titles to which their descent may entitle them, especially since potlatches are now prohibited and titles have lost their social significance.[11] Even before potlatches had been prohibited Mrs Latasse, of Tsartlip, whose parents had died when she was a little girl, failed to receive any title, and consequently bore only her childhood name, until she was thirty-two years old. At that point a sister whom she happened to visit during a potlatch at her old home, near Duncan, conferred on her two titles, one her mother's, Lateetlia, to be used in Duncan, the other her Saanich

---

10   According to George Kwakaston, the Cowichan people stem from "immigrants who moved down from the prairie lands at the headwaters of the Cowichan River" at some (unspecified) time in the past. He noted further that they learned to fish on reaching their new territory; before migration "they had lived by hunting only"; Jenness, "Saanich Notes," 271. –Ed.

11   An amendment to the federal Indian Act officially banned the potlatch in 1885. The prohibition remained on the books until 1951; Kew, "History," 167. –Ed.

grandmother's (mother's mother's) title, Swateesia, for use on the Saanich Peninsula. The sister merely invited all the principal women attending the potlatch to her house, and Mrs Latasse, mounting a high platform in front of it, threw strips of a goat wool blanket down to them to confirm their acceptance of her titles.

As this modern incident suggests, each House possessed two sets of titles, one for women only, the other for men. Every bearer of a title, man or woman, was a *siem*, a noble, and the children of nobles normally became nobles also in due course; the parents, or, if they were dead, the grandparents or near kinsfolk, gave a potlatch for each child and invested it with a title before or about the time it attained puberty.[12] Occasionally, however, a few children were passed over, either because their parents and kinfolk had fallen on hard times and could not afford the expense of a potlatch, or because some calamity had left the children without near kinsfolk who were able, or willing, to take an interest in their welfare.[13] Unless, through their own efforts, they later succeeded in gathering together enough food and property for a potlatch, these children never acquired titles, never attained the dignity of nobles, despite their birth, but swelled the ranks of the common people who attached themselves to various Houses for protection.

Contact with Europeans in the nineteenth century brought about a great change in the status of the nobles. Previously, no native unsupported by a considerable body of kinsmen and relatives could gather enough food and presents to hold a potlatch and entertain many guests for two or three days. It was therefore hopeless for a commoner to aspire to noble rank unless his skill as a hunter and fisherman, and his prowess in war, combined with a talent for leadership, attracted a body of retainers who were willing to work for his advancement and to support his right to some title, whether the right was real or fictitious. Such cases must have been comparatively rare; thus it was far easier to descend in the social scale than to ascend. But when Europeans abolished slavery,[14] the change furnished a labour market as open to the ex-slave and commoner as to the noble. This enabled one man to purchase with his year's wages as much food and goods as a whole village could have gathered previously in one year. As a result, commoners, and even ex-slaves, began to rival the nobles in the number and magnificence of their potlatches, and to assume titles to which they had no legitimate claim. This inevitably led to much fric-

12 Since the term *siem* carried an implication of mature years, these children were designated *see-ehl*, not *siem*; they became *siem* only in later years, generally after they had given potlatches on their own accounts.

13 There must have been numerous instances of this kind after the terrible smallpox epidemics that ravaged the population in the late eighteenth century, [and again at the start of the nineteenth].

14 Rather than being abolished, it is more the case that slavery among Northwest Coast peoples "withered away" during the mid to late 1800s, in large measure a result of the "cessation of warfare and the consequent end in the supply of new slaves"; Donald, *Aboriginal Slavery*, 244–45. –Ed.

tion and jealousy, but the helpless nobles could no longer uphold their old authority or stem the new economic and social currents that swirled around their doors. Before the end of the century every Indian, as an old man sadly stated, could assume a title and become a noble, if he wished, even though ancient prejudices still lingered and the upstart might be ridiculed behind his back.

Just as the manor lords of the Middle Ages upheld their state with a body of freemen and villeins [serfs], so the Houses of the Saanich Indians required the services of many commoners and slaves. It is almost impossible at this late date to calculate the numerical proportions of the three classes, notables, commoners, and slaves, but a rough guess would make the ratio 3:7:2. The slaves, who were at no time numerous, were either captives taken in raids or the descendants of such captives; but the origin of the commoners, who seem to have made up more than half the population, is less clear. The Saanich themselves account for them by the following legend, narrated by David Latasse, of Tsartlip.

> X̱e.ls, the great creator and transformer, created human beings in various places from some kind of earth, but he fashioned the stomachs of the women from bands of cherry bark so that they might expand during pregnancy. At Duncan he created a man called Hayletha, at Sooke another man named Tayakamat, with a wife, daughter, and a maid for the daughter. The girl and her maid walked from Sooke up to Duncan, where they spied on Hayletha as he talked with a female image he had made from rotten cedar; for Hayletha was lonely, and whenever he left his home to hunt or fish he would leave his distaff and the wool he spun on it in the hands of the image, as though it could spin it for him.
>
> After he had gone, the girls slipped into the house, spun the wool, and hid in some bushes before he returned. Hayletha was delighted at the industry of his image, and the next time he went out left more wool for it to spin; but this time the girls spun the wool and burned the image. He was sorely puzzled when he found only its ashes, but called out at last "I don't know who you are but come out and let me see you." The girls came out from their hiding place, and Hayletha married Tayakamat's daughter. From their children sprang the groups of Indians around Duncan, while the Sooke Indians are descendants of Tayakamat's other children. Later X̱e.ls created at Malahat a man named Hwan'am and his wife, and from this last couple came the Malahat and Saanich Indians. In the earliest times all alike ranked as nobles, but after they began to raid and enslave one another some of the nobles married their slaves, and the offspring of the mixed marriages became the commoners.

Whether, as this myth suggests, they were the offspring of nobles and captives, or of nobles who had been unable to keep up their stations, or of refugees and settlers from other districts—and it is probable that their number were recruited from all three—the commoners relied for security in their daily life on the protection of the nobles, and therefore attached themselves more or less closely to the different Houses. In many cases they seem not to have been assigned rooms or space in the long houses where the nobles dwelt, but to have erected small dwellings of their own a few yards away. While they might regulate their lives very much as they pleased, they were expected to man the canoes of the nobles, to assist in netting of deer and salmon, in the felling of trees and construction of dwellings, and generally to support their Houses both in peace and in war. In return, their Houses protected them from enslavement by other villages, and aided them in times of need.

Below the commoners were the slaves, who slept in the same houses as their noble masters and were distinguishable only by their poorer dress and greater activity. Men slaves did most of the hunting and fishing, gathered the firewood, helped in the felling of trees and making of canoes, and paddled their masters' canoes on ordinary excursions, but not on ceremonial occasions, or in war. Women slaves, who were valued as highly as men slaves, prepared and cooked the food, gathered clams, roots, and berries,[15] collected large quantities of cedar bark and rushes, and made from them clothing, baskets and mats.

Some slaves were the children of slave parents; others were captives taken in raids. The latter, when they lost their freedom, lost also their earlier names and were given new ones, occasionally derisive,[16] but more often terms taken from their places of capture or slave names current in the House of their captors. They might be addressed by these names, but a nobleman generally called his man slave "my younger brother," and a noblewoman called her female slave "my younger sister."

Slaves belonged to the individual nobles who had captured, purchased, or inherited them, but were subject to orders from other members of their owners' Houses, particularly from its leading man. Though absolutely in the power of their masters, they were seldom ill-treated, or even punished, their owners preferring to sell them to other villages if they were lazy or incorrigible. A certain nobleman on Mayne Island, who was killed later by a Saanich Indian, is said to have bruised and lacerated his slaves frequently by launching his canoe over their bodies; but this was exceptional and widely condemned. Generally speaking, they had the status of servants, and were often highly trusted and esteemed. They ate from the same dishes as their masters, shared many of the same pastimes, even obtained guardian spirits at times, and participated in the winter dances. Their heads were flattened in infancy like those of other Indians, and their children played with their masters' children, boys with boys and girls with girls.

---

15   Their mistresses helped them to gather berries, since this was an enjoyable pastime.
16   A famous Saanich warrior named one of his slave women "Worm," and afterwards married her.

Nobles rarely married slave women until the nineteenth century, when the social system was breaking down. A woman commoner who married a slave became a slave herself; but a woman slave who married a commoner was regarded as free (and her children free), though it did not necessarily improve her lot. A slave might become free, too, through the death of his master, but his freedom was so precarious that he often preferred to attach himself to another member of the same House rather than risk the danger of being enslaved by some other House. Slaves captured in raids soon received husbands and wives to make them more content with their fate.[17] In most cases, perhaps, they were content, or at least resigned, for they often fought bravely beside their masters when their villages were attacked. There was indeed no place to which they could flee without being enslaved again or returned to their masters, unless by good fortune they reached their earlier homes; being allowed to fish and hunt alone, they seldom even tried to run away, though they had many opportunities, as the following Saanich story illustrates.

Two slave girls belonging to my grandfather once tried to escape. The household was camping on one of the San Juan islands, the men engaged in halibut fishing, the women in gathering camas. One of the girls said to my grandmother "My companion's back is aching terribly. She wants me to stay home and rub her." My grandmother consented, but when everyone had gone the girls launched a small canoe and fled. The next day my grandfather saw them on the beach of a neighbouring island, crying, for they had taken no food with them. He sent my grandmother to bring them back. "Why are you staying here?" she asked them. "Why don't you come home?" The girls had been afraid to return home, though they were not punished in any way.

Though rare, a few did escape. David Latasse, now nearly ninety, remembered seeing in his boyhood another old man, also a native of Saanich, who had been carried off and enslaved by some Indians north of Comox. The slave had appeared so reconciled to his fate that he became his master's sole companion on several hunting trips. On one occasion when they were setting out to hunt, he asked his mistress to put an extra amount of food in the cedar bark bag because they would be absent rather longer than usual. Then, the first night they were away, he killed his master and fled south, paddling by night instead of by day. After making good progress for two or three days he became careless, and while paddling before dark, was captured and enslaved by the people of another village. There, too, however, he worked the same stratagem and succeeded in regaining his home on the Saanich Peninsula.

...

17   This was the case also at Nootka, apparently, for John Jewitt [a British ship's armourer], received a wife soon after his capture in the early 1800s; Jewett, *Adventures*.

There was very little privacy in the life of a Coast Salish Indian; even the room he occupied in the big house was not closed off from public view. He spoke and acted as a member of a group that observed his every movement, and he sought the approval and backing of the group on every notable occasion. Tradition had established for him a definite mode of obtaining this approval; he gave a public feast, or potlatch, at which he distributed gifts corresponding in number and value to his rank and wealth, and to the importance of the event that he was celebrating. For a minor event such as the naming of a child, even a noble might invite only the people of his own village and distribute a score or more of goat wool blankets, a very insignificant outlay; but if he were celebrating the erection of a new home, or assuming a new title, he invited guests from villages all around and distributed not only most of his own goods, but others borrowed from friends and kinsmen. It was by holding a big potlatch that lasted several days and was attended by hundreds of people that a man established his fame and reputation along the coast. Such a potlatch differed very little, except in its elaborateness, from a feast that lasted three or four hours only, and was attended by fellow villagers alone. The latter could be given by any man, commoner and noble alike, but it neither increased the giver's prestige, nor raised his status in his own and surrounding communities; rather, if he were a commoner, it exposed him to ridicule for imitating men of higher rank. The Indian therefore never regarded these intra-village feasts as true potlatches, but only such as brought in guests from all around, and through their magnificence and lavish outlays enhanced the fame and honour both of their sponsors, and of the village that supported them. With rare exceptions, none but the highest nobles could sponsor them in pre-European times, because they alone could amass the necessary food and goods; but when European settlement opened up new avenues to wealth, commoners, and even ex-slaves, began to rival the nobles, and even to outstrip them in the lavishness of their feasts.

The potlatch was really a many-sided institution.[18] It was a public assembly that ratified and celebrated important events such as marriages and the conclusion of peace. It was also a social gathering at which people feasted and indulged in various games and pastimes. Additionally, it played the role of a commercial exchange; not only did it facilitate the ordinary bartering of goods, but it provided a field for investment, because the Salish Indian who gave away his blankets and other articles merely placed them out on credit, confidently anticipating the reimbursement of his capital at some future date. Finally, it furnished a public stage for the achievement of fame and honour, thus stimulating ambition and rescuing the communities from stagnation.

---

18 It warrants mention that at the time of Jenness's fieldwork, provisions in the Indian Act banning the custom of potlatching had been in effect for a full half-century. Rather than disappearing, however, the practice survived in many communities throughout this period, participants resisting the prohibition by taking the institution underground; Lutz, *Makúk*, 93–94. Arguably the best and most complete source on Ottawa's campaign to suppress the potlatch is Cole and Chaikin, *Iron Hand*. –Ed.

Though a potlatch was organized by a single noble, its expense actually made it a cooperative undertaking since kinsmen and friends were expected to help with considerable contributions. The organizer himself contributed the largest amount of food and goods, fixed the date for the celebration, issued the invitations, and arranged, in broad outline, the program. Before committing himself to the undertaking, however, he shrewdly canvassed his kinsmen to find out how far they would back him, and then calculated, in minute detail, the amount of his capital and indebtedness. He had to make certain of enough food to entertain all his guests for several days, of enough blankets, canoes, and other goods to liquidate his old debts, to pay for the services of hired entertainers, and to disburse among the more prominent of his visitors what were conventionally called gifts, but in reality were interest-free loans.[19] If, as was generally the case, he had himself contributed to the expense of earlier potlatches, he might discreetly solicit the return of those loans in order to augment his resources.

W. Wymond Walkem[20] has described how the Saanich noble issued his invitations about the middle of the nineteenth century:

A chief, having decided upon giving a potlatch, selects the most prominent and trustworthy, as well as respected, young men of his tribe, and after giving them instructions as to which of the neighbouring tribes he wishes to invite, provides them with an adequate number of blankets, to be used as I will presently describe. Choosing the largest of their war canoes, which, as is well known, are handsome models of sea-going canoes, and manning it with the very best "paddlers" of the tribe, they set out for the various Indian settlements. As they approach the first village, the visitors strike up a song. When opposite, and close to the landing place of the first village, this chorus ceases, and one of the crew, arising, commences to sing another song in a loud, moaning tone—sadness itself. The method of approaching a village for the purpose of extending an invitation to a potlatch, is well known to every tribe on the North Pacific coast, that few, if any, of the tribe run down to welcome the visitors, it not being considered the proper thing to do. On landing from the canoe, the last singer calls out the name of the chief's heir, or, if he has no son, his next of kin. The chief sends down one of his young men, and to him is given a blanket for the chief, although his name is never mentioned, for the parent is always sheltered behind the heir. After sending a blanket as a present to the chief, another is given as a present for the second

---

19   The Saanich and their neighbours demanded only the equivalent for their contributions and gifts, without addition of interest; and they sought no return at all for gifts made to the aged and infirm, to whom they generally showed much charity.

20   A medical doctor and provincial politician, Walkem's account is based on his attendance at a ẈSÁNEĆ potlatch on the outskirts of Victoria in September, 1875, ten years before the federal government instituted its ban; *Early British Columbia*, 106–19. –Ed.

chief, and so on until six chiefs are the recipients of presents. The visitors, or ambassadors, or whatever name you may call them, are then invited to the rancheria [village], and properly entertained. Then they take their leave and proceed to the village of the next tribe on the invitation list, and the same present-making is gone through.[21]

The older Saanich, and also the natives around Duncan, claimed that this method of inviting guests came to them from the Nootka Indians of the west coast of Vancouver Island, and that in earlier times no Coast Salish Indian who was giving an important potlatch would delegate a kinsman to invite his guests. Rather, he would travel round himself, accompanied usually by a son or nephew, and carry with him small bunches of cedar sticks, each about half as long as a lead pencil, one bunch for each village. He sat in the middle of his canoe, with paddlers in front and behind, and whenever he drew near a village he stood up and led his crew in a potlatch song. The villagers, recognizing him and understanding the significance of his song, quietly watched him disembark, and one of their nobles nearly always invited him into his home. Whether invited or not, he entered the house of some noble and handed him an invitation stick while his son or nephew made a short explanatory speech.[22] The noble then offered him some food, and often a contributed blanket towards the potlatch before letting him depart to deliver his next invitation. On rare occasions, the wife of the potlatch-giver travelled with her husband and delivered invitation sticks on her own account to the wives of his guests.

The Indians had no day-to-day calendar, so that any time set for a potlatch was approximate only. Some of the guests often arrived a day or more early, others a day or more late. Each party chanted a song as it approached the shore to indicate that it came in friendship, and hastily erected temporary shelters in the place their host had set aside for them. Whatever the hour of their arrival it was his duty—carried out by his assistants—to light their fires and to provide a cooked meal. Thereafter the visitors cooked their own meals, but their host furnished all the food and, once or twice, invited them to join his own people in a common feast. For this feast his assistants cooked an immense quantity of fish and camas in a long trench, dished them up into a wooden trough, and served each portion into a smaller dish. Whatever a guest could not eat on the spot he carried back to his camp.

The program naturally differed with every occasion, but the organizer of the potlatch took pains to vary the entertainment as much as possible and to plan some activity for every hour of the day. He arranged ball contests and gam-

---

21 Ibid., 114–15.
22 Some, apparently, gave the stick into the noble's hand, others threw it at his feet. Old Bob, a Halalt native, said that his family used the sticks as tallies only, and threw them away, one by one, after delivering the invitations by word of mouth. In more recent times invitations to potlatches were less formal. The potlatch-giver shouted out his invitations from his canoe and proceeded to the next village without even landing. An old Cowichan Indian who gave a potlatch that lasted for two weeks and was attended by Indians from Saanich, Chemainus Bay, and Nanaimo, as well as from Cowichan, travelled in a buggy to invite his guests.

bling games between the people of different villages, and sometimes hired a professional clown (*kweenia*) to circulate among the guests and keep them in a state of merriment. If his daughter was of marriageable age, he might fasten a swing of goat wool blankets from a rafter inside his house and invite the sons of nobles to swing her, paying each youth with a blanket and, at the end, dividing among them the blankets that had formed the swing;[23] or he might honour his young son by having relatives carry the boy on their shoulders inside a painted box while they chanted some of the family songs.

> When I was a boy my father cooperated with his kinsmen in giving a big potlatch. At one stage in the proceedings they made me stand in a box seven or eight feet long and about 12 inches wide, bearing on the outside a painting of the sun. My kinsmen crowned their heads with chaplets of Oregon grape, and raising the box on poles, carried me out into the crowd, where everyone joined in singing two of our family songs, the same two that were chanted later at my wedding. Why they did not give me a new title at this potlatch I do not know.

Often the potlatch-giver held a memorial service for a son who had died not long before. He hired two or, more commonly, four masked dancers—men who had inherited the privilege of wearing face masks (*swaiswai*) [see Chapter 12]—set up a dressing room for them in a corner of the house, and called in all his male relatives to chant the song his son had been accustomed to sing at the winter ceremonies [i.e. spirit dances], while the masked dancers waved sticks over them to allay their grief. If a daughter had recently died the wife of the potlatch-giver presided at the memorial service and called in women relatives only.

It was at potlatches that men commonly assumed new titles, for only at such times could they be sure to have them ratified by all the leading nobles of the district. A man who could not afford to give a potlatch himself for this purpose sometimes waited until a relative was organizing one, and requested a place on the program in return for bearing part of the expense.

In early times no man could afford to give a potlatch unaided. All his kinsmen in the village cooperated with him, and outside the village he often obtained support from a prosperous son-in-law. The son-in-law might arrive with several loaded canoes and camp over to one side of the village. Then one morning, when the potlatch was already in full swing, he would put out to sea, stand up in the middle of his canoe and lead all his crew in a song. His father-in-law would go down to the beach to meet him, and anchor each canoe to the shore by placing a goat wool blanket across it. After a few blankets and other objects had been thrown into the water so that onlookers might dive for them, the rest of his contributions would be carried up and piled on the floor of the potlatch house. There the son-in-law, with a dance and song, would formally

---

23   The youths gave them to their mothers, who unravelled any that were mere strips and wove the wool into new blankets.

present them to his father-in-law, and the father-in-law express his thanks in a similar manner.

The duration of a potlatch depended on the quantity of food provided by its giver and his fellow villagers, and on the number of guests. As soon as the food supply began to run low, the celebration was brought to a close. All the people gathered round a platform in front of the potlatch house (or, if no platform had been erected, inside the house itself), the potlatch-giver mounted the platform and, calling out the name of one guest after another, threw down his present. At the same time, he discharged his own debts from previous years, and paid the Indians he had hired for various duties on the present occasion. This event usually took place during an afternoon. The following morning the guests loaded up their canoes and departed for their homes.

Many Saanich Indians kept tallies of sticks to record their potlatch debts. To ease the accumulation of perishable goods in their homes, and to prevent their debts from pyramiding, they frequently discharged their obligations at minor feasts to which they invited very few outsiders except their creditors. [24]

Tommy Paul, David Latasse and Edward Jim, three Saanich chiefs from Tsartlip, wearing twill-weave mountain goat hair blankets and headdresses.

---

24   In concluding his 1875 account of a W̱SÁNEĆ potlatch, Walkem wrote that "although I have been present at many potlatches since, I never was at one where so much merchandise was given away, or where a man transformed himself so rapidly from a state of plenty into one of poverty"; *Early British Columbia*, 119. In 1936, the government proposed (but failed to enact) changes to the Indian Act making "accumulation of any property that might be used for potlatching illegal"; Lutz, *Makúk*, 94. –Ed.

6

Warfare and Feuds

In villages thus organized without definite chiefs, the nobles were able to settle quarrels among the commoners and slaves, but quarrels among themselves could be composed only by consultations and the pressure of public opinion. A disgruntled man could always take up his residence in some other village where he had close kinsmen. Quarrels between nobles of different villages, not only on the Saanich Peninsula but from Duncan on the north to Victoria in the south, were likewise patched up through the intervention of common kinsmen, and seldom resulted in open feuds. The Saanich did have feuds with Salish communities a little more remote, but they were feuds between individual nobles, as a rule, in which the villages as a whole played the part of spectators only. One noble would challenge another to approach his village and settle their quarrel by single combat; or he would send word through a messenger that he would attack his enemy in his own home. The principals then fought out their duel on the beach, while their retainers stood by to guard against treachery. The victor might kill one or two of his enemy's nearest kinsmen, and carry away a few of his slaves, but the conflict seldom became general because it was a strictly personal quarrel between the two men, and all the Salish groups accepted the rule that no one should interfere in a duel. The only weapons permissible were the spear and the club; bows and arrows were reserved for hereditary enemies like the Kwakiutl. Many natives even frowned on the wearing of elk hide armour; and all condemned the decapitation of a fallen duelist because he belonged to the same people as the conqueror.[1]

Some feuds arose from mere jealousy. More often they flared up through high-handed action of one side or the other, and a refusal to pay compensation. A party from one village, perhaps, had encroached on the fishing grounds of another, or had robbed and carried away a slave or other member. The victimized House then took up the quarrel; if the offenders were Salish from Vancouver Island or from the mouth of the Fraser River, its leader demanded redress, or else settled the affair with a duel; but if they came from other parts of the mainland, or from north of Campbell River, it organized a retaliatory

---

1   "Their spears, which are of horn, have often wooden handles of great length"; Fraser, "Journal of a Voyage," 195. The Saanich spear had a single barbed point, for, unlike the Klallam Indians south of them, they never used the two-pointed seal spear for fighting. The club was made from bone or elk horn, sharpened on the edges; and the armour from two layers of elk skin quilted to hold flat stones between them. I know of no evidence for helmets. A Sardis native, William Sepass, said that his people sometimes sewed a round stone in leather, fastened it to the wrist by a thong, and used it as a club in close combat.

raid. One or more nobles belonging to the House manned a canoe with volunteers, mostly commoners, set an ambush for some unsuspecting party of their adversaries that was fishing or gathering berries, and either killed them, or carried them off into slavery. This naturally led to a counter-raid, and the feud continued until one side or the other made overtures for a settlement, usually by marrying a noble girl from one village to a nobleman of the other. The chief victims of such raids, however, were the slaves and commoners who did most of the fishing and berry picking, and who, if not killed, merely exchanged one master and House for another.

When a noble was taken prisoner, his captors nearly always sent word through another village, and his kinsmen immediately took steps to ransom him. He thus avoided slavery and retained his noble rank, though not without some loss, for even the briefest captivity produced a blot on his record that nothing he did afterwards could entirely erase. As the following stories demonstrate, however, girls of noble rank who were taken prisoners could escape any loss of prestige, even without being ransomed, through their people arranging for their marriage to some nobleman among their captors.

Two east Saanich men who had been hunting seals near the mainland put in at an island to boil an octopus, but just when their meal was ready, four natives from Sechelt approached them in a canoe. One of the Saanich men would have let them pass, but his companion invited the strangers to share the octopus. They accepted, but carried their guns ashore with them, which so alarmed the first Saanich man that he quietly moved away along the beach. His suspicions were justified, for his companion, while dishing up the meat, was shot in the back and killed. The survivor fled into the woods and eluded pursuit by climbing a high tree; but the Sechelt natives carried away his seals and canoe, leaving him marooned.

Three days later he sighted another canoe manned by men and women whom he recognized from their speech as Victoria [Songhees] natives. At his hail they took him on board and conveyed him to Saanich, where the murdered man's widow organized a war party to seek revenge.

Three canoes set out. In one was a Saanich medicine woman, in another a medicine man from Malahat; it was their duty to capture the souls of some Sechelt natives and make their bodies follow, thus delivering them into the hands of the Saanich. Actually, near Sechelt they did sight a canoe occupied by a man and his son, and, hastily putting ashore, left the medicine man and medicine woman on the beach as decoys while they hid in the woods with their guns. When the Sechelt natives paddled close in to shore the Saanich shot them dead.

The Sechelt then organized a counter-raid that resulted in the death of a Saanich man; and the feud continued for several years. Finally, a Saanich Indian married a Sechelt girl who happened to be visiting some relatives at Nanaimo, and the two groups composed their quarrel at the wedding celebration.

...

Many years ago when the Nanaimo natives were raiding a certain place they captured a Saanich girl who was a distant relative of my husband's family. His uncle decided to ransom her; as the affair, however, seemed comparatively trivial, he did not go to Nanaimo himself, but sent two young kinsmen with a slave crew, an elderly slave woman, one or two guns, some goat wool blankets, and some baskets of camas roots. The girl's captor, who knew the young man, entertained them hospitably, and when they announced their mission said "I cannot refuse you, but you must compensate me with another slave." They offered him the elderly woman, and though he protested she was rather old, he consented to take her if they would add a certain amount of goods. Then they brought up their guns, blankets and camas roots. This satisfied him, and he let them take the girl to Saanich where she married soon afterwards the son of a notable warrior. Her kinsmen repaid the ransom price, with interest, at the wedding.

In the National Museum of Canada is a carved wooden coffin depicting a man's guardian spirit flanked by two wolves. It is the coffin of a famous Saanich warrior, Kwalahunzit, who was born a commoner in the eighteenth century and died a noble in the early years of the nineteenth.[2] Like other nobles he had several wives, two of them nobles, the others slaves; and even today there is secret friction on the Saanich reserves because the descendants of his slave wives claim the right to noble rank. Kwalahunzit's life story gives a fairly clear picture of the raiding and duelling that was taking place at the time Europeans first penetrated into the region.

When Kwalahunzit was only thirteen years old some Kwakiutl Indians carried away his father, leaving the boy and his mother dependent on the other members of the Tsawout community of east Saanich. One day his mother caught him stealing food. She thrashed him with her wool-beater, told him that such conduct would never make him a warrior, and drove him out of the village. The boy wandered into the hills on the western side of the peninsula and, when it grew dark, crawled into the hollow base of a giant cedar tree, drawing in some

---

2   As he did in misspelling the Hul'qumi'num' place name Kwalsiawahl (see Chapter 2), here, too, Jenness mistakenly rendered Kwalahunzit's name with an /r/ in the original typescript; in SENĆOŦEN, as in Hul'qumi'num', this phoneme does not occur; Montler, *Morphology and Phonology*. –Ed

moss to keep him imprisoned. Finally, the snow turned to slush, and, faint from hunger, he set out for his home, barefooted. Just ás evening fell a man discovered him crawling on hands and knees on the outskirts of the village and carried him into his mother's home.

After recovering from this ordeal Kwalahunzit made himself a bow and arrows, club and spear, so that he might train to be a warrior; for a terrible epidemic of smallpox had just decimated the Saanich Indians and crippled their resistance to the raids of their enemies.[3] His first fight was against some southern natives who were visiting relatives at the big settlement near Sidney. He and a friend attacked and killed them at sea, then upset their canoe so that their relatives would think they had drowned.

A few years later he visited with his people some notorious raiders on Mayne Island. The Mayne Islanders invited their visitors to participate in a deer hunt, but Kwalahunzit noticed that they were bathing in the sea, blackening their faces, and rubbing their bodies and hair with deer fat, which indicated that they were really preparing for battle. He warned his companions, and while the hunters were setting up the deer net, he and his people fell on them, killed most of the men, and carried away all the women and girls whom they had enslaved.

This exploit carried his reputation far and wide. It reached the Comox Indians, who challenged him several times to single combat. Every time he accepted one of their challenges he returned victorious.

A Mayne Island Indian once sent him this challenge: "I am ready to fight you. If you are not afraid of me come." Kwalahunzit mustered his followers and paddled north. As they drew near the island they saw his challenger strutting up and down the beach, brandishing his spear, and the villagers lined up behind him. Kwalahunzit shouted "I'll fight you single-handed," and the man accepted, expecting to stab him as he disembarked from the canoe. Kwalahunzit, however, leaped into the water and reached the beach before his enemy could strike at him. Both parties drummed and sang to encourage their champions, who began to fence with their spears. Gradually Kwalahunzit gained the upper hand, and step by step forced his enemy back. The man's father then rushed to his house to seize a spear, and Kwalahunzit's own warriors dashed ashore to protect their leader from a treacherous attack in the rear. Before anyone could interfere, however, Kwalahunzit killed his adversary, after which he and his warriors slew the father and several other men in the village.

The Cowichan natives once sought his help to settle a score with the Indians of Port Angeles [Klallam] after the later had massacred some

---

3　An epidemic of smallpox swept this coast about 1780.

Cowichan visitors during a squabble over a gambling game, *lehal*.[4] Four Cowichan canoes from four different villages, each manned by about ten men, put in at Deep Cove, where many Saanich Indians had collected to gather clams; and they invited Kwalahunzit, together with another Saanich warrior who had married a Cowichan woman, to join their party as volunteers. Kwalahunzit consulted his uncle, who advised him to accept if he wished to uphold his reputation, and promised to go with him. So, after bathing in the sea, and oiling his head and body, Kwalahunzit tied on his elk skin armour, and his friends drummed and sang to kindle his fighting spirit. Afterwards they drummed for the other Saanich warrior, who strutted up and down the beach in his armour, catching at the arrows that his people shot at him. The Saanich contingent then embarked in a canoe and paddled with the Cowichan natives to Sooke, where they all rested a night before crossing over to Port Angeles.

When the Port Angeles natives observed the canoes approaching they mounted with drums to the roofs of their houses while their champion, a man named Skaiyus, marched down to the beach in full war panoply to repel the invaders. Kwalahunzit kept his canoe in the background so that the Cowichans could begin the combat. While both sides drummed and sang, the leader of each Cowichan canoe sprang ashore in turn and engaged Skaiyus, who repelled them one after another and drove them back into their canoes. Then Kwalahunzit drew near, standing on the front cross-bar and leading his crew in a war song. He leaped into the water, which swirled up around his waist, parried Skaiyus' spear-thrust, and gained the beach. There he countered thrust with thrust until his opponent gave ground and turned to flee, when he speared him and cut off his head with a knife.[5] Immediately the villagers leaped down from the roofs and sought refuge in the woods, but the Cowichan natives killed several before they could escape. The Vancouver Islanders did not carry away any women and children, however, because they were their own kindred.

After becoming very old and totally blind, Kwalahunzit met his end at the hands of the Comox Indians. One of his sons, with a slave man and some women, were taking him to the fishing ground at Port Roberts when they sighted a Comox canoe bearing down on them.

---

4   Believed to be the sole Coast Salish gambling game pre-dating European contact, SLE-HÁL, *(sləhel)* "is a fast-moving guessing game" that combines "not only elements of chance, but also these of strategy and skill"; Maranda, *Salish Gambling Games*, 49. –Ed.

5   The victor carried home the head as a trophy and planted it on a stick or hung it from a cross-pole, generally near the graveyard some distance from his village to avoid being disturbed by the ghost. The prestige of a warrior depended on the number of heads he could boast, reckoning women's and children's as well as men's; but as a rule the Coast Salish slew men only, and carried away the women and children as slaves.

They paddled hurriedly to shore and the women, leaving the old man in the canoe as a decoy, fled into the woods while the son and the slave hid behind a tree. At this period the Indians had obtained muzzle-loading guns. The Comox fired several shots at Kwalahunzit, but his son fired back at them and apparently hit one man, for as they paddled away they tilted their canoe on its side for protection. After they had gone, Kwalahunzit's party joined other Saanich Indians at Point Roberts, and were followed by a canoe of Songish Indians who, however, refused to stay ashore after it became dark, but kept watch in their canoe. About midnight they heard footsteps and saw dark figures moving along the beach towards the Saanich camp, whereupon they shouted and fired two or three warning shots. The Saanich fled into the woods—all but Kwalahunzit, who was decapitated by a Comox Indian while still struggling to put on his coat. His son shot three of the Comox before receiving a bullet in his side, and split the skull of a fourth enemy when the latter stooped over him, chanting, to cut off his head.[6] However, he, too, died the next day.

Return of the Songhees War Party

---

6   The Saanich say that only the Comox and Kwakiutl, not their own people, chanted a prayer before decapitating their enemies.

7
Childhood and Adolescence

During the first few weeks of life, before its bones had time to harden, a baby lay continuously in a wooden cradle lined with shredded cedar bark, and a cedar bark pad pressed heavily on its brow to flatten the head; for the Saanich, like their neighbours, considered a head in natural form unshapely. Parents attached neither toys nor charms to the cradle, and they discouraged precocity in talking and walking, believing that a too precocious child would not survive. Yet they rejoiced if the baby smiled and laughed aloud when alone, because then it was presumably playing with some spirit. As the weeks passed by and its forehead hardened into shape, the mother often took the infant out of the cradle and let it play on the bed mats. She called it simply baby at this period, or a pet name that carried no significance. Only after the child began to talk and walk did it receive a real name taken from some dead member of its family. This name might last throughout life, but the child of noble parents discarded it later for a family title if his (or her) parents could afford the necessary potlatch; and so, also, did the man who won riches and renown through his own efforts.

Invariably if a baby died, and often when it did not, the Saanich discarded its cradle as soon as it was no longer needed, conceiving that it had become too unhealthy to use for another child. They deposited it therefore on a ledge high up on a cliff (Malahat Mountain was a favourite place), where the sun spirit would gaze on it each morning and impart some of its strength to the child. Similarly, any hair that they clipped away, whether from a child or an adult, they inserted in a cleft or notch of a tree, and covered it with bark or moss so that the tree would absorb it into its own life; and they took care to choose only a healthy tree, since, if it fell soon afterwards, the owner of the hair would die. They paid no attention to nails worn down from use; but when a milk tooth fell out, the child threw it into the sea and called to the spirit of the porpoise, the beaver, the seal, or some other animal that has strong teeth to replace the lost tooth with a strong, firm one.

Very little children ran around naked, but as they grew older they received clothes similar to those of their parents. Girls, like their mothers, bound their hair in two braids which they anointed with fat (mixed usually with certain herbs) and wrapped with cedar bark, but boys and men let their hair hang loose or tied it in a knob at the back of the head. Some female relative unostentatiously pierced a child's ears and nose before it reached its teens, and inserted feathers in the holes until they healed. Later, the feathers were replaced with shell pendants, according to the means of the parents. No charms were worn; these were permitted to hunters only. Little children were discouraged from talking too much to their elders lest they become chatterboxes all their days. Disobedience was punished with a stick.

As soon as they were old enough, boys and girls had to take an early morning plunge in the sea, winter and summer, and harden their bodies by rubbing them with yew branches after the bath. Each village appointed an elderly man to stir the boys out of bed and drive them down to the water, if necessary, with a switch. He seldom troubled about the girls, who bathed at their own section of the beach under the supervision of an elderly female. A boy occasionally fooled his mentor by bathing unusually early and returning to his bed. On very cold mornings, too, a kindly grandmother might drench him, inside or outside the house, with a basin of lukewarm water, so that he would already be drying himself by the fire when his mentor entered to rouse him for his bath. Parents tried in many ways to make their children strong and hardy; thus during a heavy thunderstorm, one mother made her little boy run naked through the woods in the hope that, just as he safely sped through the storm, so in later life he would emerge safely from every sickness.

The Saanich strictly regulated the diet of their children. They forbade them fatty foods such as seal meat, the belly of salmon, and the marrow from the bones of deer and elk; or else they permitted these foods but seldom. Even the flesh of the spring and sockeye salmon was considered too strong until a child reached its teens; the sockeye might cause nightmares, the Indians thought, whence some parents smeared their children with consumption plant seeds the first time they allowed them to eat this fish. Crab apples, wild gooseberries, and hot water supposedly spoiled the teeth (if not also the digestion); and cold water should be drunk sitting down, not standing up. The child who ate the leg muscle of an animal would develop cramps in his own legs; if he ate the heart of any creature, but especially of a duck, he would become a coward. Even the liver had its place in the list of forbidden foods; only old people, in fact, ate either heart or liver. Because ducks swell up when they are roasted before a fire, a child should avoid eating them lest his own stomach swell up in middle life. Likewise, he should avoid eating the red cod that, when hooked, rises quickly to the surface and twists itself round the line, because his own stomach might become twisted and cause vomiting. On the other hand, he should eat as much dog fish gullet as possible, because its unusual length would make him long-winded.

Once they reached their teens, girls of good [i.e. noble] families gave considerable attention to their appearance. They removed all down from their cheeks by coating their faces with a reddish paint obtained from the hemlock, all hair from their armpits by scrubbing with yew branches, and they evened their eyebrows by pulling out the longer hairs. From now on they never went out of doors unless accompanied by some female relative, and, instead of playing, they spent their days in beating and spinning wool, making small canoe mats on which their fathers and uncles might sit and kneel, stringing seed necklaces, cleaning fish, and training for all the other duties that would fall to their lot in later years. During the winters, therefore, they seldom left their homes; but on the Saanich Peninsula winter lasts less than three months, and the pleasantly warm days of spring and summer brought them many outdoor excursions for berries, roots and bark.

There is a story that long ago a young girl would not work in the house at her baskets, but insisted on taking them out of doors. As the days passed by she wandered with them farther and farther into the woods until at length she was roaming about like a wolf. Then the wolves came and took her away, as her parents discovered when they found her baskets, and tracks of wolves all around. For a long time, they attempted to rescue her, but without success. On one occasion they sighted her gathering clams on a beach, unclad, and covered with a thick coat of hair; but when they tried to encircle her she fled with the speed of a wolf. Subsequently she gave birth to many wolf pups that were able to understand human speech.[1]

Boys, of course, spent most of their days out of doors, not in pastimes only, but learning to paddle canoes, to fish, to hunt, to use an adze and steam planks, weave nets, and perform a hundred other useful tasks. Parents feasted their kinsmen on the first deer their sons shot, and on the first seal they harpooned; the lads themselves ate other foods at these feasts.

Abundant leisure gave the Saanich opportunity for many games. Restricted to girls was battledore and shuttlecock (*sekkwoiyay*) played with a wooden bat and a shuttle of light cedar wood trimmed with three feathers.[2] Girls played also with dolls, and boys with tops, but these, together with the games "blind man's buff" and "hide and seek," may have been introduced by Europeans. Of native origin was a game in which a number of children crouched under a blanket and the "out" person distinguished them by their legs. In another game the children squatted in two rows and planted a stick in front of one of their number; the child opposite had then to walk across and carry back the stick with unsmiling face, in spite of the funny grimaces, accompanied by the chanted words "*taakchenum hwehwechiemum*" (meaning unknown), with which the line of children tried to break down his gravity.

String figures [or cat's cradles] were more popular with children than with adults; I have described two in Appendix 3. There was also a juvenile version of the men's gambling game *lehal*, or "hide the stick."[3] The children lined up in a long row with hands clasped on their stomachs and a captain stationed at each end; one captain, walking along the line, stealthily slipped a pebble into a child's hand and the other guessed who held it.

Boys and young men naturally preferred more athletic pastimes, such as football and hockey. The football was a lump of wood, described by one na-

---

1   For a variation of this story, see Part II, no. 36. –Ed.
2   This is a game similar to badminton; battledore refers to a paddle-like racquet. –Ed.
3   See page 56, footnote 4. –Ed.

tive as "the hard lump of wood that grows on the outside of the balsam."
Goals were mere lines on the beach or at opposite ends of an open field.
The players threw the ball to each other and tried to carry it over their opponent's goal. Hockey (*kwokkwoialis*) resembled football in being played on
bare ground with two lines as goals, but the curved sticks served more often
to trip the players than to propel the ball. In "ring and spear" (*sesaylam*), one
man bowled along the ground a hoop of woven reeds or a perforated stone
disc, which his opponent tried to stop with an arrow; while in "ball and hook"
(*chilkem*), he rolled a wooden ball for his opponent to catch, like a salmon, on
a hooked stick. "Tug-of-war" was identical with the European game except
that a long pole took the place of a rope; if there were only two boys or men
playing, they dispensed with the stick and merely interlocked their fingers.
Less strenuous was *kukkwim*, which resembled quoits, but was played with
a piece of kelp and a number of stick tallies. The boys took up positions two
or three yards apart, and each planted a sharpened stake in the ground. One
threw the kelp, trying to impale it on his opponent's stake; if he succeeded he
won a tally, if he failed his opponent threw in turn. Whoever first stripped his
opponent of all his tallies won the game.

Boys were fond also of war games. They shot at marks with their bows and
arrows, and also with slings, though the sling was seldom if ever employed
in actual warfare. In one game, the players selected a "victim" and lightly
squeezed his jugular vein until he toppled over. In another, they lined up in
opposing ranks and attacked one another; the victors then knotted their prisoners' hair on the crown, bound their legs, and pretended to carry them off as
slaves.

It was when their children neared adolescence that parents of noble rank
conferred on them ancestral titles or names. David Latasse, who died in 1936,
had received a grand-uncle's name, *q'alekwalt'an* (no meaning), when he was
twelve years old, and another name, *sxwa'wał* (whirlwind), his great-grandfather's, two years later, when he was fourteen. He was known by his second
name until he was about fifty years of age, when he assumed a third, *st'e'ełum*
(no meaning), borne previously by his mother's father.[4] The third name served
him at potlatches and other ceremonies until his death; like other Indians, he
used an English one in ordinary life. Another old man received his name when
he was fourteen years old and never changed it, although he occasionally contemplated bestowing it on some grandson or grand-nephew and taking a new
one for himself. It had belonged to his maternal grandfather, who was more
distinguished than any member of his father's line. His father had bestowed it
on him in a special potlatch at which he was made to stand on a high platform
inside the house and throw down blankets to the assembled crowd. Poor people, of course, could not afford to hold such potlatches and give away many

---

4   This name goes to the eldest son in the family. The name *haiełwat* (thunder) goes to the
eldest daughter. *Talsit* (lightning) goes to the second son.

presents; consequently, their children retained the names that were given to them during their infancy.

…

Parents watched their children closely for the first signs of adolescence, and warned them at that period to keep away from fires, lest their lower eyelids droop and redden in later years. When a boy's voice appeared to be changing they kept him quiet inside the house for four days and gave him very little to eat or drink. Each day his mother or some female relative chanted a prayer over him and rubbed his chest (sometimes also his mouth) with a hard stone. On the fifth day she sent him to bathe, and either going or returning made him jump four times over some bushes, or perform some corresponding ritual. The details varied from family to family, but no well-born lad passed through adolescence without undergoing some rite. Poor people, however, paid little heed to their sons during this transition period but focussed their attention on their daughters.

Some old Saanich men narrated these details of their adolescence.

> When my voice began to change I was kept four days inside the house and my head and neck encircled with bands of cedar bark. Each morning about 4 a.m. my aunt roused me, and, shaking the family rattle (a copper globe with wooden handle trimmed with goat wool pendants), chanted over me four times a wordless prayer to X̣e.ls. I ate and slept very little during those four days, and from time to time I expectorated on a boulder so that I might become as hard as the stone. My aunt gave me, too, a small black pebble and told me to rub it on my mouth and breasts so that my teeth would grow straight and even and my chest hard. On the fifth morning she sent me into the woods to bathe, and on my way back to the house made me jump over a number of small bushes in my path, to strengthen my soul (*smastimauch*).

…

> I stayed in the house four days. My parents allowed me to walk around, but not to play with other children or go outside. On the fifth morning my aunt, who was a seer (*siowa*),[5] painted my face and the top of my head with red ochre, crowned my head with red cedar bark and feathers, and led me to a creek not far from the house. As we passed through the woods the feathers and cedar bark were knocked off by the bushes or blew away. Near the creek I pulled down a branch of a fir tree, and sitting astride it, facing the rising sun, rubbed the ochre from my face with its needles, while my aunt chant-

---

5   See page 21, footnote 22. –Ed.

ed a prayer; the bough, when I slipped off it, carried the prayer high into the air. Four boughs I bestrode in this way before bathing in the creek. Then my aunt said to me: "You have finished, my child. You will have a long life. But take this black stone and rub your breasts with it every time you bathe. It will prevent any swelling of your nipples." She did not make me jump over any bushes, because there was no idea of my becoming a medicine man.

...

During the four days I remained in the house I expectorated frequently on a big black stone. On the fifth morning an aunt painted by face with red ochre and sent me into the woods for the day; then in the evening when I returned, she told me to wash off the paint in the sea. Three times I walked into the water up to my knees and walked out again; the fourth time I sat down in the water and washed.

...

During the four days I was kept in the house my aunt, who was a medicine woman, chanted over me, morning and evening, praying that X̱e.ls would make me strong. Since she wished me to become a medicine man, she placed blackberry bushes under my sleeping mats (not ferns, as some people do), made me lie on my back most of the time, and forbade me to talk. On the fifth morning she led me outdoors, told me to strip, and, pointing to a blackberry bush, said "Jump over that bush and back four times." I jumped over the bush and back four times, while she drummed and chanted a prayer; had I fallen, she would have known that I would not live long. She then sent me to bathe in the sea, where a male relative scrubbed me with blackberry bushes after my bath.

The Songhees generally paid little attention to adolescent boys, but an elderly man on their Esquimalt reserve, Jimmy Fraser, underwent a similar ritual during a visit to the Indians of San Juan Island when he was about seven years old. One morning while he was there an old medicine woman painted his face and chanted a prayer over him, shaking her rattle; and she repeated the chant in the evening. Following her instructions, the boy left the village early the next morning accompanied by his father, and ascended a mountain. Near its summit he climbed up the sunny side of a tree as high as he dared and rubbed the paint from his face with its branches, saying as he let them fly upward again, "Thank you, *siem*." He left on this tree the cedar bark towels with which the woman had painted his face, and, climbing a smaller tree in the grove, swung from tree to tree, Tarzan-like, until he was exhausted and had to rest on the ground. Next, he and his father sat astride some small saplings and let them swish skyward up their backs; then, with his arms shielding his face, he ran as fast as he could through the thick brush until he fell. After thus carrying out all the old woman's instructions they bathed and returned to the village, which they reached at dusk. Next morning, she seated the boy, his father, his mother and his sister, on a bench, and after shaking her rattle and chanting, announced to his parents "The soul of your son has climbed very high. He will therefore live to a ripe old age."

A girl's four-day confinement differed in no essential respect from a boy's, except that her seclusion was more rigid, and the prohibition against her eating and drinking was enforced more strictly. If her mouth became too dry she might moisten it with water drawn up through a tube, but not swallow any of the liquid. She passed the long hours spinning wool or making baskets, forbidden in some cases even to lie down at night, though she might rest against a post. Her mother, an aunt, or, if the family could afford it, one or perhaps two medicine women, painted her face each day and prayed X̱e.ls to grant her health and long life; or occasionally they painted it on the fifth day only, and made her rub off the paint with cedar boughs as she went through the woods to the bathing place. After her bath, too, they scrubbed her body with yew boughs (or with blackberry bushes if she was to become a medicine woman), and rubbed it with a smooth black stone to preserve its shapeliness. Then the girl deposited at some sacred rock (i.e. a rock that legend said had once been a human being),[6] or in some other place designated by her attendants, the fern leaves on which she had sat in the water, and the yew boughs or blackberry bushes with which she had been scrubbed.

Every girl, even one of slave parentage, underwent the ceremonies outlined above, though the details varied slightly in almost every case. Families of high rank announced their daughter's coming of age with special entertainments, partly to enhance the family prestige, and partly to improve the girls' chances in the marriage market. Some even postponed the most striking entertainment for weeks, and even months, after the first seclusion, so that it might coincide with some potlatch or other public function that would bring together a large crowd. Below is a description of such an entertainment, held towards the end of the nineteenth century in Cowichan Bay, though it might have occurred equally well on the Saanich Peninsula.

> The debutante's family partitioned off two corners of the house with goat wool blankets. One room concealed the girl, the other served as a dressing room for the medicine men who had been hired to stage a performance. At the entrance to their room two watchmen with painted faces stood guard to announce when they would emerge. Along the side of the house opposite the rooms were benches crowded with spectators, women with sticks in the front row, and a mixed audience behind.

---

6   For one of many instances, see Part II, no. 1. –Ed.

The leading medicine man began to chant from his room, and the audience became silent. He stopped suddenly, and recommenced; then, as the women in the foremost row beat their sticks on planks in front of them, the four medicine men filed out, each carrying a forked stick, shuffled around the open arena in the middle of the house, and then retired to their room. An old man whom they had stationed in the audience immediately announced what the show would be, and drew attention to four long narrow stones that had been placed in the middle of the floor. Hardly had he finished speaking when the watchman again called on the women to beat their sticks, the medicine men re-emerged, and, shuffling forward one behind the other, picked up each stone (after the usual three feints) in the fork of his stick. Amid deep silence the leader then leaped about and sang while his three companions walked round him. As soon as he stopped all four began to leap and sing, and the women pounded their sticks again and joined in the chant: "The stone is my toy. I am going to play with it." This act ended after a few minutes, and the four men retired with the stones to their room.

Presently the watchman signalled the women for the second act. The medicine men shuffled out, their leader hiding a black stone against his breast. He hurled it to the floor, recovered it, and retreated with his companions to his room.

At a command from the old man in the audience, two swift runners dashed out to the middle of the floor, leaped about to the beating of the women's sticks, and sped through the doorway to seek a certain shrub in the woods. The audience relaxed as soon as they disappeared, but became silent and attentive again when the beating of the sticks heralded their return. Each leaped through the doorway with a shrub in his hand and a wreath of fir boughs round his head. While they stood in the middle of the house adjusting their wreaths, two women led forth the girl from her room and seated her on a pile of goat wool blankets. The runners then "swept" her with their shrubs and retreated into the room of the medicine men.

Again the watchman called the audience to attention, the sticks resumed their pounding, and the medicine men reappeared, their leader carrying his stone and each of the other three a basket of water, which he laid on the floor after shuffling round the arena. Their leader then planted his stone beside the baskets, and, as the sticks became silent, "drilled" a feather into it. The stone screeched with his drilling, and the feather stood firmly upright. When he threw the stone into one of the baskets it floated on the water, while the feather rocked slowly like a sail. He threw it into the second basket, and the third; each time it floated as if it were a boat. Then he gathered it up, his companions recovered their baskets, and the four men retired to their room.

For the fourth time the watchman gave the signal. Two men went forward and sat down, one on each side of the girl. The medicine men approached, wearing blankets round their shoulders, and their leader laid a mink skin on the ground in front of her. As he held it by the tail the skin (worked, presumably, by hidden strings) crawled toward her as if alive; but when the two women beat it with fir branches the man hid it under his blanket again and retired to his room.

Once more they came out, each carrying in his hand a hard, dried fish. The leader held out his fish to the girls, who bit off a small piece and dropped it into the hand of one of the women. The second medicine man offered his fish, then the third and the fourth. Each time she bit off a fragment the mink under the blanket of the leader emitted a loud squeal. Thus the drama ended, and the medicine men retired from the scene.

The old speaker in the audience now rose and, after thanking the people for their attendance, called out the name of a certain noble, who was to receive one of the blankets on which the girl had been sitting, the blanket in this case being a token of a canoe which would be handed over later. He named also other old men who were to receive blankets. The girls gave them their presents, then mounted a high platform that had been erected at one end of the house. From there she threw a huge pile of blankets to the floor, and the men and boys in the audience scrambled for their possession.

At Esquimalt, the Songhees kept the girl indoors for four days, and, if they could afford it, screened her behind goat wool blankets and hired two professional women attendants. Each morning these women sat, one at the foot of her bed and the other at the head, shook their rattles over her and prayed X̱e.ls to grant her happiness and long life, after which they rubbed her breasts with a pebble and painted her face, making the patterns different each day of her seclusion. At evening they prayed over her again and then left her. On the fifth morning they repainted her face for the last time, removed the curtain, and summoned the people for whatever ceremony the parents had arranged. When this ceremony ended the girl carried into the woods all the cedar bark towels with which her attendants had wiped away the paint each morning, and hung them high up in some tree, climbing up only their sunny sides. Then she drew down a branch, rubbed her face with it once, and sent it swishing upward. Descending, she climbed a second tree and did likewise, then a third and a fourth, until the two or three girls who had followed her announced that her face was clean again. The Indians believed that if one of the branches snapped off, or if she allowed the paint to harden on her face, she would die young. Finally, she bathed in the sea or in some pool and returned home.

Annie Bob had been a professional attendant of girls at their 'coming-of-age' ritual; she described the ceremony in her district [Halalt] for high-born girls as follows:

> The girls fasted in the house for four days, working at anything she wished, but forbidden to lie down either by day or by night. Two women attendants crowned her with a goat wool headdress, tied a belt of red dyed cedar bark round her waist, and painted her face each morning with red ochre. They did not rub her body with a pebble, however, or make her expectorate on a stone. All through the day they remained with her, but at night they slept in their own homes.

> Early on the morning of the fifth day they repainted her face and prepared her bath, which was in either a water-tight basket or a canoe; sometimes, especially for a canoe bath, they screened off a special room. When everything was ready they led her, shaking their rattles, into the main part of the house and seated her on some blankets, themselves sitting on either side. The villagers trooped in and took their places, and, to the accompaniment of stick-pounding and singing, four boys danced back and forth towards the girl, each pretending to offer her some object. The first boy pretended to offer her a forked stick, the second a shell, the third a stone, and the last a basket. Their dance usually lasted two or three hours, after which the two attendants, singing and shaking their rattles, conducted her to her bath and the people dispersed.

> During the bath the attendants dipped a cedar bark doll in the water and lightly beat the girl, to make her unafraid when suitors sought her hand. After washing all the paint from her face they led her back to her seat and sent a messenger to summon the villagers again. The girl's father shouted "Scramble for the blankets" (that screened off the bathroom); and men, sometimes boys also, tore the blankets into sections and divided them up.

> As soon as this turmoil had ended the two attendants began to sing and shake their rattles while the audience beat time with sticks; then, taking a special comb, with four preliminary feints, two toward the crown and two toward the sides of the girl's head, they combed her hair and plaited it in two braids. Occasionally some family would tell their son to go and sit near her, thus silently proclaiming himself her suitor; but no one at this time paid any attention to him, least of all the girl.

> Two young boys now advanced, each carrying a male dog salmon painted red, and, with the usual preliminary feints, extended them towards her mouth. With each corner of her mouth she bit off a fragment and dropped it to the floor; the boys gathered up these fragments and deposited them on the roof of the house for the crows.

> This ritual feeding of the girl marked the end of the ceremonies.

Her father paid the women attendants, the six boys, and any others who had played a part in them. If he was wealthy, he feasted all the villagers; if not, they quietly dispersed to their homes. The girl broke her fast after her family had eaten and was freed from further confinement. The first time she went out in the canoe again, however, the two women attendants had to go with her.

From the time of her "coming out" no girl or woman might enter a man's fishing and hunting canoe, or a canoe that was used in warfare. Neither might she walk on any fish weir, or touch any tools or weapons used in fishing, hunting, and war. Periodically, each month, and throughout pregnancy, she refrained from eating halibut and black cod, foods which were forbidden to all sick people; and she avoided also the meat of seal, bear, certain waterfowl, flounders, and all varieties of salmon except the humpback.

Parents occasionally married off their daughters within a few days of their coming out. More often they waited a year or longer until the girls became more mature, and their own finances less straightened; for both the coming out ceremony and the marriage often involved considerable expense. During the interval, maidens remained in semi-seclusion, weaving wool, making rush mats, and busying themselves with other housewifely duties, but never leaving the house unless accompanied by some female relative.

Youths likewise intensified their training in all manly pursuits. Not only did they hunt and fish with their elders, but they learned to fence with spears and clubs, so that they might defend their villages from attack, and take part in raids and forays.

As they were nearing adolescence, both boys and girls began to attune themselves for contact with the world of spirits. For boys especially, this required growing accustomed to the many hardships they would eventually meet in their quest to obtain a *saila*, or guardian spirit. Instead of eating twice a day as usual, for example, they often ate in the mornings only and went to bed fasting. They were expected to gain warrior spirit guardians whose war songs they might chant when going into battle, and also when dancing at the winter festivals; and to seek other spirits which would preserve them from sickness and rescue them from sudden dangers.[7] Since these spirits revealed them-

---

7   The practical endowments bestowed on adolescents by spirit guardians were not limited to these few; nor was it certain that any power at all, let alone any particular power or powers, however desirable, would result from a quest. The W̱SÁNEĆ (and their neighbours) knew of numerous spirits, some benefitting their possessors in moments of crisis, others in workaday aspects of life, notably hunting, fishing, and canoe-making. These were mainly the spirits of visible entities such as animals, birds, and fish, and of forces of nature (so to speak), including the sun and winds. However, only certain of them, primarily mythical beings, were most apt to confer medicine (shamanic) power: the knowledge to cure illness, or to inflict harm on others, and then only by dint of the seeker's long and arduous preparation. While spirit patrons also inspired an individual's performance at winter dances (see Chapter 12), it bears mention, as Homer Barnett cautioned, that "winter dancing ... was independent of spirit seeking for utilitarian purposes"; Barnett, *Coast Salish*, 146–68; see also Suttles, "Central Coast Salish," 467. –Ed.

selves only in solitude, parents encouraged their adolescent sons to wander much alone,[8] and even sent them out to isolated places in the woods or on the mountains, where, by fasting and purifying themselves for two or three days, they would qualify for a supernatural visitation.[9] The following recollection, from west Saanich, illustrates the general character of such experiences.

When I was about twelve years old my grandfather said to me: "You see Mt. Newton yonder?[10] If you act aright you will find something near its summit. Follow a small creek up its slope until you reach a pond near which are some circles of stones. The Thunderbird dwells in a deep cave within the high bluff behind the pond. Bathe in the pond, rub your right side with a bundle of yew boughs and place them under one of the stones. Rub your left side with another bundle and place it under the next stone. Rub your right shoulder, your left shoulder, your right arm, your left arm, your right leg, your left leg and your back until bundles of yew underlie all the stones in a half-circle. When you have done this lie down and sleep; but next morning bathe again and complete the circle."

I carried out his instructions, noticing as I placed my bundles under the stones fragments of other yew branches which my own grandfather probably had deposited there some fifty years before.[11] As I looked around after my second bath I heard a loud whirring above my head, and many leaves floated down to the ground at my feet. Looking up I saw a giant bird—the Thunderbird itself—soaring out of sight in the sky. Alarmed, I hurried home, but that night, as I slept in my bed, the Thunderbird entered me and taught me two songs.[12]

---

8   As with boys, girls generally acquired a spirit before marriage. Unlike them, however, it was usual for a girl to be accompanied in the woods by a female relative, and for both to be "afflicted at the same time by the same spirit, for a person can be afflicted repeatedly;" Jenness, "Saanich Notes," 171–72. According to Barnett, a girl's "ambition was not to get an occupationally helpful spirit as much as it was to make [herself] industrious and attractive for marriage"; *Coast Salish*, 150. –Ed.

9   Prominent WSÁNEĆ men, Jenness has written elsewhere, "forced their sons to fast in solitude for several days that they might obtain guardian spirits. Probably such fasting was universal among the Coast Salish in early days, but had dropped out of fashion by the middle of the nineteenth century, except for those who desired to become medicine-men;" Jenness, *Faith of a Coast Salish*, 41. –Ed.

10   Mount Newton stands near the centre of the Saanich peninsula, north of the Tsartlip reserve –Ed.

11   On a rocky flat in the interior of Saltspring Island are several stone circles that may have been set up by Indians fasting. The present-day natives seem to know nothing about their origin.

12   Strange sights and sounds were to be expected in searching for tutelary helpers; as a result, youthful seekers were ordinarily warned not to be afraid, or to turn their backs and flee, upon encountering something uncanny. Equally important, elders warned the young that if they heard a *saila* speak to them they should not answer, but stand and listen; moreover, they should never tell anyone what the *saila* said, lest they lose its guardianship, or fall ill. To illustrate this point, David and Mrs Latasse recounted a recent case in which a man went to church on a Sunday morning and received communion. In the afternoon, while he was on his way to Malahat, he heard a spirit

The first I sing before I begin my dance at the winter festivals, the
second while I am dancing. Neither has any significant words.[13]

A few months later, again at my grandfather's bidding, I climbed up
the slope of Malahat Mountain, bathed in a pond, then slept. About
midnight I awoke, and feeling very thirsty, groped my way in the
darkness to drink from the pond. Just as I was dipping up the water in
my cupped hands a loud cry echoed near me and made my hair stand
on end; and as I drank the cry echoed a second time. I returned to my
fire and lay down again; and while I slept two songs, both wordless,
came to me, though I do not know to this day what spirit entered me.
These songs too I have sung at the winter festivals.[14]

speak to him. He answered it, and on reaching home told someone what it had said. A few days
later he became very ill, for the spirit was offended. The medicine man cured him, but told him
that his illness had been brought on by his own folly; Jenness, "Saanich Notes," 175, 202. –Ed.
13   The power that a *saila* confers comes to be embodied in a "power (or spirit) song," SYEW-
EN (*syəwən*) in SENĆOŦEN. –Ed.
14   Anthropologists have written extensively on the active quest for guardian spirits among a
host of indigenous American peoples. With reference to the Coast Salish, however, Michael Kew
observed that "spirit power may [also] come to an individual unsought or unannounced, perhaps
giving strength or aid in unknown ways"; "Coast Salish Ceremonies," 476. –Ed.

8

Marriage, Childbirth, and Death

A youth may marry any girl of his own or other village, provided she was not his sister, his first cousin, or his second cousin.[1] To avoid his marrying beneath his social level, however, his parents generally arranged the match themselves, and the youth merely fell in with their wishes. They combed the list of eligible girls in the neighbourhood, and, selecting the one that seemed most suitable, sounded out her parents to discover whether their son was acceptable. When assured in that regard, they sent him to announce his suit publicly by fasting just inside the door of her house until such time as her people invited him in to eat. If the latter highly approved of the match, they usually invited him in after a few hours; but if the suitor was unexpected or unwelcome (for occasionally a youth acted on his own initiative, or his parents sent him out without making preliminary enquiries), they ignored him for two or three days, then quietly advised him through some kinsmen to go home; or else they kept him in suspense for a still longer period before they finally accepted him.[2] In rare instances, an unwelcome but obstinate youth succeeded in winning his suit by fasting so long at the doorway that the girl's parents became alarmed lest he should die and make them liable to heavy compensation. Once he had been formally accepted—that is to say, invited inside the house and fed—the youth hurried home to notify his parents, and returned with his kinsmen a few days later to claim his bride.[3]

On the Saanich Peninsula, as in other, perhaps all, Coast Salish districts, custom demanded that the bridegroom should travel for his bride by canoe, even if she lived in the same village. The youth and his kinsmen, therefore, loaded two or three canoes with blankets and other goods and paddled to the bride's home. As they approached the shore, the head of his House, if a nobleman, stood up in the foremost canoe and chanted the family marriage song.[4] Disembarking, they marched up to the girl's house; there, bride and bridegroom sat side by side on a pile of blankets while elderly kinsmen of both families gave them wise counsel. All then sat down to the wedding feast, after which the bridegroom's people brought up their blankets and other goods for the bride's father to distribute among his kin.

The bridegroom and his people seldom departed immediately after the feast, but remained a day or two in the village, enjoying the hospitality of relatives and friends. When the time came for them to return home the bride's

---

1   For a list of the terms of relationship, see Appendix 2.
2   One man said that his father had fasted ten days inside the door of the girl's home.
3   The breach of custom or expectations in such matters is a common theme in Salish tales; for instance, see Part II, no. 31. –Ed
4   In one family, the song ran "This world is going to be mine."

father sometimes led his daughter down to the canoe, wearing a wooden face mask (if he owned one), and shaking a rattle, an honor to his son-in-law that called for liberal payment. The young couple took their places in the middle of the canoe on a pile of blankets provided by the bride's father; behind them sat the slave girls whom he often sent along to be her maids. Then the bridal party paddled away, chanting a song.

A year or so later the bride's kinsmen, travelling in two or three canoes, paid a visit to her home, bringing many presents for the young couple, or, more correctly, repaying the bride-price they had received at her wedding. Families always tried to balance these payments so that there would be no financial loss on either side, and consequently, no loss of prestige. Hence, they kept strict account of their obligations, even though years might pass before they succeeded in liquidating them all.

> When I was about eighteen years of age my kinsmen sent an aunt to Victoria to arrange a match for me with a Songhees girl. She approached the girl's parents, who consulted their relatives first and then gave their consent. As soon as my aunt returned with this news, four of my uncles launched their canoes and took me to Victoria, where three of them stayed at different houses while the fourth kept me company just inside the girl's doorway for two days and a night.[5] During that period we neither ate nor drank, but quietly sat there, wrapped in our blankets until darkness fell, when we lay on the ground and slept. In the late afternoon of the second day the girl's father told my uncles that I had fasted long enough, whereupon two of them led me right inside and brought me some food. My bride and I were then seated side by side on two piles of blankets her people had provided, and four old men preached to us, telling us that now we were married we should be faithful to one another and live in harmony all our days. After these sermons my kinsmen brought in the bride-price—forty sacks of flour, a large number of blankets and other things. We stayed there that night, but early the next morning the blankets on which we were seated during the wedding were carried down to my canoe, and my father-in-law led my wife down, shaking his rattle and chanting a song. My own people, who had already embarked, chanted their two marriage songs "I come down from the mountain," and "The nobleman begins to sing," as my wife stepped into the canoe. We paddled away to their singing.

---

5   Jimmy Fraser, an old Songhees Indian from Esquimalt, said that among his people, the youth generally sat just outside the door, which was shut against him to test the sincerity of his suit; and that whenever anyone came out he would beg "Open the door for me." If he became cold or very tired he might take shelter in another house, provided some one temporarily took his place, because if it remained vacant his suit was cancelled. After two, three, or four days he was invited to sit just inside the door, and the girl's people began to prepare for the wedding. He watched them for a time, then returned home to make his own preparations.

...

When I was old enough to marry, my parents, who lived then at Co-miaken, on the Cowichan River, sent four relatives with a present of food to the house of a girl in Clemclemaluts, three miles away, and asked them to propose a marriage. The girl's parents silently laid the food at the back of the house and consulted their relatives, after which they fed the four envoys and let them depart without any message. We knew, however, that they had agreed to the match because they did not offer to pay for the food. A few days later, therefore, I myself poled up to her house taking three goat wool blankets, one to sit on and two to wrap around my shoulders. For four days and four nights I sat or lay just within the entrance. Then four old men led me right inside, and transferred my blankets to the shoulders of two old kinsmen of my bride. At the same time, they sent word to my parents that my probation had ended, and invited them to attend the wedding.

My parents sent two men ahead to lead me into the portion of the house occupied by the girl's immediate family and followed in their canoe with a number of relatives. I was conducted to a bench at the side of the room, while my bride sat on a pile of blankets in the middle of the floor. Ten of her relatives came in: eight of them carried her blankets, the other two led her by the hand and seated her beside me. My own people arranged themselves behind us, and my parents, stepping forward, paid these ten relatives and handed over the bride-price. They paid one hundred goat wool blankets and one hundred Hudson's Bay blankets, besides other things, all of which were distributed among my bride's relatives. The latter then carried down to my canoe the blankets and other things which she was to take with her, and my people polled us down to Comiaken.

Next day my parents-in-law came down in two canoes to our house, bringing a quantity of food, and I invited all my neighbours to come in and share it the day following. Several of my relatives during this feast made speeches, thanking my parents-in-law for the food and expressing approval of the match.

Our marriage occurred shortly before the end of the winter, and my wife had become a dancer just at the beginning of that season. It was therefore rather dangerous for her to marry before it [i.e. the spirit dancing season] closed, but by chewing consumption plant seeds and rubbing them on her body after each morning bath she escaped unharmed.

In both these instances the bridegrooms were of noble rank. Below is a commoner's account of his marriage.

When I was a young man and found a girl to my liking, I did not ask any of my relatives to arrange the match for me, but just went over to her house and sat in the middle of the floor. Her parents were annoyed and told me to go home; but I refused, and sat there fasting for four days and four nights, afraid to leave lest they should lock the door against me. On the evening of the fourth day they gave in; they led me to the fire, cooked some food, brought the girl to eat with me, and sent me home. The next day my people gathered all the goat wool blankets they possessed, piled them into a canoe, and escorted me to the house to bring away my bride. Neither going nor returning did they chant any songs, nor did her father escort her to my canoe; for we were commoners, and did not possess any rattles, face masks, or marriage songs. Instead my people simply carried the blankets into her house and brought her away, with her sack of potatoes and bag of dried fish, as soon as her father told her to leave. However, a few days later her people brought a lot of food and blankets to my home and feasted all my relatives.

After my first wife died I sought the hand of my present one. Neither she nor her parents wanted me, so when I began to fast in her house they smuggled her away to Victoria and told me she might never return. She did return, however, sometime later, and I sued for her hand again. Her parents locked the door against me, but I waited outside all one night and when they opened the door in the morning, I slipped in and sat down against a post in the middle of the floor. The girl took refuge in her uncle's corner of the big house, but after two days her parents yielded and fed me until she consented to marry me.

As is evident from the above accounts, post-marital residence was patrilocal; the young husband took his wife to his father's home and was there slotted a room for himself. Though there was no real courtship prior to marriage, and the young couple might never have seen each other before their wedding, the lack of privacy in a big house and the numerous residents were in some measure a safeguard; for a man could not abuse his wife, nor she neglect her duties, without incurring the condemnation of the whole household. Always in the background, too, was her family, which would certainly resent any ill-treatment, and in the last resort might offer her asylum and marry her to someone else. The social code enjoined strict chastity both before and after marriage, and the great majority of the Saanich lived up to this code. If a woman proved unfaithful, her husband might cut off her nose and mutilate the soles of her feet without interference from her kin, or he might divorce her by sending her back to her people; and he might kill her paramour without starting a blood feud, if he had the courage to attack him. Such provocations, however, seldom arose. Only the principal nobles could afford more than one wife; and their wives came from different districts, and occupied separate rooms.[6] Even slave women and girls received the same protection as others. A mistress who could overrule her lord might conceivably ill-treat them, though the community would certainly condemn her; but the masters were too jealous of their own prestige to consort with slave women, or to permit their molestation by any outsider.

...

Since a childless marriage was considered a calamity, the birth of the first child occasioned great rejoicing. The expectant mother kept away from all fires as much as possible, though she might cook for her husband if it was absolutely necessary. Women often tried to diagnose the sex of the still unborn child. A girl, they thought, lay more quietly in the womb than a boy, made the left breast a little larger than the right, and the mother a little more prominent behind than before. Those who wanted boy babies deposited boys' toys in certain creeks and drank the water, chewed wild gooseberry leaves and certain other plants, and permitted intercourse only during the first twelve days after the oestrus [i.e. menstrual] period. To facilitate delivery, they chewed various herbs, and drank decoctions from a certain moss that grows on rotten wood or from a fungus of the family *Clavariaceae*.

A mother often delivered herself, all alone, in some corner of the house, screened off by mats. In every village, however, there was at least one woman who was prepared to serve as a midwife. She knelt, either in front of the kneeling mother (who generally grasped a stick) and held her head, or else she kneeled behind her and pressed downward on the womb. If labour was prolonged, a medicine man might be summoned to pour warm oil on the mother's head and whisper "You shall give birth. You shall complete the act for which you were prepared in the beginning of time." The midwife cut the cord of the newborn babe with a shell knife, bound it with sinew, and buried the afterbirth. After washing the baby with warm water, she rubbed it all over with fat or oil, wrapped it in sphagnum moss or shredded cedar bark, and laid it in the cradle with a cedar bark pad pressing heavily on its forehead. Then she washed the mother in warm water, squeezed the liquid from her breasts, and, if the milk was slow in flowing, applied a hot poultice of yarrow leaves (*Achillea millefolium*).[7] The mother rested from four to six days, after which she was free to bathe and resume her household duties.

A mother oiled her boy's navel string until it dropped off; then she carefully wrapped and concealed it where it would never be shaken or disturbed, believing that any disturbance would make the child restless, and perhaps in-

---

6   I failed to enquire whether they were expected to fast inside the doorway for each wife, but consider it very improbable.

7   The Saanich denied the use among themselves of elderberry rind poultices reported by Charles Hill-Tout among the Squamish.

sane. If the first child died, the parents called in a priest who, with the parents, faced the rising sun, and, raising the baby three times in his arms, placed it in the arms of the mother, shook his rattle over her and prayed the sun spirit to let her next child survive. Taking the dead babe in his arms again, he repeated the rite over the father and then buried the child. Some of the Saanich thought that the soul of the dead infant was reborn in the next child, but others would not commit themselves definitely on this point.

Twins aroused a feeling of superstitious dread for which no explanation was forthcoming. Their hair was never cut short lest they sicken and die. For several months the parents were prohibited from embarking in a canoe lest they offend the spirits of the fish and mammals in the sea, and they had to live apart from their fellow men, preferably in some lonely spot where the rising sun would shine on their cabin each morning. During these months the father hunted land animals to support himself and his family; but he also spent much time in bathing and purifying himself, so that in the end he often became an influential medicine man.

Women who wished to bear no more children interred the afterbirth from their latest child just outside the door where people would step over it; or they buried it at the waterline on the beach. A few, in desperation, stood in cold water up to the armpits immediately after delivery. Some tried to make themselves sterile by drinking a decoction from a yellow moss that grows on fir trees, or to induce an early menopause by drying on the sunny face of a mountain a tube of kelp that contained a little of their blood.

...

Just as childhood and marriage ceremonies varied slightly from family to family, so there were variations, too, in funeral rites, although the ideas behind them remained essentially uniform. However beloved a man had been during his lifetime, from the moment he ceased to breathe he became an object of deep fear because his shade, or ghost, was credited with power to inflict paralysis on any one with whom it came into contact [see Chapter 9]. A mysterious contagion attached itself to the man who made the coffin, to the "undertakers" who handled the corpse, to the mourners who attended the funeral, to the house and bed in which the deceased had breathed his last, and, most of all, to the widow he left behind him. The ghost had to be expelled from the neighbourhood of living beings, and everyone and everything that had been associated with the corpse had to undergo purification. At Halalt, twenty miles north of the Saanich Peninsula, the Indians burned all the dead man's tools and weapons, even his canoe; but the Saanich were content to burn only a few of his moveable possessions, to leave others beside the grave, and to divide the rest among his sons and mourners.[8] They made no distinction between a

---

8   The Songhees, and probably other Coast Salish Indians, occasionally reserved some of the

dead nobleman and a dead slave except that they sometimes avoided the expense of a coffin for a slave by wrapping the body in a mat.

Families had their own cemeteries, some of them on small rocky islets a short distance off shore. There the Saanich deposited the coffins, without regard to their direction, on the bare rock, or on horizontal logs, and weighted them down with stones. Elsewhere they sometimes set them in trees or on top of low posts carved and painted with red ochre. Nobles of high rank were buried occasionally, not in boxes, but in canoes, which then became the repositories of other members of the same families until the canoes rotted. In the nineteenth century the Saanich, like other Coast Salish, built a few grave houses, roofed usually with cedar bark, in which they piled the coffins, one on top of another; but they claimed that this custom, and also burial in the ground, were post-European. They seemed to have no recollection of cairn burials, although a few cairns have been found on the peninsula.

When my first wife died, a cousin made a coffin for her while some of my female relatives dressed her in her best clothes. A priest chanted a wordless prayer to X̱e.ls before they laid her in the coffin with her knees bent up close to her chin; then, while he prayed again, I leaped four times over the foot of the coffin, turning counter-clockwise after each leap, so that the ghost of my deceased wife might not follow me and bring swift death to any woman I might marry later. With other mourners I followed the procession to the graveyard, where the priest prayed again and all who had taken an active part in the funeral rites chewed some plant he had given them to ward off infection. Afterwards we returned to my house, but I was instructed to keep away from the others and to sit in a corner by myself. The priest dried some salal and Oregon grape bushes before the fire, and when darkness fell, set them ablaze, swished them over the heads of the mourners and round the walls of the house, and hurled them outdoors, banishing my wife's ghost with them. The others then ate and drank as usual, but I received from the priest only a dried salmon. He made me bite off and drop into his hand four morsels, which he afterwards threw on top of the roof for the crows; and he told me to turn my back on the people before eating the remainder, because if I ate facing them I might draw away the souls of some of the children and cause their death. He then placed blackberry, thistle, and other sharp plants under my sleeping mat to ward off any sorcery, and cautioned me to lie on my back, not on my side, to spit, not on the floor, but on a black stone he had planted close to the fire, and to remain in the house for four days.

Early the next morning the same priest painted the faces of all the

<hr>

property to burn or give away at some future potlatch, when they also chanted one of the dead man's songs to honour his memory.

mourners except me and led us down to the beach, where he stationed me about twenty yards away from the rest. Softly chanting a prayer, he trimmed each person's hair and burned it in a fire, whereupon each of the mourners bound round his head a chaplet of salal, blackberry, or Oregon grape. Finally, the priest lined them all up, and, chanting his prayer, marched them to the water's edge and back four times before commanding them to throw away their chaplets and plunge in. They were then free to go about their usual occupations; but I, whom he forbade to bathe, confined myself to my house.

Four days after the funeral the priest painted my face also with red ochre, prayed over me, and sent me into the woods to bestride four fir branches and rub my face with them. Next I sought out four moss-covered stones and rubbed the moss off with my cheeks. Then I bathed in a creek on the mountainside and returned home before night, since it was dangerous for me to be outside after dark.

On the following morning he led me outside and made me strike with my axe four times, then cut four times with my knife; after each stroke he chanted a prayer. Finally, he led me to the beach and, after four feints, each followed by a prayer, made me enter the water. Thus he freed me from all contagion. Thenceforth I could hunt and fish and perform all my usual tasks, although for several weeks longer he would not allow me to talk to any children or to eat in company unless I turned my back; and for a whole year he forbade me to eat seal, octopus, ducks, sockeye salmon, and cod. About ten days after the funeral he carried into the woods the black stone on which I had been expectorating, and left it beside some pool that had been a bathing place of medicine men long ago.

In most communities there was not only a professional coffin maker, but also a priest who specialized in marriage and funeral rites, and, with the assistance of his wife, acted as undertaker. Every priest was free to vary the ritual within certain limits, so that the funeral just described was different from many others. Some priests inserted spoken words into their prayers, and addressed them to a vague sky god,[9] not to X̱e.ls, whom many regarded as

---

9   This "vague sky god" doubtless refers to *ci'cəɫ sie'm*, the diety of which Katzie elder Peter Pierre spoke in recounting a mythic cycle of creation to Jenness; as Pierre explained at the time, Katzie cosmogony rested on an ancient and indigenous monotheistic principal. Among other groups, however, Jenness's informants claimed that the concept of a high god was a foreign accretion of relatively recent vintage, introduced, according to one (William Sepass, of Sardis), by Christian missionaries, and to others, by emissaries from aboriginal groups resident elsewhere. Exemplifying the second view, Albert Westly told him that "the Nanaimo Indians heard of Tciltcitsiem [*sic*] over 100 years ago, before the white people came," noting that "someone visited them in the middle of each summer, made them gather in a circle and sing 'Don't do anything till Siem tells you.' While singing, they looked up and pointed to heaven." Anthropologist Wayne Suttles has identified a likely non-missionary source in the nineteenth century Prophet Dance, a post-contact messianic movement that diffused westward into Coast Salish territory from the

primarily a spirit of the sea. Some burned consumption plant seeds in the house fire for several evenings to drive away the ghost, and kept the widow or widower in confinement for eight days, instead of only four. All, or most all, insisted that the corpse should be carried feet foremost out of the house, through a window or hole in the wall, but not through the door, lest the souls of the survivors follow after it.

Old David [Latasse], a priest on the Tsartlip reserve, adopted the following procedure. He and his wife washed and dressed the corpse, and before laying it in the coffin, raised it four times while he prayed X̱e.ls to "receive his child." He invited various people to attend the funeral as mourners, and arranged for them to receive certain presents later as payment, since most Indians avoided funerals through fear of the ghost; and he painted the head, face, and blanket of the widow or widower with red ochre. Strong men, relatives of the deceased, carried the coffin with cedar ropes to the family cemetery where they laid it on the ground, or set it on low posts. The priest chanted again his prayer to X̱e.ls, burned beside the coffin some of the deceased's favourite foods, or some possessions that he had especially prized, deposited nearby a few of his tools, and sent all the mourners away to bathe and scrub their bodies with yew branches. At evening he drove the ghost from the house by "sweeping" its walls and inmates with burning twigs of fig, salal, and arbutus, and arranged a new bed for the widow or widower, placing spruce boughs covered with diatomaceous earth under the sleeping mat of a widow, and blackberry under the mat of a widower. For the latter, he prescribed also a chaplet of blackberry branches. He instructed them not to approach the fire or touch any tools or utensils for four days, and to eat nothing but dried fish or dried clams. They were also to remain very quiet in a corner of the house except that once a day, they should go into the woods and bathe in some fresh water pool. On the fourth day he assembled all the household, prayed over them, and singed their hair to mitigate their grief. He then led the widower and sons to their bathing place on the beach (his wife [Mrs Latasse] substituted for him with a widow and her daughters) and made them dive into the sea while he chanted his prayer. The widower's blackberry chaplet floated away on the water. Henceforth he was free to go out in his canoe and resume his everyday life, though counselled to keep very much to himself for some weeks. The old priest said that if the widower (or widow) bathed in the sea or entered his canoe before this ceremonial bath, painful lumps would develop on the insides of his legs. For their own protection, the priest and his wife, the maker of the coffin, and the men who carried it to the cemetery, all slept over blackberry bushes for four days.

---

interior Plateau. Before this, religious belief among the W̱SÁNEĆ and their Vancouver Island neighbours focussed on the sun, the Transformer X̱e.ls, and on an array of spirit beings; Jenness, *Faith of a Coast Salish*, 88; "Saanich Notes," 166; Suttles, *Katzie*, 6; "Plateau Prophet Dance," 377. –Ed.

George Kwakaston, an elder on the Koksilah reserve, near Cowichan, described several variations and peculiarities of funerary practice in that place. To begin, three or four people in the community were hereditary undertakers, three or four others inherited the knowledge of the ritual for widows and widowers, and still others for the feast to the dead. All received small payments for their services. Prayers were addressed to the shade or ghost of the dead, not to any deity. If a man slipped and fell when helping to carry a coffin, he would die within a year. Widow and widower had to keep away from the Cowichan River for eight days through fear of spoiling the run of salmon. The widower, but not the widow, rubbed the ochre from his face with saplings. Finally, no one might stand or sit in front of the widow, or speak to her, for eight days.

On the neighbouring reserve at Quamichan, a nobleman, Johnson, similarly distinguished professional undertakers (*shusqwoiath*) who dressed the corpse, and sometimes carried it, feet foremost, to the grave, from the priests (*qoqweals*) who purified the house and the mourners. Nobles, he said, hired two priests to shake their rattles and chant a prayer— "You came from a woman's womb. Return now to your home."— before the corpse was carried from the house, to lead the procession to the cemetery, and to chant another prayer at the grave. There the mourners deposited all the dead man's property, burned his bedding and broke up his canoe. Only his [wooden] face-mask and rattle, if he possessed any, were kept back for his eldest son, who inherited also his share of the house and weir. The dead man's name was dropped from use for about two generations. After the funeral, all the mourners returned to the house and waited outside while five or six priests swept the interior with burning branches of Oregon grape; then they, too, entered and were purified in the same way while they pounded the boards in front of their benches to drive away the ghost. The widower (or widow), whose hair was cut at the nape of the neck, remained in his room for eight days wrapped in an ochre-sprinkled blanket, sleeping over some prickly plant such as Oregon grape, and eating only small quantities of dried fish with his back turned to the wall. The first time he ate, a priest made him bite off four fragments to be thrown on the roof for the crows. At the end of eight days the undertakers brought a tub of water into the house and bathed him, after which he was free to resume his ordinary life. Common people and slaves, the old man added, were buried in the same way, but with less ceremony.

Old Bob and Annie Bob, the elderly couple from Halalt, described in some detail their funeral rites as follows. Both, it should be noted, were commoners.

> The nearest of kin painted the face of the dead man (or woman), wrapped him first in a goat wool blanket, then in a rush mat, and carried him out, head foremost, through the door (only in more recent times through a hole in the wall) to an island near the village, where they laid him on the ground and burned his property, even his canoe.

No chants were sung, no prayers recited. On returning to their homes, all the mourners washed the paint from their faces with heated urine.

The next morning, before daylight, the mourners went up to the dead man's house so that the priest (*thitha*) might clip off their hair at the nape of the neck. Then they bound chaplets of blackberry vines and feathers round their heads and, marching to the beach, lined up in a row with the priest on their right. While the latter intoned a brief chant, they marched into the sea and back again, still facing the water. The second time he chanted they shouted as they entered the water; the third time they washed the paint from their faces; and the fourth they dashed right in, threw away their chaplets, and, turning round, raced for their homes without looking back. Some then gathered branches of the Oregon grape to dry beside the fire in the dead man's house, and in the evening all the mourners gathered to sweep the house with the flaming boughs, burning in the fire at the same time some seeds of the consumption plant.

The widower (or widow, for both followed the same regime) was considered impure for eight days. He slept on the floor on a bed of blackberry vines and other prickly bushes from which the thorns had been removed. His pillow was a stone with feathers strewn round its edges, and beside it was another stone on which he expectorated. Anyone who spoke to him addressed him from behind. Each morning he wandered away and bathed in every suitable pool, but not in the sea. If he came upon a stone like the one on which he expectorated, he carefully stepped over it; but he avoided stepping over any solid log, because then his next wife would soon die. Before returning home at evening he rubbed the paint from his face with fir branches, and the priest, chanting a prayer, repainted his face when he entered the house.

During the first four days he neither ate nor drank. On the fifth the priest offered him dried dog salmon sprinkled with red ochre. He bit off four fragments to be thrown to the crows and ate the rest, with his back turned to the inmates of the house. During the next three days he ate only dried fish.

On the eighth day his temporary bed was thrown out, and the priest instructed him, with the customary three feints, to use his knife and axe again. This ended his period of mourning.

Little children wore bracelets and anklets of goat wool for a time after a parent died, but underwent no other restrictions.

The Saanich often gave a feast to the dead, but it was neither obligatory, nor was it held at any definite time. When given two or three days after the funeral it was a very minor affair, intended mainly to comfort the relatives. More often it was held some months later, a favourite time being the autumn, after close of the salmon season; and then the consolation of the relatives was subordinated to the actual feeding and propitiation of the dead man's ghost and of all his friends in the world of ghosts.[10] The family hired a priest to light a fire within the house and to burn ceremonially some food to which the deceased had been partial during his lifetime. Mrs Latasse, whose husband David had often officiated at this rite, said that the priest should burn first some fish, whose crackling would summon the ghosts, then a little food for the person recently deceased, and finally some food for all deceased members of the community. He should not burn all the food lest another member of the family die soon afterwards; and he should warn away little children and ailing persons lest their souls be abstracted from their bodies and they too perish.

Some Coast Salish priests used indifferently any kind of wood for the fire provided it was thoroughly dry, but a Quamichan woman at Cowichan thought it should always be cedar, because its loud crackling served to summon the ghosts. In her community the priest was always a woman who had inherited the rite from her predecessor. She lit the ceremonial fire and walked around it, summoning the dead person by name to come and eat. After allowing due time for it to arrive she took up a bowl, and, walking half-way round the food (which was commonly laid out on boards), poured water on the ground for the ghost to drink; then, after another brief interval, she threw half of the food into the flames; the remaining food she carried home to share with relatives and friends. The ghost naturally invited all its friends in the ghost-world to share the feast, just as the deceased during his lifetime would have called in his neighbours.

At Halalt, according to the Bobs, the feast was usually held two or three months after the funeral. The priest held up some of the food, silently offering it to the ghost of the deceased, and laid it on the pile of wood. He deposited a second offering for the ghosts of deceased relatives, and a third for the ghosts of all the dead. When, finally, he lit the fire, all the spectators turned their backs and hastened away.

A widower sometimes remarried within a year of his first wife's decease, but even if his second wife was a widow, he had to lay suit to her publicly by fasting inside her door. A widow, after a lapse of about two years, usually tried to marry a kinsman of her first husband who would be interested in the welfare of her children; if there were no kinsman, she returned to her parental village, taking her children and property with her.

---

10   Cowichan elder George Kwakaston thought it preferable to hold the feast on the fifth day after death, the day after the ghost, which at first wandered aimlessly near its former home, joined the host of ghosts.

9

Man and Nature

The earth seemed to the Saanich to be a flat expanse of land and sea over which brooded the sky, which was just another land like this one, possessing water and trees, and supporting animals and human-like beings. The river that flowed through sky-land was the Milky Way, the northern lights were ice floes that drifted in the water and were lit up by the departing sun, and the winking stars were the light of people's eyes. The Indians gave names to many of the stars; they called the Great Dipper the elk, the Little Dipper the bullhead, the Morning Star the day-bringer, Orion's belt, which they imagined were six men in two canoes hunting ducks, was known as *papayahtil.* Two girls once married stars, the legend ran, and they told the Indians about sky-land after they returned to earth.

The most powerful human-like beings in that land were the sun (*sqoqw-al*), which was female, and the moon (*sqelts*), which was male.[1] The Indians prayed to the sun, just as it was rising, for the girl entering adolescence. Each family had different words, but their general tenor was "May this girl be strong, enjoy a long life, etc." Prayers were also addressed to the sun for the person who was being initiated as a dancer at the winter dances. Before his morning dip, too, many a man would walk four times up and down the beach, praying "I rely upon you to help me this day. I trust you to guide me in all my undertakings and look for your protection." Then he dived into the water. In this and the last instance, a few Indians addressed their prayers to Xɛ.ls—i.e. Haylse, the Transformer—the majority to the sun.

Only the sorcerer prayed to the setting sun, just before its last rays vanished. If he had a grudge against a man he would say "Give me your protection as you have this day. Relieve me of so-and-so who is causing me trouble. Take him from me." These were not the exact words, but approximate their general tenor; the exact formula was a secret. The sorcerer prayed thus four evenings in succession. His enemy would fall ill soon afterwards.

David Latasse affirmed that now and then the sun caught an extra-large cod, and only by a desperate struggle succeeded in killing it. During the struggle the sun was eclipsed through the cod passing in front of it, whereupon he and his family summoned to its aid the swiftest of all birds, the humming-bird, chanting "Go up, hummingbird; go up, hummingbird."[2] What caused an eclipse of the moon he did not know, nor did he concern himself greatly with the event, because the moon was definitely less powerful and less important than the sun. However, another Saanich Indian, Louis Pelkey, from Tsawout,

---

1   In SENĆOŦEN, SḰEḴEL (*sqʷəqʷʃl'*) is "sun," ȽḴÁL,J (*ɫqélč'*) is "moon." –Ed.
2   Johnson, a Quamichan Indian from near Duncan, said that the cod was eating the sun but that his people paid little attention.

flatly rejected this explanation of the solar eclipse. To him, it denoted the impending death of some nobleman whose soul was already darkening the sun's face, while a round light near the sun (a sun-dog) signified that the Comox Indians were approaching and would shortly cut off some people's heads. Under this earth, some of the Saanich thought, was another land about which, however, they could say little because it was more shadowy and vague than the sky-land above.

Between earth and sky roamed a giant eagle-like bird whose flapping wings created the thunder and whose blinking eyes were lightning flashes. Chain and forked lightning, however, marked the movements of a dangerous snake. Rain and wind were produced by certain of the superhuman beings or spirits in which this earth abounded. The winters grew more severe until they reached a maximum, then became milder, following a weather cycle whose length the Indians confessed themselves unable to determine.

Each entity on this earth, even things that Europeans class as inanimate, consisted of a soul—*smastimauch*—enclosed within a corporeal frame. Man was unable to change his frame, but this was not the case with many things; a deer, for example, might conceivably transform itself into a stump, or a fish into a stone.

> Once when my uncle was fishing for spring salmon in Cowichan Bay he felt a fish tug strongly on his line. It struggled all the way to the surface, then suddenly changed into an apparently lifeless stone, which he kept, and thereby became a wonderfully successful fisherman. I myself had a similar experience in the same bay. My salmon too changed into a stone, with the result that I caught over one hundred fish in that one night. But instead of leaving the stone in the boat, as I should have done, I wrapped it in a sack and concealed it in a hole in a bank. When I searched for it later it had disappeared, having reverted, no doubt, to a fish and returned to the water.
>
> ...
>
> On Saltspring Island, a hunter shot a buck, which fell on its back with its four legs in the air. When he walked up to it, however, he found only a stump pierced by his shot. A few weeks later, when he returned to the same place, the stump had disappeared, having changed back into a deer.

In the dawn of the world all animals, birds, and fish were human beings, but the powerful Xe.ls transformed their outward shapes without depriving them of their souls. Whether or not there were trees in those earliest days the Saanich could not say; but trees, too, they believed, possessed souls, and even wept whenever one of them was blown down by the wind. In far-away lands, fish, and perhaps other creatures, reverted to their human forms and lived in villages similar to those of the Indians; thus the salmon were fish during the migration season, and human beings all the rest of the year. Mrs Latasse said that there is a mother fish, larger than the usual one, in every species, and likewise a mother animal and a mother tree; Indians travelling far from land have occasionally seen the mother cod and the mother salmon near some mysterious island. She stated also that there are male and female specimens of every plant, that the male grows straighter, taller, and with fewer branches, the female being stubby and round, and that only the male plant should be used for medicines. Whether her ideas prevailed generally or not I did not discover. No Saanich denied to the sea a soul, or hesitated to appease it in stormy weather by a prayer.[3]

In addition to a soul and a corporeal body, all creatures, including man, possessed a shadow or reflection, *keahenettan*, visible in sunlight and moonlight, and as some thought also, in clear water. Naturally, this shadow resembled in form the body. So, too, did the soul, according to Mrs Latasse, who stated that it was very small and transparent, and that it normally dwelt in the heart. She and her husband, David, thought that human beings (and perhaps other living creatures) must possess two souls, one of which remained constantly inside the body, giving it vitality, while the other, responsible apparently for thought or consciousness, sometimes wandered away—for instance, in dreams.[4] This wandering soul was visible only to medicine men. She herself saw one occasionally, and then she knew that she would receive a visitor the next day, an Indian if the soul appeared red, a white person if it appeared green. At death, they concluded, the body and the shadow perished, the soul that gave the body vitality also perished, but the soul that gave rise to consciousness lingered near the grave and wandered abroad by night to hunt and feast. It was no longer a soul, but a ghost, *spalkwithe*, which fed on the souls of food, travelled in the souls of canoes, and generally passed a ghostly replica of its former existence inside the body. Instead of partaking in its principal meal in the late afternoon, it dined now two or three hours before daybreak. Not infrequently it assumed the form of the small owl which the old couple also called *spalk-withe*;[5] and because this owl frequently haunted their settlement, and ghosts were dangerous to living beings, people would carefully close the roof boards of their houses as soon as darkness fell, and burn in their fires the seeds of the consumption plant to drive away the ghosts. They were convinced, however, that many a ghost, or disembodied soul, was reborn in the same family, ex-

---

3   Likewise, forces of nature, including winds and thunder, no less sun, moon, and stars, possessed souls. –Ed.

4   David and Mrs Latasse used the same word for both aspects of the soul—in his notes, Jenness's renders the common term *smastímaux*—and believed that each dwelled in a man's heart, not his brain (*smatkən*). He recorded the words for shadow, and a being's outer form, as *k'eəhent'.en* and *stíuk*, respectively; "Saanich Notes," 154. –Ed.

5   In SENĆOŦEN, the screech owl is called SPELKIȽE (*spəlqʷitˀəʔ*). In his notes, Jenness transcribes the word for ghost (and its owl counterpart) as *spəlkwiθe*. It has yet a third meaning: "human corpse." –Ed.

plaining in this way the frequent likeness of a child to some ancestor.

Tom Paul, the next-door neighbour and kinsman of this old Tsartlip couple, did not agree with them concerning the afterlife. Man, he thought, had one soul only, which at death commonly assumed the form of a larger owl, *seetenuch*.[6] It was the shadow that became the small owl which sometimes flew inside the Indian houses, to talk with medicine men.[7]

Different again was the belief of Edward Jim, another old Saanich Indian who lived on the Tsekum reserve, on Patricia Bay. He postulated a shadow, a soul that resided in the heart and was visible in water or a mirror, and a mind, *shalli*.[8] At death, the mind became the little owl, the shadow became a ghost, while the soul haunted the spot where the dead man had fasted and obtained a guardian spirit. There it lingered until it was reborn in another child of the same family. Each family had its individual stock of souls, which were not transferable; hence the total number of souls was limited.

There was similar disagreement among other Coast Salish natives. In one case, Albert Westly, of Nanaimo, differentiated between the *cwali* (soul), *sititc* (or *smustiux,* mind or vitality), and *keahenettan* (shadow.) The soul sometimes leaves the body and may be recovered by a *cnem* (medicine man). At death, the shadow disappears, but the *cwali* becomes a ghost (*spalkwitha*), haunting the graveyard and appearing to people in dreams; however, it may also be reincarnated in a grandchild. If a ghost suddenly touches someone it leaves him [or her] with a twisted tongue; without the attention of a *cnem* or priest (*thitha*), such encounters may result in death.[9] By contrast, Johnson, from the Quamichan reserve, held that at death, the soul generally went to dwell in a shadowy land very much like its old home, and only rarely underwent reincarnation. He told the following story to substantiate his belief:

> A man whose wife had died refused to return to his house, but mourned beneath her grave for four days and four nights. On the fourth night he saw her alight from her coffin, adjust her blanket and walk away from the grave. He tried to seize her in his arms, but she eluded

---

6   Paul said that the man who has the big owl (*ci.tenux*) for his *saila* (guardian spirit) is a good deer hunter. ĆIYTNEW̱ (*čiitŋax*ʷ) refers to the great horned owl. –Ed.

7   Paul related the following story to illustrate the connection between shade and owl: After the whites came to Victoria there lived at Musqueam two brothers, one of whom was in the habit of riding into the city, getting drunk, and riding home again, singing loudly. After he died his brother heard singing one night, and recognized his brother's song. He went out, and saw his brother's horse going to the stable, with a big owl riding on its back. As soon as the animal entered the stable the owl disappeared; it was his brother's soul. Jenness, "Saanich Notes," 164. –Ed.

8   On the SENĆOŦEN word for soul, see page 11, footnote 9; mind (or thought) is X̱ĆENIN (*x̌čəŋin*). –Ed.

9   Westly claimed that people might use the same word for ghost (*spalkwitha*) as for graveyard. (In Hul'q'umi'num, the word for graveyard is *shmuk'wélu;* its SENĆOŦEN equivalent is *šməlqʷelə.*) He also said that some doctors become familiar with ghosts and may derive power from them; they even learn to speak their language; Jenness, "Saanich Notes," 153 –Ed

his grasp and glided along in front of him until they reached a lake. Without hesitation she walked on its surface, and he followed safely in her footsteps. Beyond the lake he lost her in a crowd of people who were rejoicing and playing games. Someone came up to him and said "what are you doing here? You are not dead." And he answered "I followed my wife." Two messengers brought his wife to him, and the people, gathering round, said "Since you love her so dearly you may take her back again. But you must not touch her for four days and four nights." The man and his wife returned to their earthly home and for two days he kept away from her. On the third night, however, he crept beneath her blanket. Then she arose, adjusted the blanket and glided away far in front of him; despite his utmost effort, he could not keep up with her. She crossed the lake to the other side, but when he tried to follow her he sank beneath the surface and drowned.

There was not one Indian who did not dread meeting a ghost, or shade, believing that the mere touch of one induced illness, often partial paralysis. Ghosts, they said, live happily by themselves and wander abroad only at night, walking with a slight stoop with their faces concealed or everted.[10] They do not like living beings to discuss them, and a man should never mention them before starting out to fish or hunt lest they keep all the fish and game away from him. Now and again they have helped an individual Indian; there was an old man, for example, who would merely draw his canoe up on the beach at nightfall and walk around while the ghosts of his dead relatives filled the boat with firewood for him. (They must have been the shades of dead relatives who had been very fond of him.) However, their presence in the vicinity was usually dangerous, and the mere touch of one occasioned a sudden cramp, causing paralysis to set in unless the victim had recourse to a medicine man who massaged the affected area with deer fat, a treatment that made the blood circulate again.

A medicine-man who was summoned to treat a sick girl announced that the ghost of her father had passed along the road outside and looked at her longingly, wishing to take her with him. Her face was already becoming paralyzed, but the medicine man rubbed it with fat every day and cured her.

...

[Louis] Pelkey's son was playing in the woods and came in with his face and limbs twisted and paralyzed. His father went to an old woman who was a *siowa* [seer]. She took her ochre, deer fat, goat wool and a feather and sat down near the boy. "I shall paint my face four times," she said, "and if he doesn't straighten out the fourth time his

10 Mrs Latasse explained that you can tell a [guardian] spirit (*saila*) from a shade (*spalkwithe*) because the latter always stoops and conceals its face, whereas the former walks upright.

case is hopeless." She dipped her feather in the ochre and started to paint her face, announcing that she was going to depict the *spalk-withe* that the boy had encountered. She chanted a song all the time she painted her face with what suggested a person; then she rubbed it off with her goat wool and painted it another pattern to the accompaniment of another song. She did this four times. The boy's face straightened at the fourth song. She rubbed him with deer fat, and he sat up and asked for food.[11]

An Indian on Brentwood Bay reserve [Tsartlip] abused his wife right up to her death. He did not go through the proper purification ceremonies after her funeral and was always afraid of his wife's shade haunting him. Once he went out after dark, pulled an apple out of his pocket and began to eat it. This is against all rules—for the smell of food out-of-doors after dark attracts the shades. Suddenly his wife's shade snatched the apple out of his hand. He turned quickly—his mouth and face became twisted; his hands began to grow paralyzed. He hurried home and his father hastily summoned a medicine man, who worked an hour over him before he was able to cure him. The medicine man received five dollars.[12]

---

11   On hearing Pelkey's tale, Johnson, Jenness's Quamichan informant, explained that the child was probably attended to by a *thitha*, not a *siowa*, since the latter were clairvoyants, not healers. In addition, he pointed out that it was surely her patient's face, not her own, that she painted. According to Barnett, however, a *siowa* might be consulted when a "patient was oppressed by dreams of the dead or by ghosts which he could see or feel"; Ibid., 248; Barnett, *Coast Salish*, 211. –Ed.
12   Jenness, "Saanich Notes," 159. –Ed

10

Guardian Spirits

The preceding chapter is the last portion of the manuscript Diamond Jenness completed. As noted in the preface, he intended to write on three additional topics: guardian spirits, illness and medicine, and winter (spirit) dances. To that end, the present chapter offers an account of spirit beings inhabiting the W̱SÁNEĆ world. Chapter 11 focuses on medical practice and practitioners, and Chapter 12, on ceremonial dancing. In order to preserve as much as possible of Jenness's perspective and style, these chapters draw heavily on passages as he composed them in his field notes.

...

As they prepared to seek the help of spirit guardians, adolescents were cautioned never to speak to anyone of their quest and its outcome, above all, what it was they saw and heard when a *saila* came to them in dreams. Breaching this cardinal rule, it was thought, threatened loss of the tutelary's help, be it fortune in fishing, fearlessness in battle, or any other "power" which, in Jenness's words, "aided him in his yearly round."[1] That said, wide-spread participation in winter dancing—best described as ritualized enactments of their spirit helpers—meant that the identity of a person's *saila* rarely remained secret for long. This accounts, in good measure, for the extent of knowledge available to the Saanich, and to all Salish peoples, about the constellation of spirit beings that formed part of the natural world around them, their particular reputations for bestowing certain kinds of favours, and the experiences, both good and bad, that family and friends have had with them.

During his stay on the Saanich Peninsula, Jenness recorded information—in some cases little more than names, in others, detailed descriptions and accounts of personal encounters—on upwards of four dozen spirit beings. David and Mrs Latasse supplied the bulk of this material. Most of these beings had up-island analogues, although his informants in the Duncan and Cowichan areas also spoke of a few others. These spirits are divisible into groups based on the niche to which each belongs in the broad scheme of existence: species of plants and animals; celestial bodies and terrestrial phenomena (i.e. forces of nature); and spirits whose truly extraordinary features best fit the mythical realm. There are also two cases whose classificatory ambiguity properly place them under the title "other." Only the spirit beings about which Jenness's notes provide substance beyond their simple enumeration are presented here.[2]

---

1   Jenness, *Faith of a Coast Salish*, 41. –Ed.
2   Unless otherwise indicated, the following material is from Jenness, "Saanich Notes," 193–96, 202–19. –Ed.

Plants

Siahahhao—Camas Bulb. Indians gather this bulb between November and January to roast for food. A woman often gets the *siahahhao* spirit when she has been working hard on mountain goat blankets. Mrs Latasse said that an old man helps her sing her song at the winter dance, but gave no reason for this. One morning, after performing her dance, she would go out, very early, and gather a whole basketful of the bulbs in an amazingly short time, because the spirit helped her. People "afflicted" by this spirit are very lively, and appear to be wide-awake.

Animals of the Air, Sea, and Land

Qaqai'yaqanna—Blue-bottle [blow fly]. This *saila* is said to make a man a good hunter, for it endows him with keen scent.

Səmsəmai'a—Yellow-Jacket [common wasp]. A woman who was digging clams far out on a tidal flat uncovered a nest of yellow-jackets. They flew all around her but did not sting. Afterward, she became a strong *cnem*—medicine woman—and attributed her powers to this experience.

Crow. A woman at Esquimalt has this *saila*. She paints her face black when she performs at the winter dances. When other people hear the crow cry Ka Ka, she hears it speaking intelligibly.

Hummingbird. The spirit of this tiny bird is very powerful. It makes the man who possesses it a great warrior, one who is both quick and sure afoot.

Hi'kok—White Owl. When it flies, this spirit emits a light. Mrs Latasse told of going home one very dark night when she saw a light moving ahead of her. It settled on a stump, whose outline it lit up clearly. She moved off the road and passed it. Next day she had a terrible pain in her side, a common occurrence following an encounter with a spirit being. Her husband David's nephew, who was a medicine man, drew the spirit out of her side and kept it to add to his own medicine powers.

Shópship—Nightingale. The name s*hópship* seems to be used for two different spirit beings. Its better known manifestation is the nightingale, or a similar "night bird."[3] It is said by some to emit a light while in flight and to bring its votary good luck. Mrs Latasse once encountered *shópship* as she and a young girl were walking in the evening to a neighbour's house. A light flew over their heads and the girl said "There is thunder." The elder knew better. Her

---

3 In SENĆOTEN, the word ŚOPŚEP (*šapšəp*) denotes "night bird power." –Ed.

encounter with the spirit left her with a pain in her side strong enough to keep her in bed for several days. According to this same informant, *shópship* is also a mythical rabbit, one that crawls along the ground on lizard-like legs.

A 'tceq—Crab. The crab *saila* is associated with medicine powers, although it is not often encountered.

In his youth, Edward Paul's father was wandering in the mountains. He came to a pond and bathed in it. As he went on he heard a strange noise and thought "There must be a terrible thunderstorm coming." He came to another pond and discovered that the noise came from a multitude of crabs that crawled over one another, making a noise like steam from an engine. Instead of walking right into the pond he ran away, frightened. That night the master of the crabs came to him and said "Why did you run away? Why did you not come to me?" "I was frightened," the youth said. The crab answered "If you had come to me I would have made you a powerful medicine man. Even though a man had died you could have called him back to life." As it was, the youth received no power because he had run away. No one else is known to have seen these crabs, but when the youth told his people about them they remembered having heard about them.

Blackfish [probably Killer Whale].[4] This is a powerful spirit, and desirable to acquire because it brought success in catching fish and other marine animals. Someone who saw a school of blackfish might dive into the midst of them in order to obtain it as a *saila*.

A man who lived at Gordon River (near Sooke) before the smallpox came went out constantly to get a spirit, but secured only unimportant ones. Still he tried, hunting continually, but without success. At last he went down to the beach. There he saw a number of canoes, and smoke, and what seemed to be people moving about. He sat down and watched. Presently the canoes moved off and became a school of blackfish, which lingered near the shore. He was sure there had been smoke and that someone was around, so, after waiting for a time, he went over to the place. There, on the beach, were seals, sea lions, porpoises, octopus, cod, fish in fact of every kind. Not knowing to whom they belonged he waited without touching them, then retreated into the woods and slept. In the morning the fish were still there, and still no one had appeared. Not daring to touch them, he went home. There, at night, the Blackfish spirit appeared to him and said "Hence-

---

4   Jenness did not collect a W̱SÁNEĆ name for this spirit; at Koksilah, however, George Kwakaston gave it as *kaƚlanamatsan*; Ibid. 217. The Hul'qumi'num', word for killer whale is *q̓ullhánumucun*; its SENĆOŦEN equivalent is KELŁOLEMEĆEN (*q̓əlláləməčən*). The name for porpoise, or blackfish, is QONED (*kʷánət'*). –Ed.

forth you shall catch in abundance all the fish you wish." After that the man could catch anything. He would go out with a small net and catch a huge cod in it; the fish would make no attempt to escape.

Once this same man decided to hunt whales. He invited a number of strong young men to accompany him and they paddled away. They sighted a whale, and he drove his harpoon right into its heart. He got on to the whale's back to change the rope on the harpoon preliminary to towing it. His companions, however, suddenly left him and paddled away. There he was, marooned on the whale's back. With his knife he cut out a large square just behind the dorsal fin to sit in, and bored a hole through the fin to hold on to, so that the waves would not wash him off. However, the night was calm. He dreamed that he was to order the whale to take him home. In the morning the whale suddenly shivered. The man struck up his whaling song—the chant used by whalers to make the wounded whale go to some creek to die. Immediately, the whale moved steadily towards a creek near the man's village. As soon as it entered the creek it died. The man got off it, and entered the village, interrupting the wailing of his relatives who were mourning his supposed death.[5]

Skwanelεts—Fish (or Fish Master). This powerful spirit is known to haunt certain places, principally where there is turbulent water. Tom Paul knew of an elder years ago who saw a rainbow that was composed of fish, each only about four inches long. It was *skwanelεts,* and naturally enough, it made the man a wonderful fisherman.

While she was out trolling for fish in Cowichan Bay, Mrs Latasse pulled over at a point of land to rest. Remembering how she had been haunted by the screech owl spirit when she was a little girl (as her father had been before her), she was looking into the trees on the point when she heard three drums deep down in the water, one deep-toned, another higher-toned, and the third so high-toned that it was barely audible. It was the fish spirit, *skwane.lεts* [*sic*], playing in its home. Had she gone back to the spot repeatedly she would probably have heard it drumming again and become sick. She might have done this if she had wanted to become a medicine woman; she would have returned again and again to the place, bathed there and kept her body clean by eating herbs, etc. The fish spirit is very powerful. The medicine man who has it can find lost or stolen objects or lost people. He can also identify wrong-doers. With a crowd gathered round, he takes a towel (formerly shredded cedar bark) and twists it into a hoop. After singing his song he throws the hoop to the floor, where it wriggles

5   Jenness, "Saanich Notes," 200. –Ed.

like a snake and moves straight to the thief. The Indians wear down on their heads at dances so that they can see.

Sk'aθk'e'nikun—Mole (or mole-like creature.) This being has a sharp, pointed nose and lives in the hollows of fallen trees. If someone is lucky enough to catch one, it should be killed, carefully wrapped in a mountain goat blanket, and then kept in a box. This will make the person immensely rich. Baptiste Paul, Tom Paul's son, caught one in a trap but, failing to recognize what it was, threw sk'aθk'e'nikun away.[6]

Sxaiyakwas—Raccoon. George Kwakaston said that at winter dances at Koksilah, the man who possessed this *saila* chanted the following song: "*kwalacas kwasxaiyakwas*," "Coon shot me."

Stikaia—Wolf. The wolf spirit is closely associated with hunting, although its *saila*, as recounted in the story below, may endow other, potentially more beneficial, powers.

Kulaxunzit's son Xe·xa (the one whose powder horn was struck) went into the woods to get a spirit. He caught two wolf cubs in their den, and carried them away to a hut of twigs that he erected, though pursued by the parent wolf. Before night a whole pack of wolves surrounded him and tried to burrow their way in; but wherever they dug he emptied a few drops of urine from his urine box and so kept them out. All night he kept the pups while he made for each a harness. In the morning he let them loose. The mother wolf ran up and sniffed them without disturbing the harnesses and the entire pack disappeared.

Still Xe·xa wandered through the woods, seeking now the wolf spirit. He came upon a female wolf that had a bone caught in its jaws and was foaming at the mouth. He knelt in front of it and chanted "*He θa'skwa, he θa'skwa*"—"I will take it, I will take it," meaning "I will accept any spirit you wish to give me." As he chanted these words he held now his right arm, now his left, before his eyes after the manner of a medicine man chanting over a patient. Then he went up to the wolf, took the bone out of its mouth and continued up the hill. The wolf went up the same hill by another path. As he climbed he heard someone chanting "*He θa'skwa, he θa'skwa*." He said to himself, "That is my song." Suddenly he came upon the wolf he had relieved standing in the centre of the pack singing his song. He shouted to

---

6   Ironically, Jean Baptiste Paul found his "fortune" in an entirely different way: as a professional wrestler, competing under the names Red Indian Warrior, and Chief Thunderbird. His career lasted twenty-five years and brought him an international reputation, if not great wealth; http://www.firstnations.de/development/coast_salish-yos.htm. –Ed

them to let them know he was near, not feeling sure how they would receive him. Then he lost consciousness. As he lay there the wolf spirit entered him. When he recovered consciousness he went home. After this he became a medicine man. Also every morning the wolves would drive a deer past his house into the water.

Later X̱e x̱a's wife had twins and the family had to live alone for two months. When the twins were seven months old one became very ill and in fact died. X̱e x̱a took it from its mother's arms, wrapped in a blanket, and sang his wolf song over it for about three hours, calling on the wolf spirit for help. The child began to perspire and recovered completely.

Tetc.kən—Mink. A man living on Kuper Island was said to have the mink *saila*. It made him a successful deer hunter.

Frog [Frog Master]. This is a lucky spirit to encounter, for those who have it as their *saila* are able to acquire every type of food without trouble; the food appears in their baskets unasked.

A young man was out seeking a spirit. His people had been fishing. He got out of the canoe and started to walk home through the woods just behind the beach. Presently he saw smoke drifting through the trees and discovered a tiny beach with a small swamp in the woods just behind. He noticed canoes on the beach, and people who all walked with a peculiar limp. They were carrying large cedar bags filled with dry fish from the beach to the swamp. As he drew near they vanished. He sat down beside the canoes and bags, not daring to touch the fish till someone returned. He waited for hours, but no one came. Then he went back into the woods a short distance and slept. As he slept a man touched his shoulder, said a few words to him, and passed on. The youth stayed out several more nights, and on each night the same man visited him. He then discovered the canoe people were frogs.

In later life that man always had plenty of fish and was continually feeding the people. He kept his dry fish hung up in cedar bags, as others did. In the morning, when six or ten people would join him as he sat outside his house, he would call to his wife "Bring us out some dried fish, but be sure to leave some in the bag." When one bag was becoming empty he distributed from the second, then the third; by the time his last bag was drawing low the first would be full again, replenished by the frog spirit.

Xamalitsa—Frog (or "glistening frog"). This spirit is rarer than the Frog Master, and brings even greater fortune to those who meet it. Known by its distinctive cry, one that sounds like that of an infant or young child—wa wa wa.

According to David and Mrs Latasse, its body is frog-shaped but glitters, as if strewn with pearls—most beautiful. Anyone who kills this being should place it in a hole in a large cedar tree and then cover it over with plenty of fragrant leaves. These leaves then turn into anything you wish for—mountain goat wool, for instance, or any other valued commodity. (In another version of *xamalitsa* protocol, the body must be wrapped in goat wool.) Whenever you visit the spot, it is necessary to leave a little wool, etc., behind. A poor person who finds this frog soon becomes rich enough to afford giving a potlatch. Anyone who was jealous of his good fortune and followed him to the hollow tree would see nothing, because he does not carry the spirit within him.

Louis Pelkey offered a different take on x*amalitsa*. He said this unusual being has a huge stomach, one that is full of goat wool blankets that Salish people have discarded. It can be heard crying (like an infant) in the woods, now here, now there. If a person succeeds in capturing it, he should kill it, cut open its stomach, and put the remains in a box. Then, whenever he wants a lot of blankets, he has only to put one blanket on top of the box, and in the morning there will be a pile of them in place of the one.

Differing again was Tom Paul's point of view on *qamali'tca* [*sic*], describing this creature as a tiny, infant-like being that haunts woods and swamps. (At Quamichan, Johnson likened it to a mythical hybrid: a frog that appeared human from the shoulders up.) Occasionally a man will hear it cry *huwe-a*, just like a baby. Then, if he is wise, he will search for it, though the sound seems to have come from here, now from there. Should he see bubbles of froth on the water he should take them up in both hands and place them at his waist, for they will help him in the search.[7] Paul said that after finding *qamali't-ca,* the person should take it home, kill it, wrap the body in a mountain goat blanket and keep it in a box. Then wealth will pour in upon him; he will get everything he wants.

Not everyone who meets this spirit is rewarded with fortune.

> A young cousin of Mrs Latasse was wandering in the woods up towards Shawnigan Lake [south of Duncan] when he heard what seemed to be the cry of a baby. He went on and saw *hamala'tsa* [*sic*], the glistening frog, but not having heard of it before he left it and went away. That night, *hamala'tsa* visited him and said "Why did you not take me?" "I was afraid," the youth said; "I have never heard of you." *Hamala'tsa* said "You shall live to be an old man, but you shall always be poor." He is still living, very poor and crippled.[8]

For some people, however, x*amalitsa* lived up to its reputation.

---

7 Its distinctive sound, together with Tom Paul's additional details, seem to identify *xamalitsa* as a spring peeper, WEXES (*wáxəs*) in SENĆOŦEN. This suggests that its counterpart is probably SXE‚ÁNEW̱ (*sxəʔénəxʷ*), the bullfrog. –Ed.

8 Children are advised against being afraid of spirit beings they encounter; see page 69, footnote 12. –Ed.

A Nanaimo man who was sick in bed felt something heavy on his leg and kicked it off his bed. It cried wa wa wa. He told his wife to see what it was. She saw something that looked like a frog, and, taking two sticks on which she had been roasting ducks, threw it outside over a bank. When she went back into the house and told him what it was he sent her out to find it again. The creature had disappeared. She returned and told her husband it had vanished, and he sent her to bring in the sticks she had used to throw it away. On the tips of these sticks were golden stains left by the creature. The man wrapped them in goat wool and hid them away. Later he became very rich and was able to hire a hundred *swaiswai* dancers for a potlatch he gave.

Sinałke. The Coast Salish knew of several serpentine beings, each powerful and often dangerous to encounter. Moreover, as its SENĆOŦEN name suggests—SINEŁḴI (*sínəłqiʔ*), "flying lizard"—it may actually be no ordinary reptile, but rather one belonging to the mythic realm. S*inałke* endowed people with medicine powers (see chapter 11), but sometimes conveyed mundane gifts on those who acquired it as a guardian.

A young man went out continually on the water to seek a spirit and failed because he probably did not strike the exact places where the spirits were. He determined to try his luck along the shore. Near Sidney he found a pond, and in the pond [was] the largest snake he had ever seen. He killed it, then felt anxious as to whether he had done right or wrong. He did not know whether it was *sinałke* or not. That night the snake spirit visited him and said "I am not vexed at your killing me. Now do as I tell you. Take my body and cut it into four parts. Bury one part at high tide level at a certain place near Cowichan, another on Saltspring Island, the third and fourth at certain other places I designate. If you do this then, whenever you want fish, go to the water off those places and you will catch all you want." The man obeyed the snake's instructions. Thereafter he and his people always caught fish in those places, as the Indians still do to this day.

S'kaiyep. Like s*inałke,* this being is a powerful and dangerous snake-like creature, one whose spirit is closely associated with blood, as well as with medicine power; its name in SENĆOŦEN—SḴÍEP (*sqəyəp*)—refers to "power using red paint." When postulants seeking a *saila* encounter this being in the woods, either by day or night, it may come to them in the form of a large man with a snake-like face. On hearing its song, its "victim" falls ill and only fully recovers upon being initiated as a dancer. Appropriately enough, those who represent this spirit at the winter dances paint their faces red.

Not long ago, s*kaiyep* drew away the soul of a Saanich girl. Night after night she had the same dream about a man, and at last the man—*skaiyep*—took her soul to a lake far away so that it could not return. A medicine man discovered what was wrong with the girl and recovered her soul; but by that time it was so weak and lifeless that the girl did not survive.

...

A young man went out to seek a vision. One day when he was alone he shot an arrow idly into the air, to see how high it would go. The wind carried it into an open glade in the woods, from which there rose a cry, as from a woman "O, you hit me." The lad thought that he had shot some woman and was afraid to go and look. At last he mustered up his courage and went closer. Instead of a woman there was a brilliantly coloured snake writhing on the ground from an arrow that was stuck in its neck. The youth watched it for some time, but was afraid to extract his arrow and at last left it. Two days later he told a companion about the strange thing he had shot, and the two youths went over to examine it. The snake had gone, and his arrow was lying on the ground.

A month later the same youth saw something moving in the bushes and shot his arrow at it. Again something cried out, and again he thought he had hit someone. "Did I shoot you?" he called out; but there was no reply. He went to examine what he had struck. His arrow had pierced the head of another snake, just as brilliant as the one he had shot before, but with different colours. He watched it writhing for a time and left it, as he had left the earlier one, to go and tell his people. But when they visited the place with him this snake, too, had disappeared, and his arrow rested on the ground.

Some weeks later something knocked him unconscious. Then a snake appeared to him and said "You should not have been afraid of me. I am the greatest *siowa* [seer] in this land. If you had withdrawn your arrow and killed me I would have given you great power and made you the richest person in the country. If a man has lost something he valued, stolen by some enemy, you could have shot your arrow into the air and it would have penetrated the shoulder of the thief, no matter how far away he was; and if he tried to remove it, his hand would have stuck to it until you came and accused him of the theft. Also, if one man used sorcery on another, you could have traced the sorcerer in the same way. But you left me. So now I am going to grant you only a little power. You have seen my colours. Whenever you make a canoe, a box, or anything, decorate it with the colours that you have seen on me."

Celestial Bodies and Terrestrial Forces

Fire Spirit. David Latasse's grandfather was afflicted with this. Three times fire spread all round his grave and left it untouched. Those with the fire *saila* put their hands in the fire while dancing and are not burned.

Lake Spirit. There are certain places—one is the bridge over The Gorge, near Victoria –where the water rises and foams at certain times; this is where the lake spirit resides. It is a favourite *saila* of women. A mother might take her daughter to such a place and make her bathe. At night the girl would see a female spirit and learn a song. Afterwards, she would always have quantities of mountain goat wool, obtained without effort thanks to the spirit. This enabled her to give many potlatches. Men, too, met this being.

> Old David's father once came to a strange lake where he noticed the water boiled and foamed at intervals. After watching it for some time from the shelter of a dead cedar tree he gathered some wood for a fire, stripped off his clothes, crawled out along a log and was ready to dive in when the water foamed again. The moment it began he dived, expecting to strike something. Instead, the water foamed furiously— the lake spirit was giving a potlatch and throwing out mountain goat wool. He came out of the water, lit his fire, and slept. Then the lake spirit visited him and taught him a song. Later he held a big potlatch at which he gave away huge quantities of mountain goat wool and a few mountain goat furs for the old people. Another time he returned to the spot, split the dead cedar tree, and tied up its branches, as a mark. He then told his son to go there in order to obtain a spirit. But when his father died very soon thereafter, David did not go.

Sea Spirit. This spirit brings ill fortune. It looks like a human being and has long hair like a woman. It is visible only in places where there is a great riptide. People who have seen it have soon died, or lost some members of their family. An Indian saw it near Sidney three years ago and has since lost two of his children. He saw a black object on the water that looked like the back of a man's head—one always sees the back of its head first. Suddenly it turned and he could see just a little of its face, for most of it was covered by its long hair. Frightened, he rowed as fast as he could for shore, giving up his fishing for the day.

Łkɛls—Moon. This is said to be a wicked spirit. Johnson, of Quamichan, said that no one had moon as a *saila*. Others say that those who do meet it will gain nothing. A propos of its reputation, a person who exposes himself naked to moonlight will become paralyzed. Even sleeping with moonlight shining on your face makes a person ill.[9]

---

9   Jenness, "Saanich Notes," 180. –Ed.

Simshathet—Sun.[10] As a guardian spirit, *simshathet* brings its possessor good luck, as it did for David Latasse's father. He acquired this *saila* while walking up from Victoria to a little lake on Saanich Peninsula.

> A rock protruded from the lake. Thinking the rock did not look natural, and as it was nearly evening, he first laid sticks for a fire near a big cedar, then stripped off his clothes and swam round and round the rock until his body became chilled (as is necessary when seeking a spirit). Afterwards he lit the fire and slept beside it. Now the sun rested at this rock during certain hours of the day; it was the sun's house. So the sun spirit visited him that night and said to him "You shall be very wealthy. Everything you touch shall turn to money." Just at this time the white men were building the Caribou road,[11] and David's father could not make enough canoes to meet the demand for them. He made and sold them all the time, became very wealthy, and gave many potlatches and had many slaves. Eventually a certain Cowichan man became jealous, and shot both him and a slave wife in the woods as they were travelling to visit some friends. No one knew who the murderer was until long after, when the man boasted of the deed to his son.

Slale'kwal—East Wind. The spirit of the east wind brings rain and mild weather in winter.

> Once when a strong north wind had brought much cold and snow the Indians, unable to hunt, approached an old man who had been afflicted by *slale'kwal*, the spirit of the east wind. He danced and sang until the perspiration rolled down his face, then said to someone, "Go outside and see if there is any change." The man went out and returned to report "No change." Again the old man danced; and again there was no change. A third time he danced till he was almost exhausted. Then a man reported "the fog is lifting and rain from the east is falling!" So he mitigated the weather.

Tanwok—South Wind. Tom Paul said that a person whose *saila* is the south wind chants these words at the winter dances: "*niłala sicen kwakta-a-a* (repeated), *stemy kwakta-a.*" (It must be I dreamed about the south wind. That is what I dreamed.)

---

10   George Kwakaston distinguished between the spirit he called *səmshathet*, "sun" and *skweal*, "day" or "daylight." In Hul'qumi'num', the former is *sháathut*, the latter *skweyul*; their SENĆOŦEN equivalents are SḴEḴEL (*sqʷəqʷə́l*ʹ) and SȻÁȻEL (*skʷičəl*), respectively. –Ed.

11   This is probably a reference to the 650 km-long Cariboo Wagon Road, a project initiated in the early 1860s to facilitate transport to gold mining areas in the remote Cariboo District in the British Columbia interior; http://www.thecanadianencyclopedia.ca/en/article/cariboo-road/ –Ed.

Sqolqwolcan—Whirlwind. One day, Tom Paul saw a whirlwind swirling leaves up into the air. On top of it was what looked like ducks. That night the whirlwind came to him in the form of a man, rather unremarkable in appearance, who taught him a power song. George Kwakaston related the story of another encounter with this spirit, one that turned out very differently.

> A man called Skwahalem went deer hunting up the Cowichan River. He had just crossed the river when he saw a whirlwind, *qwolqwolcan* [*sic*] toss everything into the air. *Qwolqwolcan* is a powerful *saila*, like a huge lizard with three long fins on its back. Skwahalem picked up a stick and tried to kill it, but when he struck the ground there was nothing. He struck three or four times. Then he fell unconscious. When he came to his mouth was bleeding, and the *saila* had disappeared. He was so weak that he had to leave his gun behind and crawl to the river, where he tumbled in and floated down to his fishing weir, beside which he had a house. He bumped against the weir, made his way to the house, and lay there three days, all alone. On the fourth day he felt stronger, so he got into his canoe and went down the river to drive the salmon into the weir. He had just started to drive them when he happened to look round and saw what appeared to be a wave behind him. He paddled ashore, then waded out into the water to intercept the monster that was coming, apparently a huge porpoise. Three times he struck it with his two-pointed spear, but its body seemed as hard as a rock. Feeling strange, he stumbled ashore and fell. When he recovered the porpoise had gone. With difficulty he paddled up to his weir, where he merely tied up his boat, being too weak to drag it ashore, and rested in his house.

Soqwa'as—Thunder. Appearing to people as a man-like being, sometimes with six heads, the thunder spirit lives in a cave whose walls are hung with food of all kinds, weapons, and various other things. Few Salish have encountered *Soqwa'as*. One who did was David Latasse's great grandfather; this happened sometime in the past when the man

> wandered away into the woods after his people had been ravaged by enemies. He came to a place that was being swept by powerful winds which he was sure came from Thunder. He pressed against the wind, which every now and then blew him back several paces. Still he pressed on, often crawling, until he lost consciousness. When he came to he was in Thunder's house. Thunder said to him "What is it you want?" He replied "My enemies have driven me out. I have come to ask your help." Thunder pointed to all the things on the wall and asked him what he wanted. He saw a human forearm with a cord attached to one end that it might be used as a club. "I want that," he said. Thunder gave it to him.

Old David himself was sick for a long time. Then he dreamed that the thunder spirit came to him and said "Do you want to get better?" David said "Yes." Thunder said "I will cure you. Roll up your shirt." David rolled it up, and one of the spirit's six heads bent down and licked every painful spot in David's chest, while the spirit chanted a song. It chanted a second song and licked his chest with its second head. It licked with its six heads, to six different songs, and vanished. David felt very much better when he awoke and began to sing the songs that Thunder had sung.

...

A woman at Halalt has the thunder spirit. About the end of last year, she became sick and called on Thunder to heal her. That night there was a terrific thunder storm which did a great deal of damage; among other results it lifted the house in which she was living right off its foundations. The people blamed her for the storm.

When this woman was initiated as a dancer for the first time, four owners of *swaiswai* masks were hired to dance for her. Two old women led the new dancer out, two *swaiswai* dancers preceded her, and two followed, all singing one of her family songs to the accompaniment of two drums beaten by two other men. It was a magnificent initiation.[12]

Hwa'ta'c'an—Rainbow. As the following story reveals, this spirit makes it recipient physically strong.

A man who was out in a canoe during a great storm saw a rainbow just before his canoe capsized. He clung to the side of his boat till he lost consciousness. When he came to his canoe was right-side up, and facing him sat a strange man. He wondered at first if he were delirious, then thought "how did my canoe become right-side up?" His companion said nothing, and the Indian was afraid to speak, and feeling very weary, laid his head on his arm and slept. When he lifted his head again his companion was gone.

Later his canoe capsized in another storm and he swam till he fainted. When he regained consciousness the man was on a beach beside his canoe and the same stranger sat facing him. As before, the Indian dared not speak, and the stranger suddenly vanished. The stranger was the rainbow spirit. Afterwards the Indian, who was not a big man, found himself possessed of great strength. He did not dance at the winter dances, though his injection by the rainbow spirit entitled him to do so.

---

12   For other encounters with Thunder, see Part II, nos. 26 and 45. –Ed.

Mythical Beings

Musti'mux—Mermaid. There was no mention of this being on the Saanich Peninsula, but farther north, in Cowichan territory, George Kwakaston and Johnson each identified it. As expected, mermaid takes hybrid form, half-human above the waist, half-fish below. While their description does not include long hair, like the sea spirit, she is said to be dangerous to meet.[13]

Qwe'qxwq—Wood Chopper. This spirit appears as a diminutive man, about four feet tall. Tom Paul nearly got this *saila* when he was a boy. He had gone into the forest to gather spruce gum, and had already collected a little in his pail, with his hatchet, when he heard three chops and the crash of a falling tree. He ran home and told his people.

Siε.yε'—Timber Giant. This spirit has a human body and a very long, pointed chin, stands only about three and a half feet high, but is broad-shouldered and very powerful. It travels around with a club, knocking down trees. Usually associated with endowing great physical strength, it was Timber Giant's song that David Latasse's uncle sang when he led a fight that ended with the massacre of Comox warriors. He had met *siε.yε'* in the woods and used its song to hypnotize his enemies.[14] Skwahalem, the same man whose story of encountering *sqolqwolcan,* whirlwind, is recounted above, also claimed the mythic Timber Giant as his spirit guardian; one day, as he was walking towards the Chemainus River,

> he came upon some trees that had recently been uprooted. He thought he was rather late to see the timber-being, *sie'ye,* in action, but hadn't walked much farther when he came upon a little man about four feet high with kinky hair, like a negro's. Skwahalem picked up a stick to kill him, but as he struck *sie'ye* leaped behind a tree. He struck at him three or four times, but each time avoided the stroke and finally disappeared. Afterwards, Skwahalem received a vision and got *sie'ye* for his *saila.*

Skun'kun—This monstrous spirit being takes the form of a large animal, half-seal, half-dog, that lives in lakes. It howls like a dog, then gives a cry like a human being.

When Old David was a youth he accompanied his uncle to the San

---

13   There is a SENĆOŦEN word for "mermaid"—SḴITEU, (*sqítəw*). The Hul'qumi'num' word *smustímuxw*, "body of a person," may be the source of the name given to this spirit by Kwakaston and Johnson. –Ed.

14   In his work on the Katzie, Jenness wrote of the existence of two timber giants; *siε.yε'* itself, a *saila* capable of making its possessor very powerful, and *sε'sq'əc*, "an ordinary creature unable to confer any power"; *Faith of a Coast Salish*, 61. –Ed.

Juan islands. There they caught more fish than they needed, so, following the usual custom, his uncle told David to take some of them to some old people who were camped some distance off. David carried one basket of fish and two slave women carried others. As they were going through the woods they heard a cry like that of a human being and stopped to listen. One of the slave women said "Someone is lost in the woods. Shall we answer?" David said "No, can't you feel your face burning?" (a sure sign a spirit is near), then they heard a sound like the barking of a dog. They hurried on, not wishing to be attacked by the spirit.

S*kalathan*—Warrior. *Skalathan* is a fearsome spirit, one that instills in its protégés a craving for blood.[15] It takes two people to hold down a man with this *saila* when he becomes violent. One way to calm such a person is to make a small incision at the side of his wrist and let him drink his own blood; then he becomes well. Tom Paul denied that all young men tried to obtain the warrior spirit; only some actually succeeded, the rest receiving other spirits' help in fishing, hunting, and so on.

Along similar lines, Albert Westly, of Nanaimo, spoke of *skalskalathan*, a being that comes in a nightmarish dream and causes a person to want to fight.[16] At the winter dances, those who have had this experience perform as *skalathan* dancers. There are four new dancers in Nanaimo this winter [1935–36], he added, all *skalathan*—three of whom are women.[17]

David and Mrs Latasse said that there was another entirely different type of warrior spirit: s*palkwithe*, or ordinary shades (ghosts) of the dead. Unlike the ferocious and blood-thirsty s*kalathan*, this spirit, they explained, tends to be cowardly and relies on stealth when approaching someone at night. It carries a spear, and like its name-sake (screech) owl, makes hooting sounds. If it repeatedly visits a person in dreams, it causes sickness.

> A boy at Esquimalt had been sick; to cure him his people made him a dancer. They brought him up to Malahat to give his dance. Mrs David went inside to watch him. His song was so pitifully girlish, and he danced so mincingly, that her own warrior spirit caught her and rendered her unconscious. Every boy had to get warrior spirit; it didn't matter which kind. The only difference was a slight one in the song. The shade kind would say "I am s*pałkwi´θɛ*. Mrs David got this warrior spirit one night, while she was in the house. Her husband David laughed at her, saying "So the spirit would not come to you in the woods!"

15 The SENĆOŦEN word S̱ḴOLEŦEN (*sqə´łəθən*) means "invisible wild person." –Ed.
16 In the Hul'qumi'num' language *squlquluthun* means "dream"; its SENĆOŦEN equivalent is ḴEL,ḴEL,OŦEN (*qəl'qəl'aθən*). –Ed.
17 Jenness, "Saanich Notes," 222. –Ed.

Tsinkwa—Lightning Snake. This being is sometimes depicted as a two-headed snake capable of flying through the air. It is associated with thunder and lightening because it travels through forests and knocks down trees during thunderstorms. Finding one of its scales confers wealth. Johnson told of an occasion when he went up a mountain right after a heavy thunderstorm to look for deer.

> He saw many trees that had been struck by lightning. Finally, he saw something shining on a felled tree, something small that kept changing colour. He took a stick and lifted it off, laying it on the ground; then lifted down a second, similar object just above it. When he turned to pick them up, however, they had disappeared, and though he searched for a long time, he could not find them. They were scales of *tsinkwa.*

Xwáł'təp—Snake-Bird. In SENĆOŦEN, the word X̱OLTEP (*xʷaltəp*) refers to a "flying snake." Even so, this spirit is generally described as a bird, albeit a bird that resembles a seal. Said to be about two feet long, black in colour, and with a wrinkled face, it crawls along the ground or swims in streams and ponds as a snake might, but also flies. Forbidding appearance notwithstanding, it is reported to have a pleasant voice that sounds like the song of a bird. Those who meet it suffer severe pain in the side, the usual result of encounters with powerful and monstrous beings of this type.

> A certain bird, *hwaltap* [*sic*], hovered around the house of an Indian and his wife, and every time it cried their son went into a trance. The parents said "We must make him a dancer, or else we shall lose him." They gathered all the people together to beat and sing, and set the boy out on the floor to dance. As he danced he rose two feet or more into the air, alarming the people who caught hold of him and made him sit down. After a time, he said to his mother "Take good care of my wife if I go away and do not return." Then he rose to dance again, clad in the skin shirt decorated with many fringes that they had made for him. The people tied a rope round his waist to hold him to the ground, but he rose irresistibly into the air, his legs crossed and his arms out-stretched, and out through the roof, where the ropes fell from him. Circling higher and higher, and flying like a swan, he finally disappeared.
>
> His mother wept. The dancing season came to a close and summer made its appearance. She slept with her daughter-in-law to protect her from other suitors. They gathered a quantity of pitch and *qathmin* [consumption plant], filling many baskets, and distributed it to all the other families in the village, telling them that if the youth reappeared they should light fires outside their houses and burn the *qathmin* and another sweet-smelling plant.

The dancing season came round again. Always the people were listening for the youth's return, but for a long time he did not appear. Finally the Cowichan people heard him; they set fire to the pitch outside their houses, threw in the *qathmin* and another sweet-smelling substance, and beat with their sticks. The youth passed over them and alighted at his own home; his parents had prepared a room for him where he would be out of sight. He entered his room; but his features had changed, his stomach had disappeared, and feathers were growing out of his flesh. The villagers peeked at him through holes in the wall. Gradually he shrivelled up and died, for his *hwaltap saila* was too powerful.[18]

...

Albert Westly's daughter was picking berries in the state of Washington. Being very dusty, she went to a pool below a high cliff to bathe. While she was bathing she saw some sticks fall into the water, and, looking up, saw three "men" on top of the bluff. Soon after she became ill, and remained so for a long time. Then one Xmas, just at the beginning of the dance season, her father asked her what was the matter with her. She said "Don't ask me, father. I'll come and tell you when I need you." Two days later, in the dance house, she became "crazy" and began to dance and wave her hands wildly. Her father and other dancers gathered round her, chanting and shaking *kutcmin* [deer hoof rattle], and quieted her. Then they wrapped her in goat wool blankets to make her perspire—to get the badness out of her—and initiated her. Her *saila* was *hwaltap* [*sic*], which comes from the Yokwiłteł [Kwakiutl].

Other

Hwani'tum—White Man.[19] The father of a man named Kansimo was said to have obtained the spirit of the white man long before any white people arrived on the Pacific coast. When he performed during the winter dances he would sing two songs. The first ran: "*hwani'tum tena.*" (I am a white man.) The second, *ho ho ho ho ho*, was accompanied by motions as though pulling up an anchor. There was another man, this one at Blaine, in Washington, who had this same spirit. The words to his dancing song were: "It will be fun when the white man comes to my place."[20]

---

18   Ibid. 221. Katzie elder Peter Pierre informed Jenness that while some Salish people on southern Vancouver Island represented *xwáł'tap* at winter dances, "none of them possessed more than the echo of the spirit's power." In fact, he continued, *xwáł'tap* was not a guardian spirit associated with these groups, but had been borrowed from non-Salish peoples by way of Comox intermediaries; Jenness, *Faith of a Coast Salish*, 61. –Ed.

19   WENITEM (*x*ʷ*ənítəm*) is SENĆOŦEN for "Anglo," or "white man." –Ed.

20   At Katzie, Jenness recorded the story of another unusual *saila*: Locomotive. "When a half-

Stəlmexən. Mrs Latasse mentioned this spirit, but is uncertain if it is a true spirit. If it is, it is an evil one since it mainly afflicts drunken women, although men get it occasionally as well.

---

breed Indian living near Abbotsford claimed it during one of the winter dances, the other Indians laughed at him. He insisted, however, that it enabled him to control the weather, because a locomotive goes everywhere through rain and sunshine"; *Faith of a Coast Salish*, 48. –Ed.

11
Illness and Medicine

Contagion through contact with shades, as noted in Chapter 9, was but one of several classes of illness known to the Saanich and other Coast Salish groups. Each had prescribed methods of treatment, some widely available to laypersons, the others being the customary purview of professionals. In the first case, every family had its quota of secret remedies for ordinary complaints that were handed down from one generation to the next.[1] For treating wounds, for instance, a family in west Saanich made the patient drink what it regarded (probably quite correctly) as a deadly poison: i.e. crushed shell slugs, adding some other medicine five or ten minutes later. They claimed that the treatment quickly arrested throbbing of the wound and induced healing. Apart from secret remedies of this kind, there were others known almost universally. Thus for tonics, many natives drank warm infusions of mint leaves, or the leaves of the wild rose, or bearberry leaves [*Arctostaphylos uva-ursi*] that had turned red. To cure colds, they induced a perspiration by drinking a hot infusion of the leaves of *Micromeria douglasii* [yerba buena].[2] Still another remedy for colds was to chew arbutus leaves, while arbutus sap, diluted with a little water, was considered to be a cure for measles. The fine roots of *Achlys tripphylla* [deer-foot or vanilla-leaf], pounded between stones and brewed in water, was a panacea for smallpox, for fish bones lodged in the throat, and for choking that occurred when eating berries. For haemorrhage of the lungs some natives drank the red liquid that forms at the base of rotten oaks. Bearberry bark was a common laxative, but still more widely used was devil's club (*Fatsia horrida*). One prescription for obscure stomach troubles was the dried and powdered cone of the skunk cabbage (*Lysichiton camtschatcense*) steeped in water, while the root of the same plant was a specific for rheumatism. There was even a prescription for preventing hair from turning gray: pound up the dried tails of the dog fish, stir them in oil from the same fish, and when the solution has settled, rub the clear liquid in the hair.[3]

Maladies of a more serious nature fell into one of three main types: contamination from contact with spirits, both the shades of the dead and other ethereal beings such as those described in the preceding chapter; an errant soul; and sorcery. Diagnosis and treatment required the expertise of a specialist. Certain cases were typically attended to by a *thitha* (priest), someone whose knowledge was principally an inheritance from generations past. Others, usually those posing graver or immediate danger to a patient, called for a *cnem*,

---

1 More often than not, it was women who acquired and passed on this practical knowledge; Barnett, *Coast Salish*, 209. –Ed.
2 Fraser River natives occasionally substituted snowberries (*Chiogenes hispidula*).
3 Jenness, "Saanich Notes," 258–59. –Ed.

a "medicine man" (or shaman) able to call on powerful spirit helpers gained through a prolonged and arduous regimen of fasting and bathing in remote places, followed by a period of training under an experienced practitioner.[4] In describing medical practice among the Katzie, on the lower Fraser, Jenness observed that there was a certain degree of overlap in what each was able to do. Nonetheless, "speaking broadly, the two functionaries differed in a way familiar to us from our own society; the priest was the expert in preventive medicine, while the medicine-man was the regular practitioner of the healing art."[5] This characterization was equally pertinent to the Saanich, as it was to their up-island neighbours. According to Tom Paul, priests comprised a special class of medicine men who specialized in removing shades that obsessed human beings and made them ill.

Suppose a person is ill. A *cnem* is called in. He kneels on the floor about five feet from the patient, shields his eyes with his arm, taps on a board or on the floor with a stick and sings his medicine song. If the illness has been caused by some piece of bone or other object shot into the patient by another medicine man, the *cnem* is capable of removing it; but if it has been caused by a shade he has not the necessary power. He will then say "You had better call in a *thitha*." The priest comes, kneels down like the *cnem*, but closer to the patient, and instead of shielding his eyes, keeps them steadily fixed on the patient while he taps the floor with his stick, paints a certain pattern on his face in red ochre, and sings his song. If this has no effect he rubs the paint from his face with a cedar bark towel and paints another pattern on it, then he taps the floor and sings again. He may sing five or six songs before the patient opens his eyes and looks up. Then he knows that he has come to grips with the shade and that the sick man is reviving. He paints his face again, and also the patient's face, and sings another song, then throws in the fire *qathmin* [consumption plant] seeds and other herbs or roots as food for the shade, to make it go away. Generally, too, he gives the patient an herbal remedy. Like the *cnem*, he might have to perform over the patient night after night before he effects a cure.[6]

In addition to exorcising shades, priests tended to the widow and widower for four days after the funeral, painted his or her face with red ochre in accor-

---

4   Apprenticeships were expensive, ranging, according to David Latasse, from $200 to $300 in the 1930s. They usually lasted from one to three months, during which time the aspirant lived with the medicine man and received instruction during the hours of daylight only. Tutors could tell their protégés had been visited by a spirit, for this helping spirit always hovered around them thereafter, and was visible to another medicine man; Ibid., 227.

5   Jenness, *Faith of a Coast Salish*, 68. –Ed.

6   Jenness, "Saanich Notes," 246. Elsewhere, Jenness writes that "In some cases the Indians first called in a priest because his services were less expensive, and the priest himself, when a cure lagged, advised the summoning of a medicine man"; Ibid. –Ed

dance with prescribed patterns, looked after their food, and drove away the shade of the deceased. Likewise, the priest looked after the new dancer who had to undergo exactly the same treatment to ward off contagion during his or her initiation as a spirit dancer. When first given food, the widow, widower, or new dancer bit off four morsels and dropped them from the mouth (the food was always dried salmon, or at any rate dried fish or meat). These morsels were said to carry the taint away from the eater's person, after which he could eat freely. Similarly, the priest forced the widow to make four feints before using a knife or an axe again, or going into the water.[7]

As with priests, both men and women might become a *cnem*, though it was said that few young women did so because of the forced solitude and corporeal privations the process entailed. For much the same reason, young men were usually discouraged from embarking on the quest before reaching physical maturity.[8] In order to maintain the purity of mind and body the undertaking demanded, postulants were instructed to chew certain herbs and drink the purgative juice of devil's club bark instead of water, to eat little more than roots and herbs, bathe frequently in cold lakes or streams, and to daub themselves with deer fat. They were also enjoined to avoid thoughts of the opposite sex, let alone engage in physical intimacy, important reasons why those seeking medicine power ordinarily did so before marriage. This last injunction may explain, at least in part, the unfortunate outcome of the following incident, recounted by David Latasse.

> About seventy years ago a man at Duncan went out into the woods in the hopes of becoming a medicine man. He did not tell his wife what he was doing, and she did not like his staying away from home two or three days at a time, fearing that he was up to some mischief. He took no notice of her reproaches. One day he told her he was going to the store; but when he failed to reappear after two days his wife organized a search for him. The search party noticed a fire in a place where they had never seen one before and went to investigate it; but as they drew near the fire disappeared. They went up to the spot, and found the man lying unconscious, his body covered with blood and many snakes crawling round him. They whipped the snakes away and carried him home. As they drew near the house he regained consciousness and said to them "Why did you drive those people away? They were making me a powerful medicine man. You have done harm to me, not good, for now I shall die." He lingered a few days, then died.[9]

While it was possible that nearly any spirit might become the helping spirit

---

7   Ibid. –Ed.
8   Katzie elder Peter Pierre was surely the rarest of exceptions in this regard, claiming to have begun his initiation, under his mother's tutelage, at the age of three; Jenness, *Faith of a Coast Salish*, 65. –Ed.
9   Jenness, "Saanich Notes," 167. –Ed.

(*saila*) of a *cnem*, a select few—beings known to inhabit deep, dark lakes and similarly forbidding places—were said to be most closely associated with the profession.[10] These were chiefly serpentine creatures, each one especially powerful and potentially dangerous to anyone who encountered them; two of Jenness's Cowichan informants described these beings as *slelekam*, "monsters."[11] David Latasse identified *skaiyep* as the snake spirit most commonly obtained; even so, humans who met *skaiyep* and others of its ilk were invariably bloodied, as happened to the ultimately luckless husband in the preceding account, and on occasion, were struck unconscious. Equally potent, and supposedly harder and more perilous to acquire, was *sinałke*, sometimes depicted as a two-headed snake. Adding further to its fearsome reputation, Latasse said that this spirit's poisonous breath might trigger bodily contortions and paralysis in anyone unfortunate enough to inhale it. Moreover, *sinałke* afflicted people with a sickness called *stceł*, caused by contact with a mat-like slime which it produced and deposited in water; failure to wash it off immediately allowed the slime to penetrate into the bones, leaving victims very ill.[12]

Louis Pelkey, of Tsawout, knew of a *sinałke* that inhabited Ganges Harbour, on Salt Spring Island; he said it resembled a dog fish and met the approach of humans by squirting blood from its mouth.[13] Tom Paul told of a successful encounter with a mildly less noxious manifestation of this snake spirit.

> Many years ago a [Saanich] man who was training to be a *cnem* went hunting in the mountains just north of Malahat. In the night he heard something pass him, and his head suddenly twisted over to one side and blood issued from him. Next morning, he went higher up the mountain. Presently he came upon some immense strawberries and, near them, *sinałke*, coiled up like a big rock. Drawing back, the man prayed, then drew a hair from his head and shot at the creature. Returning to the village, he stayed in David Latasse's house in Brentwood for a fortnight, for he was very sick, *sinałke* having entered his body. At the end of two weeks the spirit in him became strong and he recovered. He was now a full *cnem*, though to increase his powers he received a little training from another medicine man. He then took the name Tcilkeam, after the celebrated character who had also received power from *sinałke*.[14]

---

10   David and Mrs Latasse said that medicine power might also be obtained by sleeping on the grave of a renowned warrior. They claimed that David's nephew had done this; but when Mrs Latasse asked him if it was the grave of her grandfather on which he had slept, the nephew would not say, for it was taboo to tell. Such a medicine man would go out before dawn, or after dark, and pray in the woods to the shade of that warrior for help. No one should see or hear him; Ibid., 154.

11   Ibid., 228–29, 241–42. In their Hul'qumi'num' dialect, "monster" is *st' leluqum* its SENĆOŦEN equivalent is S̱ŦÁLEḴEM (*sx̌éləqəm*). –Ed.

12   Ibid., 249. –Ed.

13   Ibid., 214.

14   Ibid., 211.

The *cnem* used physical manipulation to treat ailments such as pain and inflammation, massaging affected areas to induce the discharge of accumulated blood or other infecting substance, or sucking out the malignant agent with his mouth. Some informants claimed that only practitioners with strong medicine power were able to apply a third method, using their hands to draw (or cup out) offensive matter from the patient's body. This matter usually consisted of a piece of bone, a strand of hair, or some other small object visible only to the *cnem*. Once extracted, the *cnem* disposed of the contaminant, sometimes by vigorously blowing it away.[15]

The presence of foreign matter often signalled the work of a sorcerer, some shaman having resorted to magical means to inflict intentional harm. David Latasse's experience offers a case in point.

> During a visit to Esquimalt, a medicine man magically drove into his body a long strand of hair. David felt it the moment it entered him. He had a severe pain in his side and nearly fainted. Knowing that some medicine man had attacked him, he summoned all his energy and returned home to Brentwood Bay [Tsartlip]. Mrs Latasse sent for a *cnem* from East Reserve [Tsawout], and another from the couple's own village. The local *cnem*, who, unlike his counterpart, had never received proper training, was nevertheless so jealous that he almost refused to attend. The Tsawout *cnem*, as the more powerful, should have led in the rattling and singing, but to avoid any friction he let the Brentwood Bay man rattle and sing first. He followed with his own medicine song, and massaged David with deer fat, which entered his body and drew out the strand of hair. He told them what it was, but did not show it to them. David recovered, but for some time afterward he had a pain in his side.[16]

In addition to illustrating another form of sorcery, the next recollection also reveals the evil-doer's motivation in seeking to inflict grave harm.

> A man on the Brentwood Bay reserve [Tsartlip] married a woman's daughter, and after a time abandoned her, owing his mother-in-law some money. Unable to get her money, or to induce her son-in-law back to her daughter, she called in the help of a medicine man. The medicine man laid three traps for the culprit; he planted a powerful spirit at the man's door, a second at the beach, and a third at the graveyard just beyond. The man became very sick, and his friends, on Old David's advice, called in a medicine man from Duncan. This medicine man and David put their heads together and decided that the only thing to do was to take the patient to Cowichan and treat

---

15   Ibid., 228–29.
16   Both shamans possessed *skaiyep* as their helping spirit; their rattles were made of deer hoofs; Ibid., 249.

him there. They prepared to take the man away. At the doorstep he stopped, planted his feet down firmly and called out "You can't touch me. I am a *cnem*," which is what people so afflicted always say. After they had forcibly carried him beyond his doorstep he was able and willing to walk. When they reached the beach, however, the same thing happened again; and a third time when they came to the graveyard. After they had passed the graveyard the man seemed greatly improved in health, and he recovered entirely at Cowichan. The medicine man who took him there returned to Brentwood Bay and removed the three traps, thus enabling the man to return to his home.[17]

According to Albert Westly, of Nanaimo, lay people might also engage in sorcery.

At the winter dances, a feather from the head of a new dancer wafted into her mouth. A woman who was jealous of her pulled it out, and secretly inserted it in a coffin in the graveyard. The feather had *siekkum*, "breath," on it, the breath of the new dancer. She became ill. A strong *cnem* from Squamish was called in. He discovered what had happened. He had some new mats made into a kind of sack, which he drew over his head. The audience saw only his feet moving, now a step forward, now back. Meanwhile, his *cnem* [that is, his helping spirit] went to the coffin and recovered the feather. The *cnem*'s wife pulled off the bag, and the *cnem* held out the feather he had brought back. The patient recovered. Naturally, the *cnem* did not reveal the name of the woman who had caused her illness.[18]

A different, potentially more serious malady stemmed from the inherent nature of the soul. Apart from its ghostly transformation after death, the soul—at least that portion associated with mind, or consciousness—was understood to be separable from the living body, its wanderings at night explaining the occurrence of ordinary dreams and the special visions linked to guardian spirits. Like shades, moreover, their actions sometimes threatened a person's health. This happened when the soul failed to return of its own accord, for instance, or was waylaid by a ghost. It might also fall victim to the sorcerer's art, a shaman capturing it to weaken, or even kill, an enemy.[19] Whatever the cause,

---

17   Ibid., 250.
18   Ibid., 153. A more familiar, do-it-yourself method, was the use of poison. Mrs Latasse supplied the following recipe: Grind up a human bone, preferably a bone that had contained marrow. The simplest way is to scrape it with a file. Mix a little of the scrapings with a person's food. Soon the victim's throat will become very dry, the poison will go to his lungs and all through his system, and before very long, he will die; Ibid., 239.
19   A medicine man who captured a wandering soul sometimes imprisoned it in a container made of cedar (but not bone, as was thought to be the Haida practice). If he wanted to kill its owner he might cut the soul to pieces with a knife; this caused a quick death. A second method was to put it into a bivalve shell which, in turn, was placed in hot ashes; as the shell and its contents heated, the owner grew ever more dangerously feverish. The *cnem* in this case might escape

the effected person fell ill, typically becoming partially or fully unconscious. Only a *cnem* possessed the means and knowledge to find and restore the missing soul, and thus stave off death. Recalling an illness that had befallen his wife, Albert Westly described some general features of Coast Salish medical practice in such instances. To begin, the attending *cnem* sings his medicine song to summon his (or her) tutelary spirits; he then dispatches them to locate and retrieve the soul since spirits alone possess the power to navigate within the ethereal plane of existence.[20] However, by shading his eyes with his arms and looking into a pan of water which, by custom, is said to "draw the whole world into its compass," he is able to see where they travel and what they do. Ordinarily, he does not use a deer hoof rattle, but does so if the patient appears to be in critical condition. On the spirits' return, their mission accomplished, the *cnem* catches the recovered soul in his hands and immediately puts it inside his own chest where it is warmed and allowed to revive after its ordeal. The next morning, he restores it, inserting the soul directly into the patient's body.[21]

Jimmy Fraser, Jenness's Esquimalt informant, described a different technique for recapturing an errant soul, a practice which Peter Pierre, at Katzie, believed to have originated with Salish groups in the state of Washington.

> A youth is ill four or five months; his parents call in a *cnem*. The *cnem* says "His soul is missing." The parents and relatives bring in blankets and other things to pay the *cnem*, who undertakes to treat the case. That evening he fixes up a long kelp line under the roof of the house; to the far end of the line he attaches a human image made of cedar bark. In the morning the people gather and two men hold the loose end of the line. As the *cnem* sings and dances they pull the line, stopping whenever his song ends. After he has sung his fourth song the image slides down into the *cnem*'s hands. He clasps it against his breast, saying "I have the wandering soul. I'll keep it for a while and warm it inside my body. Then I will restore it to him." The next day he restores the soul to the youth's body.
>
> The restoration of the soul may not bring the youth back to health immediately, and the *cnem* will say "He needs to dance, that is all. His soul had a fright, or met something [e.g., a spirit] back in the mountains." The parents pay off the *cnem* and arrange to initiate the youth as a winter dancer.[22]

As was briefly noted in the previous chapter, sickness befell those who were

---

suspicion of sorcery because the illness developed gradually; Ibid., 160.

20 In Mrs Westly's case, trouble began when she saw a tiny figure—her own reflection—while peering into the water at the bottom of a deep shaft. As she lingered there, the portion of the soul her husband called *sititc* [mind, or consciousness], perhaps entranced by the image, dropped from her head and fell into the water below. Soon thereafter she fell ill; Ibid., 153.

21 Ibid. 153, 229.

22 Ibid., 189.

possessed, even briefly, by spirit beings other than ghosts. Jenness learned from Mrs Latasse that this was likeliest (though not exclusively) to occur through encounters with the more powerful of those beings, *sinałke*, for instance, or the fearsome warrior spirit, *skalathan*. She claimed to have had numerous such illnesses—typically a sharp pain in her side—owing to this cause. Her work as a midwife made her susceptible, she explained, since calls to attend a birth often came at night, the time when spirits, like ghosts, were apt to be at large around the village. As luck would have it, her work meant that the spirits were unable to remain in her body for long, being repelled by the impurity resulting from their host's close contact with women in labour. In consequence, symptoms tended to be relatively mild and short-lived.[23] Under different conditions, however, an afflicted person could be left in a more precarious state, one requiring intervention of a *cnem*. One such case, at Halalt, is detailed in Old Bob and Annie Bob's personal account.

Old Bob is a commoner. Shortly after he married his second wife, who is of *siem* [noble] rank, he went to work for a white man. One very hot day he thought he would have a swim, and, going down to a deep pool, stripped off his clothes and dived in. Deep down under the water his hand caught a log, and he heard something leaping and causing waves to break on the shore. Terrified, he hurried out of the water, climbed a bank, and looked down into the clear depths, but could see nothing. Then he put on his clothes and went back to work.

Shortly after he and his boss sat down to dinner, and his boss said to him "What is the matter? Are you feeling ill?" Bob answered "No." His boss said "You are very pale. You had better go home." Bob's mind went blank on the way home, and how he reached home he does not know. His wife asked him what was the matter with him, but he could not speak; only just as he got into bed he told her, in a whisper, to take good care of their baby. He lay in bed, asleep or unconscious, for some time, then suddenly wakened with a shout, and stiffened through all his body and limbs. His soul wandered, he said, and came to a gate where there stood a gatekeeper with a key. The gatekeeper asked him if he wished to enter, and he answered "I suppose so, since I have come here." But the gatekeeper said "You are not wanted here yet. Go back. But be very careful. Do not steal, do not slander women, do not lie. If you disobey you cannot come here when you die. Do not lose your way, or you will never find your body."

Bob lay unconscious for four days. His wife called in a local *cnem* on the second day. The *cnem* felt his pulse, but could find no signs of life, and said the patient was dead. The *cnem* was asked to find out what had happened, and the people gathered round the house with

23   Ibid., 193.

sticks to beat for him. Four times they beat for him. After the fourth time he said "Bob swam in the deep hole. The dogs of the *slelekan* [monstrous supernatural beings][24] that lives down there attacked him, and the *slelekan* itself passed over his head. It has killed him. I can do nothing." Bob's wife asked the *cnem* to paint Bob's face as a *thitha* would, with red ochre. At first the *cnem* refused, but on her insisting, and getting out the ochre, feathers, and cedar bark, he proceeded to paint Bob's face. Four times he painted it, rubbing it off after the first three times. At the fourth painting, when there was still no sign of life, the *cnem* wept and said "I can do no more. He is dead."

At sunset on the fourth day Old Bob's body moved. His wife spoke to him but he did not answer. She threw a blanket over him, and he perspired freely. After a time, Old Bob grunted, sat up, and turned towards his left. His eyes were wide open, like burning coals, and he could neither speak nor understand what was said to him. At daybreak he collapsed again and was to all appearances dead. The people decided that now he really was dead; putting him on board a canoe with his mattress, they conveyed him over to the cemetery on Kuper Island for burial.

When the coffin-bearers came to lift him out of the canoe he stirred again. They conveyed him back to Westholme and laid him on a bed inside the big house. The church-goers rang bells around him in an attempt to restore him to consciousness, but for two days and two nights he neither spoke nor closed his eyes, but only from time to time reached out for some imaginary object.[25] Two men kept watch beside him to keep him quiet. They then sent a canoe to Nanaimo to bring a *thitha* from there, and also Old Bob's aunt. When the pair arrived they sat on the bed beside him, and his aunt called for ochre, grease, and cedar bark. Just as the *thitha* was preparing to paint his face Old Bob suddenly sat up and said "Are you going to paint my face?" "Yes," said the astonished *thitha*. "I don't want you to," answered Old Bob. "Go up and get me four tiny fir trees." They sent two boys to bring the firs; two they set at the bottom corners of his bed and capped them with feathers; the other two at the top corners of the bed, capped with cedar bark dyed red with alder. Now Old Bob said to the *thitha* "I'll tell you how to mark my face. Don't make a mistake." As soon as the *thitha* began to paint his face Old Bob dropped off into a deep sleep, and slept for twenty-four hours.

After twenty-four hours Mrs Bob went over to her husband's bed.

---

24   See page 110, footnote 11. –Ed.

25   These church-goers were probably members of the Indian Shaker Church, a denomination whose practices include the ringing of hand-bells; Thom, per. comm, 10 August, 2016. Founded in Washington State in the early 1880s, the church's teachings reached Vancouver Island less than a decade later; Amos, "Indian Shaker Church," 633–35. –Ed.

He recognized her and asked for his clothes. As he dressed, the people watched him to see what he would do. All round the building was a line of boards on edge. He walked round on these and passed through the wall. His wife, frightened, ran outside to catch him, but he passed in through the wall again. As she went up to him he took her hand and led her up the hill. "Do you see so and so paddling his canoe yonder?" he asked. "No," she said, for there was not a canoe in sight. Bob answered "Well, he has two porpoises on board." Not long afterwards the very man did come ashore with two porpoises.

Bob led her to the church on top of the hill, where the people motioned to his wife to let him go. The priest held a service over him. He was very weak, but in his right mind. He had become a *siowa* through his contact with the *slelekam* in the pool. That was why he was able to walk on the edge of the boards. He believes that if people had let him, he could have walked on the surface of the water. The *slelekam* had no name, and the pool where he met it has now dried up. But for many years he retained the power of foresight. His visions came to him in bed at night. He could tell if a sick man would recover or die; if a man was going to die, people would seem to take him into the middle of the floor and jump around him. If there was a rock below the surface that kept chattering, he could hear and see it, and would tell the people to dig it up and move it elsewhere.[26]

---

26   Ibid., 241–42.

12

Spirit Dancing

On the Saanich Peninsula, as elsewhere on Vancouver Island, early December through February found the Coast Salish settled in their home villages, the pace of economic activity, like the sun's strength, at low ebb. In seeming contrast to the season's material conditions, this was the time of year when the power bestowed on individuals by their guardian spirits was felt most intensely, often to the point of inducing illness. Mr and Mrs Bob likened what they called "*saila* sickness" to a great wind that wells up in the body and threatens the sufferer's vitality and clarity of mind.[1] Treatment lay outside the bounds of a priest or medicine man's practice, although parents might consult one or the other if the patient were an adolescent son or daughter. Instead, it fell to the afflicted themselves to gain relief by channelling their tutelary, not exorcizing it, as was done with shades. To that end, nearly every evening throughout the winter months was devoted to *smiłla*, "spirit dancing," round upon round of ritualized performances in which individuals, seemingly possessed by their indwelling spirit, mirrored its essence and sang its *syawan*, the "power song," it had taught them.[2]

Dancers portrayed their spirit guardians by donning representative costumes—but not masks—and painting their faces in prescribed patterns and colours: red or black, and sometimes both. A man who had *skalathan* (warrior) as his *saila*, for instance, customarily dressed in a hide shirt and a cone-shaped leather hat decorated with human hair hanging down behind; he painted his face black. For the snake known as *qwxw'qs*, the costume was a buckskin shirt sprinkled with red ochre, a cedar bark head band with a knot at front and back, and red face paint. In the case of *skaiyep*, also a snake spirit, it consisted of a buckskin shirt like that used for *qwxw'qs*, but its dancer wore a headband made of a material other than cedar bark, and decorated with the red feathers of a red-wing blackbird; he also carried a deer hoof rattle (*kutc-*

---

1   Jenness, "Saanich Notes," 190. Along the Fraser, some Salish thought the annual surge of spirit power began in the east, usually in late October, and gradually spread westward, reaching the Chilliwack area in November, Musqueam only in January, and later still on Vancouver Island; Duff, *Upper Stalo*, 107. Among the W̱SÁNEĆ, as in other Salish communities on the island, this idea appears to have had no currency. –Ed.

2   In describing spirit sickness among the Snuneymuxw (Nanaimo), Sarah Robinson wrote that upon "Lodging in the owner's chest, the power ascends to the throat in the beginning of the winter season, to 'burst forth as sound, simultaneously taking possession and turning him into a manifestation of the power itself'"; cited in Jilek, *Salish Mental Health*, 34. In SENĆOŦEN, SYEWEN (*syəwən*) means "power song." It bears mention, however, that SYEWEN functions solely in the context of SMIŁE (*smiłəʔ*), the "spirit (or Indian) dance." Though its source may be the same, this song is unrelated to whatever practical powers and accompanying song(s) a "vision quest" might bring, and is typically bestowed at the spirit's wintertime return; Barnett, *Coast Salish*, 277; Suttles, "Central Coast Salish," 467. –Ed.

min) in each hand.[3] In addition to the costume worn, a person might carry, or produce, some other symbolic representation of his or her tutelary, one designed to create a special effect. Louis Pelkey told of a man who was impersonating *skaiyep*; blood trickled from his mouth as he danced, a depiction of how the spirit appeared to him in a vision. Another, who danced the fish spirit *skwanelɛts*, carried a pole with duck-like objects on top. While he danced and sang, four strong men held the pole; even so, the pole repeatedly jerked upward and struck the roof, the men barely able to hold on, for the "ducks" wanted to fly away.[4]

From time to time, the power of the spirit possessing a dancer took form in extraordinary ways. According to his father Tom, Baptiste Paul, who had a *saila* known to the Saanich as *sqale'k.an*—"breakers on the beach"—got an intense craving to enter the water when he danced.[5] Two men held on to him as they lead him down to the water; once Baptiste bathed, he was able to regain self-control. More impressive still is an account of a dancer possessed by the powerful mythical bird-snake, *xwáł'təp*.

> Long ago, as he was dancing *xwáł'təp*, a man flew right away and could not return, for his *saila* was too strong. He could come back at intervals, but was carried away again. His parents then set two lads at puberty on the roof of the house and when next he settled there they seized him and brought him down. He became a normal man again.[6]

Dances were public events; in some villages they were staged in ordinary dwellings, in others, in a communal dance-house. Their organization was informal, the business of seeing to basic arrangements, including provision of food for onlookers and dancers alike, being the host's responsibility.[7] With the usual exception of slaves (on which, see below), anyone who had received a *syawan* (power song) was entitled to dance. Before participating for the first time, however, each "new dancer"—*xau'sálaqał*—was required to undergo a ceremonial initiation. Compared to ordinary dances, initiations tended to be more elaborate, consuming the best part of a week and involving the services of an officiating priest, up to a dozen "old dancers" who possessed strong *saila*, and a cadre of young attendants; all had to be compensated for their time and effort.[8] Families of noble rank might engage masked *swaiswai*

---

3   Jenness, "Saanich Notes," 196, 203. In the SENĆOTEN lexicon, the word ĆEĆMIN (*kʷəčmín*) refers to a "dancer's pole with deer hooves." *Kwucmín*, in Hul'qumi'num' speech, denotes "deer hoof rattle," while on the Fraser, its Sto:lo analog is *kwóxwmal*, appropriately (and more fully) defined as "(spirit) dancer's stick with deer-hoof rattles tied onto it." –Ed.

4   Ibid. 214.

5   In Cowichan communities, this spirit is known as *hai'yeək*. When Baptiste Paul danced, he painted his face black, with red around the mouth; Ibid. 211.

6   Ibid., 198, 217.

7   Barnett notes that hosts also insured that a *cnem* was present to protect attendees from the machinations of sorcerers; *Coast Salish*, 276. –Ed.

8   The SENĆOTEN word for "new dancer" is XEU‚SOLEĆEŁ (*xəwsáləkʷəl*); its counterpart,

dancers as well, individuals whose right to use the wooden masks, and to sing associated songs, was a family inheritance. Like many potlatches, initiations thus were costly affairs, and depending on the sponsoring family's resources, might necessitate drawing on the assistance of kin and allies. This meant many commoners were hard-pressed to sponsor a child's initiation, although it sometimes happened that nobles contributed to their cause. Rarer still, one imagines, were cases of like-minded beneficence towards slaves.

A slave, all of whose masters had died, was travelling over the top of Mt Newton when he saw a fire. Thinking this was a strange place for one he approached it and discovered it blazed brightly but gave out no heat. Then he knew it was a spirit's fire, and was sick with the spirit for a long time until someone took pity on him and made him a dancer. It was the snake spirit *si′nəɬkɛ′*.[9]

Preceding pages have recounted how adolescents, particularly those of noble lineage, received parental encouragement to obtain guardian spirits.[10] For those who succeeded in their quest, and not all did, two or three years might pass before they became aware of their spirit's presence, let alone its nature, a gestational period of sorts during which the *saila* was thought to be gathering strength and gaining firm hold of its recipient. It is at this crucial point, with winter's approach, that spirit sickness developed, a condition perhaps better regarded as a malaise, Jenness's characterization of the phenomenon among the Katzie.[11] A *cnem* or *thitha*, and sometimes an old dancer, is called to examine the patient and advise the parents on a course of action. An old dancer's examination might consist of little more than feeling the sufferer's chest or hands; if they were hot and moist, it was time for the young person to dance. The youth, indeed anyone of virtually any age, who possessed a tutelary spirit and ignored the need to dance, risked suffering illness throughout the winter, and possibly at other times of the year, too.[12]

"(old) dancer," is SJEL‚WEN̲ (*sčə̓lx̌ʷəŋ*). –Ed.

9   Jenness, "Saanich Notes," 193.

10   Every nobleman's child, boy or girl, was sent into the woods at the age of about 15–17 and left to wander there four to ten days until the youngster saw a spirit. This might happen at any time of year save the coldest months. Every child had to see some spirit; but while the parents could not determine which one, they would naturally direct the seeker to a place known to be inhabited by one of the "better" (i.e. more powerful, and hence prestigious) spirits. The questing youngster bathed in many places and might come in contact with many spirits, each of which would enter and afflict him. Which to accept was the child's choice. However, sometimes a rejected spirit bothered a person greatly. If a youth had the wolf, bear, seal and warrior spirits and chose the warrior, for instance, the bear might give him cramps or pains in some part of his body. The parents would then call in a medicine man to shift the place of the bear spirit in his body—to push it round to the back or somewhere so it would stop hurting him; Ibid., 183.

11   Jenness, *Faith of a Coast Salish*, 41. –Ed.

12   Jenness, "Saanich Notes," 183. Further to this point, George Kwakaston told Jenness that despite receiving a *saila* as a youngster, afterward he never wanted to dance. He is not alone in this, he said, because the present dances are not like the old, and many or all the Indians are

A Saanich woman married a white man and now lives on San Juan Island. He did not want her to join in the winter dances. A medicine man said to her "If you don't dance you will be sick all summer; however, if you are not allowed to dance at least sing your medicine song that was given to you." One of her sons helps her to sing it; the rest think she is crazy. Her husband sits reading in his chair and takes no notice of her as she softly sings her song.[13]

In most villages, a good sign that someone was soon to be made a new dancer was when a family asked its neighbours to help with the important task of gathering firewood.[14]

Nonetheless, parents took care not to let children know in advance that they were to be initiated. Failure to keep this confidence, it was thought, might cause the *saila* to move from the chest to below the left or right ribs, and thereby make the spirit restive and ill-tempered. In view of that injunction, various preparations were necessarily made in secret, a task often entrusted to someone from outside the immediate family, as long as that person was already a dancer. The usual to-do list included recruiting the *thitha* and a group of old dancers—either male or female, as appropriate to the initiate's sex— whose principal role was to elicit the new dancer's power song.[15] They also found someone to make the costume only worn by initiates: a cedar bark headdress and belt, the latter used to pull up the youth when it was time to dance.[16] In order to strengthen the individual who was to wear them, it was customary to lay these adornments on the ledge of a high cliff, facing the sun. In more recent times, families have taken to keeping this paraphernalia at home, a change Tom Paul attributed to the theft by white people of items ostensibly abandoned out in the open. Needless to say, acquiring these important things added to the sponsor's expense; in the case of a noble family, especially one that hired *swaiswai* dancers, a child's initiation might well cost a small fortune.[17]

Jenness's primary Saanich informants, Tom Paul, and David and Mrs La-tasse, offered descriptions of the event itself that differed in certain details, yet were largely similar with reference to basic structure and procedure.[18] (Much

---

Christians. In the old days practically everyone had a *saila* and danced. If they did not dance they became ill. Those who dance today at Cowichan, he added, merely choose what they will represent in the dances; they do not have real guardians, obtained in dreams; Ibid., 219.

13   Ibid., 171–72.

14   Ibid., 173.

15   Sometimes the sponsor tries to recruit old dancers in pairs: for example, two who have the powerful serpentine *saila* called *qoxoqs*, two with *shopship*, "night bird," and perhaps two with *skaiyep*; Ibid., 173.

16   Some hats were made of cedar mixed with goat wool and long hairs that trailed down the wearer's back; Ibid., 178.

17   Tom Paul told Jenness that local Indian agents sought to cut back the scale of initiation ceremonies on the grounds that their expense was wasteful; Ibid.

18   According to Homer Barnett, Paul "never became a dancer [himself] because, by the time

the same can be said about the accounts he obtained in other areas.) The elderly couple said the ceremony commences in the evening when six old dancers entered the sponsoring family's house; immediately they approach the youth who, to this point, remains unaware that he is to be made a *χauʹsálaqał*, a "new dancer." The group's first objective is to discover the identity of the initiate's guardian spirit, and thereby elicit his *syawan*, the spirit's power song. They begin by lifting him up bodily from his sickbed—a space earlier partitioned off with blankets or mats, and in which he remains in ritual seclusion over the coming days—and carrying him round the house four times, doing so while making hooting sounds. Next, they lay him back down and, in turn, each dancer sings his own power song. If one of these songs seems to excite the youth, causing him to shout "*hu hu hu*," they know which *saila* it is that possesses him. Thereafter, only the old dancer(s) with that tutelary continue to sing, leaving the others to beat time with the wooden sticks they carry; should these others continue with their songs, it was feared, they risked confusing the youth.[19] Once the old dancers identify the *saila*, the presiding *thitha* leaves the initiate with two young men whose job it is to watch over him, day and night. This is done to insure that he not become too excited and thus harm himself. If their initial efforts failed to determine the *saila*, they leave one youth only, returning the following morning to repeat their actions of the previous night. Should their efforts have succeeded, however, they invite others from the village with the same spirit to perform their dances and songs on the following morning.

Unlike his elderly neighbours, Tom Paul said that the initiation begins at daybreak, not in the evening. He also added a detail they may well have overlooked: before anything else happens, a *thitha* enters the empty house and ritually purifies the initiate by applying paint to his face.[20] That done, the old dancers, one after the next, perform their personal dance and *saila* song. As each takes his turn, the others stand along the sides of the house and beat with their sticks. Everyone listens intently to hear any answering cry—"*ho ho ho*"—indication of the identity of the youth's *saila*. The dancer(s) whose spirit matches his becomes his "partner," remaining close to him and preventing

---

he was old enough to be initiated, his father and grandfather had died and there was no one who could sponsor him and make the necessary property distribution connected with the initiation"; *Coast Salish*, 284–85. –Ed.

19 It was not unusual for several people to acquire the same spirit, but their respective power songs were never identical, sometimes only a few words distinguishing one from another. On a related note, George Kwakaston said that a man might have two (or more) *saila* at the same time, even a new dancer. The stronger has the mastery and it is the song given by that *saila* that he chants. Should they struggle for mastery, their host retains an experienced dancer who attempts to reconcile them in some way; driving one away, however, imperils the victim's health; Jenness, "Saanich Notes," 171, 196.

20 Kwakaston's account of Cowichan practice describes the *thitha's* overall role as minimal, and does not include face-painting at the initiation's outset. In the Bobs's version, as in Paul's, the ceremony begins when a priest paints the new dancer's face with red ochre; Ibid. 186, 190.

him from confusing his own *syawan* with those of the other dancers. Once they determine what spirit the youth has, the group breaks up and are fed, for it is then about eight or nine in the morning.

That evening, Paul's account continues, the whole village gathers in the sponsor's house, old dancers sitting up front, male nobles immediately behind but in front of male commoners, women and children in back, against the walls. The old dancers again give some of their individual dances. Then two of them enter the curtained enclosure set aside for the initiate and entertain him with a story. Meanwhile, the remaining dancers line up, one behind the other; their leader holds a deer hoof rattle, and someone behind him a drum. Softly they march to the youngster's enclosure, fling open the curtain, shake the rattle and beat the drum and shout "*ho ho ho.*" [21] The initiate begins to stand. As he does, the men lift him up bodily, carry him four times round the house and then deposit him on his bed again, closing the curtains that conceal him and the two young companions whose job it is to keep him company, night and day. (At the initiation of a girl dancer, her companions are girls of her own age.) After resuming their seats, the old dancers rise and dance again for some while. There is no special order in their dancing; usually after one man or woman has danced, the next one to him, or her, stands up and performs.

Missing from Paul's description is mention of what transpires should an initiate fail to become excited by any of the old dancers' songs, a failure generally taken to mean that, as of yet, the youth has no *saila*. In such cases, David Latasse explained, the presiding priest possesses the power to impel one into him.[22] On one such occasion,

> an old woman summoned David's uncle, who was a *thitha*, to make her grandson a dancer. He mustered the old dancers as usual, but none of their songs excited the young fellow, or roused in him the least attention. Then the *thitha* went over to the fire, warmed his *kutcmin* (deer hoof rattle), returned to the initiate and shook it at his head. He did this four times, each time praying to his deer *saila* as he warmed the rattle to enter the man. After the fourth warming he suddenly struck the initiate on the stomach with the rattle. He yelled, and thereafter could not stop yelling, for the spirit had entered him, and, as usual, was making his stomach swell up.[23]

---

21 Kwakaston said that a *celmoxis* (horn rattle) is shaken over the initiate; the old dancer who does this is called *i'man*. The Hul'qumi'num' word for "horn rattle" is *shulmuxwtsus*; Thom, "Senses of Place," 311. –Ed.

22 Albert Westly said old dancers do this with their *slekkum*, or "breath pressure," much as a *saila* does when, in a dream, it teaches its power song. In Hul'qumi'num', breath pressure is *slhek'wum*; Ibid., 222.

23 In the old days, according to Jenness's Halalt informants, if a boy made fun of a dancer and imitated his actions in dancing, the parents would call in a *cnem* who shook his deer hoof rattle at him. This knocked the boy senseless. Then the *cnem* revived him until he began to shout "ho

And on another, though under different circumstances, this same uncle drove a *saila* into David's cousin, who was always becoming drunk and complaining that people paid no attention to him, although all his cousins were *siems* (nobles) and dancers. One evening when he entered the house, half drunk and complaining as usual, David's uncle said to his brother "I'll settle him this time." He bade his brother go behind the man and be ready to grab his hair; then he warmed his *kutcmin* at the fire and struck the man a violent blow in the stomach. With a yell he fell back unconscious—a *saila* had been driven into him. They laid him on his bed and covered him with a goat wool blanket. When he recovered in the early morning he wondered where he was and why blankets were spread over him. Feeling cold, he went and sat by the fire, and as he fingered the blanket over his shoulders remarked "This is not my blanket." Suddenly he realized what they were doing to him and fell back unconscious. They laid him on his bed again and called in some old dancers.

From this point onward, both renditions largely coincide, though as before, they differ on certain details. Each described the second and third days as repetitions of the first, with one noteworthy exception: in the Latasse account of events, the third evening finds the presiding priest painting the cedar house posts with red ochre; this is necessary because in the mythic past, cedar was an old man. To honour their spirits, the *thitha* then "feeds" the posts by burning tallow, mountain goat wool, ochre, and reeds in the fire. The ochre is meant to propitiate the weather, assuring its spirit will treat the new dancer gently whenever he travels in the woods. He prays to this spirit as he paints the posts, and to the spirits of the posts as he feeds them at the fire. Jenness's Quamichan informant, Johnson, spoke of the ritual feeding of house posts as well, noting that the custom ordinarily took place a day or two after the initiate's first dance, and was witnessed by members of the community who had been invited in for the occasion. The offering of food was nearly the same as its Saanich counterpart, the lone difference being that consumption plant was substituted for reeds. After praying at each post for the welfare of the youth and then throwing each offering into the fire, the *thitha* performed his own *saila* dance, the youth followed with his, and the gathered people sang. Once the youth had taken his seat, the person to his right rose to dance, and after him everyone else, in regular order.[24]

The fourth day of the initiation, according to Tom Paul, is when the old dancers stop their performances and listen for the youth's own power song, which his two young companions now urge him to sing, and try to learn themselves. If it is a difficult song, they may press him to repeat it later in the evening. At dawn on the fifth and final day, the *thitha* goes to the youth and prays over

---

ho ho," indication that the *cnem* had put a *saila* into the youngster. The parents then arranged to initiate their son as a dancer, but without the ceremony that attended a youth who obtained a *saila* in the ordinary way; Ibid., 220.

24   Ibid., 175, 185.

him. That done, he mounts a ladder to the roof of the house, faces the rising sun, offers a wordless prayer to Xe.ls, and then strikes the roof loudly with a stick.[25] He repeats this four times before descending to paint the youth's face, as he has done every morning. While this is happening, the old male dancers assemble if a boy is being initiated, female dancers if the initiate is a girl. Two bring in a tub of warm water and lay a bed of grass beside it about the middle of one side. They escort the boy outside, bathe him, put clothes on him again and seat him on the grass bed.[26] The *thitha* combs his hair and twice chants the following words: "*tackenam tackenam kwasi'yal sialem.*" (Have your drink. May it make you healthy, young noble.) After his hair is combed, all turn their eyes to the enclosure where the four *swaiswai* men are hidden.[27] Two of them emerge, wearing their masks. As the onlookers tap with their sticks, the pair, holding rattles in their right hands and fir branches in their left, dance round the room until they reach the place where the boy is sitting; they then shuffle towards him, wave their branches over his head, shuffle back, and repeat the movement four times. Finally, they dance back to their room to let the other two *swaiswai* dancers take a turn.

Two old dancers now carry the boy back into his room. Once more, the *thitha* paints his face, then offers him a salmon; after biting off four small pieces, the initiate drops them in the priest's hand.[28] He is given cold water

---

25   David Latasse noted that the *thitha* only strikes the roof when *swaiswai* dancers are to perform, as they do in Paul's recitation; Ibid. 174.

26   At Koksilah, the custom of bathing the initiate is more dramatic. On the fourth morning everyone in the village gathers; on occasion, they are joined by people from neighbouring villages. With everyone seated, the youth is taken outside, strips, and then stands inside a canoe that is to serve as his bath. Suddenly, and to him unexpectedly, two to four men on the roof each pour down on him a bucket of the coldest spring water they can find. The shock makes the youth frenzied for a few moments, but as soon as he has quieted down he dresses again and is conducted back indoors to his enclosure. While he sits there a blanket is laid over the canoe, and all the men and boys in attendance scramble to take possession of it: he who seizes the blanket is said to "own" the canoe. As they tussle, pulling from every direction, a man—likely the initiate's kinsman—enters the canoe and calls out "I will buy it." He offers to pay each individual a certain amount to release his hold on the blanket. Once this is settled, all those who held the blanket cut it into strips and divide it among themselves; Ibid. 186–87.

27   If the family has hired *swaiswai* dancers, these dancers enter the house on the evening preceding the initiation's opening day and erect for themselves a small enclosure (with blankets or mats) well away from the space occupied by the initiate; Ibid., 176.

28   David and Mrs Latasse said that this "breakfast" consists of one male and one female fish; at one time, these were freshly baked salmon. After being offered the female fish four times the boy takes a bite out of its side and drops the fragment into the *thitha*'s hand, who places it in a dish. He does the same with the male fish. As this is happening, the *thitha* prays to *skwanelɛts*, the fish spirit, to look after his son, so that he may be able to eat any kind of fish afterwards without becoming ill. If, for some reason, the prayers were left incomplete, the couple noted, the initiate will have terrible cramps in his stomach. Having bitten off the small bits, the youth then eats as much of the fish as he can. If, during the winter season, the new dancer wishes to attend a dance across the water, the *thitha* will take him to the beach and pray to *skwanelɛts* that the youth may come to no harm in his travels by canoe. There, while holding him by the shoulders, the priest pushes him three times towards the water, and the fourth time makes him go in up to his knees; Ibid., 174–75.

to drink, which he sucks up through a bone tube.[29] The *thitha* then conducts the youth to the door, and standing outside, throws red ochre (*tamał*) over his legs as he goes to emerge.[30] The boy retires a few paces, then re-advances to have his legs sprinkled again. This is done four times. So treated, the initiate heads off to the woods, accompanied by a number of youths whose job it is to watch over him. They light a fire near a creek in which the youth bathes. If his companions fail to keep watch over him it was feared that, after his bath, his *saila* might grow so strong that he would become "crazy" and lose himself in the woods. Meanwhile, the *thitha* climbs the roof once more and deposits the four morsels of salmon on top for the crows to eat.[31] For their part, the old dancers resume dancing, continuing to do so through the remainder of the morning, while two other men busy themselves making a hat for the youth of the kind his *saila* requires.

About three in the afternoon the youth is heard shouting on his return from the woods. On his way he pulls up a stout young tree—it must be uprooted, not cut down—and trims it with an axe or knife to serve as a walking stick (*qaqwa*) wherever he goes during the next two or three months.[32] Villagers again gather round the sides of the house. The officiating *thitha*, standing just inside the doorway, sprinkles the initiate's legs four times with red ochre before the youth enters, walking backward. Once inside, he turns round and then dances round the house as the old dancers tap their sticks and chant his song.[33] After concluding his dance, he retires to his room; then he, and everyone else, eats.

At nightfall, the old dancers put on their dancing paraphernalia one more

---

29 If the initiate wants to scratch his head, he must not use his fingers, but a special scratcher, made of bone; Ibid. 174.

30 Much as Indian consumption plant is used to prevent infection from a *spalkwithe* [shade], red ochre thwarts the possibility of contagion from contact with a "tainted"—that is, a pregnant or menstruating—woman; Ibid. 177. In SENĆOŦEN, "red ochre" is TEMEⱢ (*təməł*). –Ed.

31 In recounting this ceremony, Louis Pelkey explained that after the initiate bites off the four pieces of salmon, the officiant places them in the fire. On occasion, the priest places them on a stump instead, and then keeps watch. If a crow takes them away to eat, it is said that the boy will enjoy long life; if the crow ignores the morsels, however, the boy is bound to die within two years. Jimmy Fraser, of Esquimalt, reported something similar: if the salmon presented to the youth is very hard and his teeth make no mark in it, he will not live long. Only a *thitha* who harboured ill-intentions would supply hard fish, he said; Ibid., 184, 189.

32 KOĆE (*q'əkʷə*), in SENĆOŦEN, denotes "a new dancer's staff." In an addendum to his account, Tom Paul noted that his son, Baptiste, had a walking stick that was about seven feet long. Pointed at one end, it was wrapped with cedar bark and had an eagle feather at a point two-thirds along its length; eagle feathers, he explained, make a strong *saila*. The stick was pointed so that if he were sent to give a duck or something as a present to an old man or woman, he could carry it on the point; etiquette demanded the gift not be held in his hands; Ibid., 178. –Ed.

33 An initiate who fell to the floor while dancing lay as if dead, his stomach beginning to swell. A *thitha* was called to revive him by chanting, rubbing fat over the "dead" man's stomach, and painting his face with ochre until his breath returned and he began to gurgle. Onlookers then beat their sticks, and the *thitha* chanted again and shook his rattle (*kutcmin*). Once the fallen initiate cried "ho ho ho" he soon became himself again. Two young men then picked him up from the floor while a third "lifted" him by the forelock. He steadied himself on his feet and resumed his dance; Ibid., 220.

time and the youth dons his new hat and other trappings. A hired dancer with a deer hoof rattle stands at the door of the youth's enclosure and shakes the rattle. Two men lead the initiate out, one holding him by the waist in front, the other by the waist from behind. They make four feints before leading him out, then conduct him four times round the house before they leave him, standing alone, in the middle of the floor. The new dancer then performs the dance associated with his *saila*; on growing weary, he is led back to his enclosure by the same two men.[34]

It is at this point that the boy's father, or whoever is sponsoring him, calls for all the goods accumulated to pay for the initiation—blankets, guns, and other items—to be piled in the middle of the floor; only canoes, if they are too big, are left outdoors. The two men who earlier accompanied the initiate to his enclosure now lead him to a seat atop the blankets while his father calls out the individuals by name who are to receive payment. All the hired persons are paid first. The *thitha* may get as much as twenty blankets and a gun;[35] then there are the *swaiswai* men who performed and made the youth's hat, the two who led him out from his enclosure, and all the old dancers who have tapped their sticks and sung their songs. Over and above the outlay for these goods is the cost, also borne by the father, incurred in feeding participants and specta-tors alike throughout the five-day ceremony.

Newly initiated dancers remained subject to certain restrictions until the dancing season drew to a close. The main of these was an injunction against removing ceremonial face paint, and with it, against going into streams which villagers ordinarily used for bathing. Although Saanich informants were un-clear on the next points, at Koksilah, and likely elsewhere, new dancers—their status as such remained unchanged until the next year—were also expected to limit as much as possible socializing and speaking, even with family; and while permitted to participate in the remainder of the current season's dances, they were strictly barred from touching anyone's food but their own.

The informality that prevailed in organizing individual dances seems to have applied equally to settling on the evening that was to be the season's last. On that final day everyone except the new dancer bathed, but when the villagers gathered after dark in the dance house, everyone entitled to do so, without exception, participated. The following morning brought resumption of ordinary life. For new dancers, however, two obligations remained. After first depositing their special headdress and other dancing paraphernalia on a high cliff, facing into the rising sun to receive the sun spirit's blessing, they

---

34 Occasionally a new dancer seems not to wish to dance, or not to be able to do so. He just lies on his couch and will not rise. A medicine man dances up to him, chanting his song, takes a deer hoof rattle, breathes on it, and points (shoots) it at the youth. The reluctant initiate falls back as if dead, and may lie in that condition for as much as a day and a night. Only then does he rise up and dance. The *cnem* has forced his *saila* (spirit) to become active; Ibid., 184.

35 David and Mrs Latasse put the *thitha's* compensation alone at $5–20, a goat wool blanket, and all the dishes used during the initiation; Ibid., 175.

were permitted to bathe and wash away the paint they had been wearing now for weeks, or even months.[36]

...

Unlike winter spirit dancing, Jenness's notes on *swaiswai* (or *xwai xwai*)[37] masks and the customs associated with them among Salish groups on Vancouver Island are relatively spare. Most, but not all, of the details he did record—the lion's share of which were provided by Albert Westly and pertain to Nanaimo—appear as an appendix to his monograph on the Katzie.[38] Several Saanich informants spoke about the age-old tradition, however, including Louis Pelkey, who said that the people of Sooke were the first to receive these wooden masks, given as a gift by X̱e.ls. Afterwards, knowledge of them spread through marriage ties to other island groups, eventually reaching Nanaimo, where, he noted further, they are now more common than elsewhere. Halalt elder Old Bob presented an alternative story, saying that the masks originally reached his area from Musqueam, across the strait, and from Malahat, to the south. Adding to the mix, Jimmy Fraser stated that the Songhees had no *swaiswai* masks at all, the tradition being restricted to the Saanich, Cowichan, and Salish groups around Vancouver and on the lower Fraser.[39]

Questions of origins aside, all who spoke on the topic agreed that the right to perform as *swaiswai* dancers was an inheritance passed from one generation to the next within particular families. The masks themselves were made of cedar and, among the Saanich at least, depicted one of three powerful spirits: Skwanelets, Thunderbird, and Wolf. However, no two masks were the same, even those representing the same spirit. Along with the mask came entitlement to wear its accompanying costume—dancing apron and leggings made of woven mountain goat wool, with tassels of cedar bark—to use a shell rattle (*shelmaxsis*),[40] and to perform certain songs, which were also inherited. While there must have been others, David Latasse spoke of two songs in particular, one for the dead, chanted at funerals, the other for the living, performed at marriages and on occasions when family names were bestowed on sons and daughters. Offered as prayers to X̱e.ls, they were always chanted four times.

---

36 Even after bathing, George Kwakaston said that recent initiates were warned against going near fishing rivers for some time, lest their presence spoil the all-important salmon run; Ibid., 188.

37 The SENĆOŦEN word SX̱ÍX̱I (*sxʷə́yxʷi*) denotes "masked dance." A valuable examination of this dance and its associated paraphernalia is found in Suttles, "Halkomelem Sxwayxwey." –Ed.

38 Jenness, *Faith of a Coast Salish*, 91–92. –Ed.

39 Jenness, "Saanich Notes," 255.

40 It appears that Jenness (Ibid., 254) recorded the wrong word for shell rattle; in the SENĆOŦEN language, S̱YELMEW̱ĆES (*šyəlməxʷčəs*) is "horn rattle"; Montler's lexicon contains no word for a rattle made of shell. Thom has explained the item in question is comprised of large scallop shells strung on a ring of cedar; per. comm. 10 August, 2016. In Hul'qumi'num', this ceremonial object, used in masked dances, is called *kwunémmum*. –Ed.

As kinsmen related through their mothers, he noted further, his own songs, and those of Edward Jim, of Tseycum, were practically indistinguishable.

Westly told Jenness that at Nanaimo, *swaihwai* [*sic*] masks depicted five spirit beings: beaver, raven, spring salmon, sawbill duck, and *spalkwithe*—the "night owl," or shade. This last had been his own until it was destroyed in a fire. On learning of the loss, a Musqueam elder made him another, this one symbolizing the sawbill. As with spirit dancers, the performances of *swaiswai* dancers portrayed the beings their masks represented: thus raven jumps up and down, spring salmon pretends to fight, beaver slinks around, and so forth.[41]

Hiring *swaiswai* dancers for potlatches and other occasions, as noted previously, was an expensive proposition, unaffordable for all but the upper echelons of society. Indeed, David Latasse claimed that dancers could demand any sum they saw fit since much prestige attached to their performances. Along similar lines, Westly said that dancers either performed a lot, or a little, depending on the pay they expected to receive, or so he was advised at the time he received his mask and costume. Moreover, it was customary that dancers at Nanaimo, and probably elsewhere, had to be hired in pairs, homage, it seems, to the legendary pair of brothers who were the first people to perform in *swaiswai* mask and costume in that community. A grand potlatch might employ as many as twenty dancers, a modest one, two or four. From time to time it happened that a man holding a feast might only be able to muster an odd number of dancers, making it necessary to even things out by hiring a so-called "half-*swaihwai*," said to be the possession of a single local family, and in view of its derivation, of lesser status than was accorded proper *swaiswai* dancers. At once anomalous and useful, Westly recounted the story of its origin:

> A Nanaimo man named Kauexxan made two masks, one for himself and one for his sister. Every morning they walked down to a bluff wearing their masks, laid them aside, and sat there all day. At evening they donned their masks and marched back to their home. Two young men who were spearing cod with shuttles and spears passed this bluff day after day and saw them. One said to the other "Those two do nothing with their *swaihwai*, make no use of them at all. Why don't we buy them with our fishing gear and some fish? They will then have fish to eat, and we can make more spears and shuttles for ourselves." So they traded. The new owners, who were Nanaimo River men, said to one another "We will use our masks as the Musqueam people use theirs. They shall be real *swaihwai*."[42]

41   Ibid. 256–57.
42   Ibid. 254, 257.

Part II
Myths and Tales

Myths of X̱e.ls (Hayles), theTransformer[1]

(1) X̱e.ls

Told by Peter Pierre, Katzie

X̱e.ls, the creator of man, has been seen by Indians, but not often. Stories about him were too sacred to tell to children. It was X̱e.ls who taught people how to make bows and arrows and to hunt. How he himself arose is not known. He always called the Indians his brothers. He appeared as a fine-looking man, with shining garments.

A foolish young man once conceived the desire to kill X̱e.ls. He took his mussel shell knives and began to sharpen the big bone of an elk with them. Someone came up to him—X̱e.ls himself—and said "What are you doing?" "Oh, I am just waiting for that fellow X̱e.ls whom they say will be coming along soon." "What is that you are using?" asked X̱e.ls. "Those are my mussel shell knives. I am going to cut X̱e.ls' throat with them." "What are those things you are making?" "Those are bones I am sharpening to set in the ground and lame him when he comes along; then I will cut his throat." "Let me see those knives," said X̱e.ls. The man handed them over. X̱e.ls clapped one over the man's ear on one side, and the other over the other ear. The man was delighted. "Give me those bones," said X̱e.ls. He slapped one bone into each of the man's ankles. "That is fine," said the man. "Now jump," said X̱e.ls. The man became a deer with pointed ears and long legs. "Let me fix your eyes," said X̱e.ls. "Oh no," said the man, "My eyes are big and round enough." "Well, you should be food for generations to come." That is how deer was created.

At the bottom of Saanich Bay is a rock that is uncovered at low tide. On the land above is another rock. The former was a married woman with whom the latter, a man, was in love. He followed her secretly when she went to bathe and was peering through the long grass when X̱e.ls turned both of them into stones.

At Kuper Island, seven lads went swimming, and, when they came out of the water, lay down on the beach. X̱e.ls made them stones. At Sooke he turned a halibut and cod fish into stones. So, too, Siwash Rock near Vancouver.[2] Up the Fraser somewhere is a man spinning goat wool on a loom, in stone, near a mountain.

A hunter launched his arrow at a deer. Just as he fired he saw another arrow, shining like a ray of light, speed in front of his and strike the deer, while his

---

1   The forty-five stories presented in Part II were selected from a body of nearly one hundred Jenness collected on Vancouver Island and on the lower Fraser River. This material comprises the first third (pp. 2–99) of his "Saanich Notes." The remaining two-thirds consist of general ethnographic material, including the notes used to complete the concluding three chapters of Part I. –Ed.
2   The Squamish name for this rock is Skalsh.

own missed. He went up to the animal and, seeing no one near, replaced the shining arrow in the wound by his own. X̱e.ls appeared. "Give me my arrow." "Where is your arrow?" The man answered, "I shot this deer." "Very well," said X̱e.ls, "open up the carcass and give me the heart." The man opened it up, grumbling, and refused to give up the heart. "Very well brother," said X̱e.ls, and helped him put the carcass on his back, then left him. The man went home, entered his house and said to his wife, "There is a deer outside." She fed him, and, after looking outside, came in and said "Where did you say the deer was?" He went out to look but found it turned to rotten wood.

(2) X̱e.ls and the Origin of Death
Told by Louis Pelkey, Tsawout

Raven said to X̱e.ls "There are too many people. The smoke of their fires hurts my eyes. It would be better if people should die." X̱e.ls said "Alright." Thereafter people began to die; that is how death began. Later, Raven went hunting and shot an elk. He was carrying it home when X̱e.ls met him, in a changed form, and said "What is that you are carrying?" "O, it is something I got." "I would like a little of the fat." Raven answered, "Who do you think I am hunting for? It is for myself and my children. I am not giving any of it to other people." X̱e.ls said alright and went away. Raven carried his booty home and threw the pack down at the door. His youngest child was crying for food as usual. Raven said to him "What are you crying for? Do you want something to eat?" and he threw the heart of the elk, which he was carrying on his breast, at the child's body. It turned into a white stone that struck the boy on the heart and killed him. Raven examined the body and said to his older child "Run and ask your uncle to change the arrangement of things and restore my child to life." But X̱e.ls answered "I can't change things twice," and refused.

(3) X̱e.ls Changes the Land and Sea
Told by David and Mrs Latasse, Tsartlip [3]

X̱e.ls was going around changing the earth. Raven and Mink went with him. At one place Raven said "the capes here should extend farther into the sea so that people would have farther to go round; and they should lie farther apart—exactly a day's journey. Then each day the people would camp on a point and I could follow them and gather up the food they have left." X̱e.ls made it so. Then Mink spoke up: "The sea should retire farther; then I could come down and gather fish and clams." X̱e.ls kicked the sea back. Mink said "farther still." X̱e.ls kicked it again. "Farther still." Again X̱e.ls kicked it, so

---

3   Jenness collected numerous stories from David and Mrs Latasse. However, his notes do not attribute any of these stories to either one or the other elder. In the circumstances, both are credited in these pages. –Ed.

now when the tide reaches lower and lower levels each day these levels mark the forward steps X̌e.ls took as he kicked back the sea.

(4) X̌e.ls Makes the Boss of Trees
Told by Louis Pelkey, Tsawout

Xe.ls made people of differently coloured clays; that is why the Indians are brown, and Europeans white. In the first days there was only one man. He was lonely and wept. The mucus from his nose took shape as a baby girl, whom he married later.

People heard that Xe.ls was going around changing things. The clams heard of it and said to one another, "We had better go and hide at the low tide mark." They started off. The parents travelled faster than their children, who had only reached the half-tide level when Xe.ls appeared and changed them all to clams. That is why you find the big clams at the lower-tide level, the but-ter-clams at the half-tide.

Pitch used to go fishing before the sun rose, and retire to the shade before it became strong. One day he was late and had just reached the beach when he melted. Other people rushed to share him. Fir arrived first and secured most of the pitch, which he poured over his head and body; Balsam obtained only a little; and by the time Arbutus arrived there was none left. Arbutus said "I shall peel my skin every year and have a good wash to keep me clean." But just then Xe.ls appeared and said "You shall all be trees, and Fir shall be your boss." So now the arbutus sheds its bark every year, and the fir has more pitch than any other tree.

Raven sought nothing but refuse, so Xe.ls made him black and changed him into a bird, saying "You shall always eat refuse."

(5) X̌e.ls Helps the People
Told by Louis Pelkey, Tsawout

At Pender Island there lived a man named Kwinakus, whose legs were cov-ered with long hair.[4] Whenever he shouted the hair shouted with him, inten-sifying his cry a hundred-fold. One day he was catching young perch in his canoe. He filled the bottom of the canoe with grass, turned it on its side so that the small perch, two or three inches long, would enter the grass, then tipped it right side up, bailed out the water, and extracted the fish from among the grass. (A few Indians still do this.) Kwinakus turned his canoe right side up and shouted. Just then X̌e.ls and his companion Mink were coming round a hill. Mink said to X̌e.ls "There must be a great number of people here." X̌e.ls said "We'll see." Kwinakus saw X̌e.ls approaching and said to himself, "That

---

4   In a later story (no. 30), the name appears as Kwinus. The SENĆOŦEN word ḰINEȻES (q̫ʼinəkʷəs) refers to all types of body hair save whiskers and pubic hair. –Ed.

must be X̱e.ls." When X̱e.ls drew near Kwinakus said "You have come, my grandson." X̱e.ls was well pleased at being addressed so politely; Kwinakus told him that they could not cross over the narrow channel where he was fishing because of the strong current. X̱e.ls said "I'll soon arrange that." He picked up a piece of bark and a stone, laid the bark on the ground in front of him, placed the stone on top and stamped on it. Immediately the channel became dry land. Water, however, was seeping through it. X̱e.ls picked up the bark and stone again, told Kwinakus to place his canoe beyond them, so that they would be on the right side, placed some clay under the bark, and stamped down the stone on top of it again. Now the channel was completely sealed by dry land.

Kwinakus said further to X̱e.ls "We cannot get fresh water here, for though there are two pools, some monster attacks us when we dip our pails." X̱e.ls said "I'll amend that." He took a pail and dipped it in one of the ponds. Immediately a giant devilfish [octopus] caught hold of him and dragged him under. He called to Mink "Come and help me;" but Mink answered "Why don't you turn the devil-fish to stone." X̱e.ls, who was unable to disentangle himself, called out again "Dive and bring me my knife. I'll call you my older brother, and you shall live longer than I." Mink dived with the knife. X̱e.ls cut off all the arms of the devilfish, then drew it up to the surface, and flung the different parts of the monster to various parts of the country, naming them Sooke, Clallam [sic], Pender Island, etc. So now devilfish are found in all these places. He threw the body of the fish to Clallam; that is why the devilfish there are larger than in other places. Only the Fraser Delta he omitted, because devilfish there would spoil the salmon fishing.

(6) X̱e.ls, Raven, and Partridge[5]

Told by Edward Jim, Tseycum

Raven and Partridge went out to spear herring. Raven was successful, but Partridge caught nothing. Partridge's children ran down to the beach to meet their Uncle Raven when he returned, but he only splashed them with water and said "Run home. I caught nothing, but your father has plenty of fish." The children went home, and since their father had caught nothing, they had to go to bed hungry.

Early the next morning Partridge went hunting and sighted an elk. He shot an arrow at it. As it flew through the air another arrow followed close behind, like a streak of fire. Partridge hurried forward and examined the animal; there

---

5   The bird Jenness identifies here as partridge is, in all likelihood, grouse. The former are not native to the Americas. The Ruffed Grouse, however, perhaps the species in question, is commonly (if mistakenly) referred to as partridge; http://www.hww.ca/en/wildlife/birds/ruffed-grouse.html?referrer=https://www.google.ca/#sid14

were two arrows in its body. He drew them out, laid them on the ground side by side, and proceeded to cut up the carcass. X̱e.ls approached and said to him "Where is my arrow?" "It is here" said Partridge, and handed him the arrow. "Give me the heart of the elk," said X̱e.ls. Partridge gave it to him. Then X̱e.ls helped Partridge to lift the carcass onto his back and said to him "If your load becomes too heavy shake it a little and it will become light again." Partridge thanked him, and by shaking his load a little whenever it became heavy, reached home without any trouble. His children were delighted, and, taking the fat of the elk, roasted it in front of the fire.

Raven heard the noise they were making and smelled the toasted fat. He said to his family "What are Partridge and his children doing?" They did not know, so he sent his eldest son over with a few herring to give to his Uncle Partridge. The child knocked at the door until he was tired; when there was still no answer, he returned home. Raven sent his second son, with the same result. Then he sent his wife, but she, too, could not gain admittance. Angrily, he shouted "You are all lying. Give me the herring; I'll take them over myself." He knocked and called to his nephews, "My nephews, here are some herring for you"; but no one would open the door for him. Then he ran to his canoe, lay down under it out of sight, and ate the herring himself. After he had eaten the last one he bit his thumb until it bled, and going home, he told his wife that his nephews had been so excited over the herring that one of them had bitten his thumb.

The next morning Raven went hunting. The same thing befell him as befell Partridge; he shot an arrow at an elk, and another arrow sped like a shaft of light behind his own. When he approached the carcass the strange arrow was lodged in its flank, but his own had fallen short and was lying on the ground. He pulled out X̱e.ls's arrow, threw it on the ground, and inserted his own in the wound. Just then X̱e.ls approached and said "Where is my arrow?" "It is lying there," Raven answered, "You missed." X̱e.ls picked it up and said "I just want the heart." But Raven answered gruffly "You can't have it. I want it myself." X̱e.ls stood and watched him dress the animal. When it was ready he even helped to load it on Raven's back; then he said to him "If your load becomes heavy just shake it and it will grow light." But Raven responded "No one needs to tell me how to carry an elk." As soon as he reached home, he threw down the carcass outside; the quiver, which he had stuffed with fat, he carried inside. His sons came running up to him; "Go and bring the elk indoors," he said to them. They looked for it, but could not find it. He then sent his wife. She, too, returned and said "I can't find any elk. There is only a stump outside." "You are like a child," said Raven. "You can't do anything." And he went out himself. His elk had changed into a stump. He rushed to the quiver to examine the fat; it had turned to moss. Even his arrows were changed, into snakes, which fell to the ground and wriggled away. Old people therefore counsel their children to be truthful, like Partridge.

(7) X̱e.ls Makes Raven a Bird
Told by Louis Pelkey, Tsawout

Satitc[6], the north wind, blew so hard that Raven, who was a big man with many children, could not keep his house warm. His children suffered from the cold. He said to Mink, who lived with him, "I am going over to the home of Satitc to steal one of his children." They paddled until they reached Satitc's home, which was covered with ice outside, though warm within. Raven snatched up Satitc's little daughter and fled with her to his home, where he seated her near a fire and told one of his boys to poke her with a lighted stick every time the wind blew strong. The boy poked her in the stomach with the stick and she screamed. After a time, the wind died down, and Satitc came over with his people to rescue his daughter. Raven and Mink kept in the house and did not go out to meet them. Satitc called out "We'll give you anything you want if you will give me back my daughter. We'll make you very rich." Raven said to his son "Poke her in the stomach again." The boy did so and the girl screamed while her father and his people wept. Satitc called again "What is it you want? We'll give you anything you wish if you will restore her to us." Raven said "I want refuse." They gave it to him, but X̱e.ls was so disgusted that he changed Raven into a bird. Mink said to Satitc "I want the box that produces calm weather." They gave it to Mink, who placed it in the bow of his canoe and went out fishing. As he was looking down into the water Satitc sent his followers to steal the box from him. Just as they were rushing to spear him, Mink dived. That is why Mink now dives after fish.

When X̱e.ls turned Raven to a bird he said "Hereafter everyone who uses bad words shall be called by your name." So now when any one uses bad words the Indians say "He must be Spa·l (Raven)."[7]

(8) The Man Who Challenged X̱e.ls
Told by David and Mrs Latasse, Tsartlip

A certain man lived so long in the woods, alone, that he obtained tremendous power and almost became a spirit himself. He thought he could do all that X̱e.ls could and challenged X̱e.ls. He threw some liquid on X̱e.ls that set him afire, yet X̱e.ls was unharmed. X̱e.ls set his challenger ablaze in the same way, but did not destroy him. They competed in other ways until the man had exhausted all his powers. Then he said to X̱e.ls "You have beaten me. Don't kill me down here, but on top of yonder mountain." They ascended the mountain and there X̱e.ls turned the man into stone. It can still be seen behind Duncan.

---

6   The SENĆOŦEN word SOTEĆ (*sátəč*) means "cold (or northeast) wind." –Ed.
7   In SENĆOŦEN, SPOOL (*spáal'*) is "raven." –Ed.

(9) X̱e.ls Creates Dog Salmon
Louis Pelkey, Tsawout

Someone kept visiting a young girl during the night and would not tell her who he was, or show himself to her parents. One night she daubed red ochre over his body. Next morning, she went down to the beach and saw her own brother trying to wash the ochre from his body. She approached him and said "You cannot wash that off. I put it on you to find out who you were. We cannot go back to our parents, for we have done wrong." Just then X̱e.ls came along. "Turn around and face the sea," he said. "Now jump." They leaped into the water and changed to dog-salmon. Now the male dog-salmon has red on its side, and the female swims near him.

Myths of How Things Came to Be

(10) Origin of Ants
Told by Johnson, Quamichan

Ants were once human beings. Today you can see them logging, and carrying wood chips. At a certain hour of the day they stop and rest. Once someone killed the father of the ants. His children cut off their father's head and dried it. When clouds began to rise in the south they carried the head outside and chanted; then the clouds retreated. Their friends wanted to see if they would reveal who had killed their father. They tied a rope around an ant's waist and pulled it very tight. The young ants, however, would not tell. Because they pulled the rope very tight, ants now have pinched waists.

(11) Dwarfs and the Origin of Sea Lions
Told by Louis Pelkey, Tsawout

Two Kuper Island men went out after seals. Their enemy, a sorcerer, made a sea lion out of red cedar, gave it some of his power, and set it on the water. The hunters saw and struck it with a harpoon. The sea lion dragged their canoe far away to the northward, farther than they had ever been. At last it stopped, but when they drew alongside the sea lion had become a lifeless log again. They extracted their harpoon, and, seeing a canoe approaching, hurried ashore, drew up their boat, and hid in the woods. The man in the canoe dropped his anchor, dived under the water, and, after remaining below for a long time, emerged with two halibut, which he threw into his boat, climbed in after them, and sat down to rest. He was a dwarf, only about three feet high, one of the people called *kwisti.mux*.[8] Again he dived, and brought up two more halibut. The hunters on shore said to one another, "If we watch for our chance when he dives, we can steal one of his halibut and make the shore again before he comes up." They did this, hid their boat as before, and watched from the woods. The dwarf came up with his two halibut, noticed that one of his fish was missing. He waved his arm around the horizon, then put his hand to his nose to scent out where the thieves were hiding. Instantly he discovered them, and, paddling ashore, went into the woods after them. The hunters tried to spear him, but he caught their spear, seized both of them, one in each hand, trussed them in the bottom of his canoe, and paddled home to his people, dragging their canoe behind his own. Like all his people, he had a very small, round mouth, and when he spoke, his speech was like whistling. They did not know how to make fire, but let their halibut rot in the hot sun before eating it. Instead of dogs they had seals. They were an immensely powerful people, though very small; but they were afraid of one thing, ducks, for their feathers caught in their throats and choked them. They intended to keep the two hunters as slaves. Suddenly the ducks attacked them. In the melee the hunters launched their own canoe and fled. They paddled for many days, and on their voyage saw several sea lions like the one that had carried them off; apparently that one had given birth to many others. They did not dare to attack them, but continued until they reached their home. But today the sea lion is brownish, because the cedar from which the first sea lion was made was brown.

(12) Origin of the Blue Jay and Wren
Told by Johnson, Quamichan

An orphan boy asked his grandmother one evening for some food, saying that he was hungry. She bade him take one of the fish that were hanging up in the smoke and to soak it in the stream; this would make it soft and ready to eat by morning. He took down a fish, wrapped it tightly round with cedar twigs, and laid it to soak. Next morning, when he went to recover it, the fish was gone. He told his grandmother, who bade him soak another fish. This he did, but went home quickly and asked her for a bow and arrow. She made them for him, and he hid that night on the bank of the stream.

Just before dawn some monstrous thing, a *slelakan*, appeared, looked all around, noticed the fish, and swallowed it. The boy called after it "Give me back what you have taken or I shall shoot you." The monster paid no attention. Again the boy shouted. This time *slelakan* looked around and answered "If you don't stop shouting I'll swallow you too." The boy shouted a third time, and the monster swallowed him.

The boy, however, was not hurt. He wandered in the monster's stomach,

---

8	In SENĆOŦEN, SIYÁYE (*siyéyəʔ*) refers to a "tiny (leprechaun-like) person." In Hul'qumi'num', however, "dwarf" is *q̓wa'qwi'stéy̓muxw*. –Ed.

and, seeing something dangling above him, shot it with his arrow. Presently the monster began to totter, and as it fell, ejected the boy, who ran home and said to his grandmother, "Grandmother, I have shot a *slelakan*. Come and see." Greatly excited, the old woman followed him and found an elk lying dead on the ground. Taking out her knife, she skinned it; and they carried the meat home, cut it up and hung it to dry in the smoke. The old woman then cracked a leg bone and began to eat the marrow. But a piece of bone stuck in her throat and choked her. "Cough harder," the boy said to her. She coughed harder, and the bone penetrated through the top of her skull. She turned to a blue jay, and, crying like that bird, flew away. That is why the blue jay now has a top knot.

The boy, left alone, sat down and wept. As he wept he sang "my grandmother, alas." Then he changed into a wren and flew away.

(13) How the People Got Salmon
Told by Johnny Claxton, Tsawout

Once there were no seals so the people were starving; they lived on elk and whatever other game they could kill. Two brave youths said to each other "Let us go and see if we can find any salmon." They embarked in their canoe and headed out to sea, not caring in what direction they travelled. They journeyed for three-and-a-half months. Then they came to a strange country. When they reached the shore a man came out and welcomed them, saying "You have arrived." "We have arrived," the youths answered, though they did not know where they were. They were given food to eat, and after they had eaten their host led them outside the house and said "Look around and see what you can see." They looked around and saw smoke from *qathmin* (Indian consumption plant) that the steelhead, sockeye, spring, and other varieties of salmon were burning, each for itself, in their houses.

The youths stayed in this place for a month. Their hosts then said to them, "You must go home tomorrow. Everything is arranged for you. The salmon that you were looking for will muster at your home and start off on their journey. You must follow them." So the two youths followed the salmon; for three-and-a-half months they travelled, day and night, with the fish. Every night they took *qathmin* and burned it that the salmon might feed on the smoke and sustain themselves. Finally, they reached Discovery Island (*kctes*)[9] where they burned *qathmin* all along the beach; for their hosts had said to them, "Burn *qathmin* along the beach when you reach land, to feed the salmon that travel with you. Then, if you treat the salmon well, you will always have them in abundance."

---

9   This island, called ṮĆÁS (*x̣̌ čés*) in SENĆOŦEN, is situated due east of Oak Bay, off the southeastern tip of Vancouver Island. –Ed.

Now that they had plenty of salmon at Discovery Island they let them go to other places—to the Fraser River, Nanaimo, etc. Because their journey took them three-and-a-half months, salmon are now absent on the coast for that period each year.

The cohoe said to the other salmon "You can go ahead of us, for we have not yet got what we wanted from the lakes." That is why the cohoe is always the last of the salmon.

The young men now had salmon, but no good way of catching them. The leaders of the salmon, a real man and woman, taught them how to make *sxwala*—reef nets[10]—and how to use *qathmin*. They also told the young men how their people should dress when they caught the salmon, and that they should start to use their reef net in July, when the berries were ripe. So today, when the Indians dry their salmon, they always burn some *qathmin* in the fire (or on top of the stove); and they put a little in the fish when they cook it. Also, when they cut up the salmon, before inserting the knife, they pray to the salmon, that they may always be plentiful.

(14) Origin of the Dip Net [The Girl Who Married a Salmon]

Told by George Kwakaston, Koksilah

A man and his wife had only one daughter whom they did not allow to work, training her to the dignity of a *siem* [noble]. One evening, someone entered her bed, but disappeared before morning. He visited her every night until she became pregnant. She could not tell her parents anything about her visitor except that he was very cold, for he was really a sockeye salmon, that became a man by night and a salmon by day. Finally, she asked him where he came from and he told her he was a salmon, and came from far away. He consented to remain with her now by day as well as by night. Then he told the people, "You have no means of catching the salmon that come here. I will make you a dip-net" (*mas.at*).[11] He made the net for them, and the Indians caught salmon with it. Then he said to his wife, "I am going to take you away with me." He leaped into the water, and his wife leaped in after him. Both became salmon. Both came back with the salmon later and the girl stayed with her parents for a time. Her parents asked them to leave their child behind when next they went away. They did, and never returned.

---

10   In SENĆOŦEN, the word is SXOLE, (*sxʷál ə?*). –Ed.
11   The meaning of the word Jenness transcribed here is uncertain; in SENĆOŦEN, "dip net" is EQIYN (*?ə kʷiyn*), and in Hul'qumi'num', it is *'ux̱thímtun*. –Ed.

(15) Thunder Helps the People
Told by Johnny Claxton, Tsawout

A girl who was trying to obtain medicine power wandered in the woods. Bathing night and morning, she nourished herself on herbs alone so that she might make herself pure. After she had done this for some years, Thunder carried her off while she was asleep and deposited her in his house. He then went off to find food for her, and discovering a whale, brought it to her. The girl became his wife, and in time bore him a child, a little Thunder.

Meanwhile the girl's two brothers had missed her, and began to bathe and purify themselves in order that they, too, might obtain medicine power and discover where she had gone. After preparing themselves in this way for three years they said to one another, "It may have been Thunder who took her away. Let us go to his house." They tried to reach his home, but a great wind blew them back. Again they bathed and purified themselves for a long time, then made a second attempt to reach Thunder's home. This time they succeeded, and, entering the house, sat down beside their sister. Presently they heard a noise outside, and, looking out, they saw Thunder dropping a whale at the door. He removed his clothes, laid them on the ground, and entered. After sitting for a time, Thunder said to his wife "I had better take your brothers home." So he took them back to their home. Thereafter he provided them with food by leaving a whale at their door in the morning, and when that was consumed by the two young men and their neighbours, a second whale, and a third.

Thunder's wife now wanted to see her parents again, so Thunder took her to her old home. Her friends visited her so often to examine her baby that Thunder became afraid that something might happen to it and to them, for the baby, Little Thunder, almost set them on fire. The girl's parents, however, did not want her to leave them. Thunder decided that he would have to take her away, and began to roar. At once the people approached the two brothers and said "Thunder has already broken down some of the houses. Let him take his wife and baby again." So Thunder recovered his wife and child. The people did not see him take them away, but knew that he must have done so when he roared right afterwards.

Now that he had recovered his family Thunder was very happy, and from time to time would leave a whale on the beach for her people. After a time, however, when he became tired of doing this, he gave the two brothers his whaling equipment instead so that they could go out and catch their own whales. He gave them, too, his fishing equipment, so that they could catch not only whales, but fish of every kind. Next he gave them bows and arrows so that they could hunt the deer and other land animals. Whenever they went out to hunt they would look up at the mountain where Thunder lived and pray to him for help. Last of all he gave them the canoe. That is how the Indians obtained their weapons and their boats.

(16) The Winds

Told by Louis Pelkey, Tsawout

Satitc, the cold north wind, was freezing up the land. Ice lay everywhere. Then Skangit, the warm south wind, said to her two sons, Stcas (southwest wind) and Tentcalux (west wind), "Let us go play *lehal* with Satitc."[12] They started out in their canoe, but at last had to leave it behind on account of the ice. Skangit stamped on the ice and caused it to crack with a loud report. She was alarmed. Her sons said to her "Do not break the ice here." They went on, and Stcas stamped on it when they reached the middle. Again it cracked with a loud report, and Skangit became still more alarmed. Skangit said to Satitc "my sons want to gamble with you and your family." Satitc said "All right." Skangit produced her two gambling sticks, shuffled them in her hands, and sang while her sons joined in with her. Satitc made a wrong guess, whereupon Skangit banged the stick he had pointed to on the ice. It cracked. She said to one of her sons "Go and bring the canoe. Soon the ice will break everywhere." She began to sing and shuffle her sticks again, but Satitc was afraid and went away, taking his family with him. Then Skangit banged the ice with her stick and it broke up everywhere; as it did, the waves came breaking through. She and her sons got into their canoe and paddled home. So now, whenever the south wind blows, it quickly stirs up the waves and breaks up any ice that has formed.

Tales of Raven and Mink

(17) Raven and Crow

Told by David and Mrs Latasse, Tsartlip

Next to Raven's house lived his sister Crow and her family. One day, Crow went down to the beach to gather clams. She found a seal that had been harpooned, but escaped, only to die later and drift ashore. She wondered how she could carry it home past Raven's house without being discovered. Finally, she gathered a great number of butter clams, put the seal in the bottom of her basket and the clams on top, and went home. The blood of the seal dripped onto her feet. Raven saw her and said "What have you been doing?" "Gathering clams." "But what is that on your feet?" "Oh, those are just stains I got on the beach." She hurried by, entered the house, shut the door tight, cooked the meat, fed herself and her children with it, and hung the remainder on the rack to dry. Then she went back to the beach to bring in the remainder of her

---

12   In SENĆOŦEN, the north, south, southwest, and west winds are SOTEĆ (*sátəč*), S$\underline{K}$Á$\underline{N}$ET (*sqéŋət*), SCES (*sčə́s*), and TEN,ĆO,LEҠ (*tənčáʔləqʷ*), respectively. On the gambling game SLEHÁL, (*sləhél*), see page 56, footnote 4. –Ed.

clams. Raven watched her pass, then slipped over to her house and asked her children what their mother had been doing. None of them would answer until at last the foolish one piped up, "Oh she brought a seal and cooked it, and hung the meat on the rack up there." Raven got a ladder, climbed up, and ate all the meat. Then he went home.

Crow returned. Her children said, "Your brother came over and this foolish child here told him about the seal. He ate it all." Crow sat down and cried. Raven heard her cry and came over. "Why don't you drum for your mother," he said, and taking the long pole used to slide the roof boards, he shifted one board over so that he could see and began to sing. Crow called him Big Nose and other names, abusing him, but he merely chanted her words of abuse, trying to make her dance. Finally, she stopped crying and he went home.

He waited a while, and when he judged Crow would be in a good humour again, he went over to her house and said "Where did you get the seal?" "Oh, I got it on the beach." "But how did you get it?" "Oh, I just sat on that rock and called it." "Yes, but what did you say?" "Oh, I just waited until the tide was coming in and called 'Come to me, come to me'; then the seal came and I clubbed it." Raven said "Oh, was that how you got it?" "Yes." Raven went off, put on his deerskin blanket, and tied round his waist his cedar bark belt, and went and sat on the rock. As the tide came in he called "Come to me, come to me, a big one, come to me." The tide came higher and higher, and he climbed higher and higher on the rock. Still calling "Come to me, big one, come to me." At last the water covered the rock, and drowned him. The waves washed him ashore. Crow saw his body floating on the beach and was glad.

(18) Deer Foils Raven
Told by David and Mrs Latasse, Tsartlip

Raven went out to hunt deer. Instead of going ashore and pursuing them in the woods, he sat in his canoe and called to them. Three or four came down. "Where have you come from?" he asked them. "From the tall trees," they replied. He did not think them fat enough, so he went farther and called for fat deer. More came down to his canoe. "Where have you come from?" "From the salal berries." They were not fat enough either, so he went on. Again he called, and more came. "Where have you come from?" "From the places where there are many blossoms." "Well, get into my canoe." Still, Raven wasn't satisfied; he thought he could get still fatter deer. He went on and called again. More deer came. "Where have you come from?" "From the berry bushes." "Get into my canoe." They got in and he paddled home. When he reached the beach he called to his wife. She came out of the house. "Bring me that," he called, not daring to name what he wanted lest the deer understand him. She did not know what he wanted. At last he became exasperated and called "Bring me my skinning knife."[13] But the deer understood this word, and upsetting the canoe, ran away.

(19) Raven and His Sisters Pick Berries
Told by David and Mrs Latasse, Tsartlip

Xwabic, the vireo (?), invited her sister birds to accompany her to pick blackberries. Raven went with them to protect his sisters. They paddled in Xwabic's canoe to the berry ground, where they filled their baskets and carried them down to the beach. There, Raven began to groan that he was sick—he had done nothing all day but eat berries. He said, "I will go up the hill and gather some moss. That may help me." He filled his basket with moss, the others loaded the baskets into the canoe, and started out, Raven steering. As they travelled a fog came up and enveloped them. Raven took bunches of his moss and laid it on the water where it swelled up and, through the fog, had the appearance of canoes at a distance. He called out "Paddle hard, my sisters, the enemy are pursuing us. Paddle hard." They paddled hard and reached a cliff. "Flee up the cliff, my sisters," cried Raven. I will stay and fight the enemy." They fled up the cliff, all but Slug, who travels very slow and therefore took shelter under a clam shell on the beach. Then Raven ate the blackberries, and poured the juice over his head to pretend he was wounded. His sisters came back after a time, one by one, to find out what had happened. He lay groaning on the beach with a stomach ache. His companions said, "What has happened." Raven answered, "The enemy beat me up terribly. See my bloody head." As they commiserated over him, Slug came forward and said, "Alas. My brother has over-eaten." "Take her away," cried Raven; "she makes me worse instead of better!" Slug, however, repeated her refrain. Her sisters examined Raven more closely and found that the blood was only berry juice. They looked from one to the other, then quietly entered the canoe and paddled away, leaving Raven to groan alone on the beach.

(20) How Mink Acquired Fire
Told by George Kwakaston, Koksilah

Mink paddled along the shore gathering crabs. After catching a number, he went ashore and ate them raw. Then he lay down and slept. On awakening, he began to wonder whether later generations of people would have to eat their food raw as he did.

---

13   The traditional skinning knife was made of bone or stone; later, hoop iron was used; "Saanich Notes," 16. The word Jenness recorded, QEJTEN (kʷə́čʼən), refers specifically to a "salmon knife." –Ed.

A little while later he met two of Wolf's children. He killed them and carried their skins to his home on a high bluff, some distance from the water. One of his family, in the course of conversation, remarked that a certain man called Yałmax possessed fire. Mink decided to get it from him. He embarked with his wife in a canoe and paddled away to find Yałmax. They came to one village; Yałmax did not live there. They reached another; Yałmax lived farther away. After calling at many villages, they came at last to Yałmax's home, and Mink stole up and peered inside. Yałmax's baby was hanging up in a cradle. Mink carried the baby away. As he fled by the first village on the way back, he told his wife to pinch the child so that the villagers could tell Yałmax who had stolen it. She pinched it, and the child cried "I am Yałmax's child." Every village they passed she pinched it, so that all knew the ravisher had passed them by.

Yałmax, seeking his child, stopped at every village and was directed farther on. He knew that it was Mink who had stolen it, because the ravisher had made the villagers sleepy. He made one man from each village accompany him on his search.

Mink was searching again for something to eat when he saw his pursuers approaching. Unable to escape, he did something to his eyes so that they appeared almost blind. "Have you my child?" Yałmax called to him. "Why, no. Look at my eyes. I couldn't steal your child, for I can hardly see." They took Mink on board and asked him, "Do you know who is holding it?" "I believe that a man round the point has it." As they approached the point he said to them, "Put me ashore here. I'll dance on the shore while you go round the point. Give me your shirts to put on so that I can dance properly." They gave him their shirts, and he sang to the wind to blow them close to shore. As they drew near, he suddenly dived overboard and fled to his home, carrying all their shirts with him. They exclaimed "Look, that was Mink himself; and he has carried away with him all our shirts."

They landed, but could not approach Mink's house because it was protected by a high bluff. Mink put on one of Wolf's skins and told his wife to beat the drum for him while he danced. Wolf looked up and saw him; "It was Mink who killed my children," he exclaimed. Mink now went inside again, and Yałmax sent a messenger to ask what he wanted in exchange for the child. The messenger offered all kinds of things, but Mink refused. Then Mink sent out his wife to tell Yałmax he wanted the thing called *kwatakwata* (fire-drill).[14] Yałmax brought it ashore and handed it over, while Mink restored the baby. So people got fire.

---

14   The word for "fire drill" in Hul'qumi'num' is *shulcup*; its SENĆOŦEN equivalent is ŚELTSEP (*šəltsəp*). –Ed.

(21) Mink Finds a Bride
Told by David and Mrs Latasse, Tsartlip

Mink went out to spear herring. He followed another man's canoe very closely, even splashing him with his spear. Presently, a whale came along, as whales always do when fish are numerous. Neither Mink nor the other man took any notice of it, but when the whale drew closer and closer, the other man paddled some way off. Presently, the whale sucked Mink and his canoe right down his throat. Mink found himself in a dark but quite roomy house. Every now and then a lot of herring would come rushing in. He thought to himself, "This is a good place to dry herring." He broke off long strips of wood from his canoe on which to string them, then made a fire with other sticks from his canoe. The whale became uncomfortable with the heat, and began to jump about, causing the fish to fall and put out the fire. Mink stretched them across the whale's stomach again and relit the fire. Again the whale began to jump about, and its heart over Mink's head swayed and bumped him. Mink said, "This thing is in the way," and he cut off the heart. The whale became still and Mink dried his fish without further trouble. He lived there for several days.

Now Mink heard the sound of drumming. The whale had drifted ashore near where a man was using an adze to a make a canoe. Mink called out, "Ho, drummer, I am inside the spouter." The man looked about, but could see nothing, no one. Mink kept calling until, at last, the man went up to the house and said "There is someone calling all the time, but I can see nothing except a log on the beach." The people went down and found that it was not a log, but a whale. They began to cut it up. Mink, inside, was unable to get out of the whale's mouth. He called out "Cut here, cut through the side." They cut through the whale's side and released him. Mink appeared to be a handsome young man. However, he did not stay, but went away somewhere.

Now the people began to cut up the fat and flesh of the whale. A certain girl said to her mother, "I want some of the meat, too." Her mother went down to the beach and got her some; but the girl choked and died. Mourning deeply, her people put her body in a cedar box and carried it to the graveyard.

That night a man who had gone outside heard a shout. "The dead has come to life." He listened and listened. Always it was the same cry that seemed to come from the graveyard. He went inside and told the people. Other men went out to listen, and finally a number of them went to the graveyard. There was the girl sitting in her coffin, and a young man, Mink, sitting beside her. She said to her parents "This man brought me to life again. I am going to marry him." They happily consented, rejoicing that their daughter had been restored to them. So Mink married the girl and they lived quietly in their home for some time. Then the people decided to move to another place, and loaded what they needed in their canoes. They took some of the boards of their houses and laid them across pairs of canoes to make a platform. Mink and his wife sat on one of the platforms.

Presently, they discovered sea anemones (sea eggs) on the bottom of the water, but were unable to get them because they had no long-handled net with them. Mink said, "Give me a basket. I will get them for you." They gave him a basket and he dived, re-emerging soon after with the basket filled. The people divided them up and ate while he returned for more. Three times he filled the basket. The fourth time he decided to stay on the bottom to avoid being observed, and ate. The people, feasting, did not remark his long absence for some time. Then they looked down. The water had cleared and they could see him eating voraciously. They said to each other, "That must certainly be Mink. Let us go away and leave him." So they paddled away. After a time, Mink came up to the surface and called to them but they were far off and could not hear him.

(22) Mink Loses His Tail
Told by David and Mrs Latasse, Tsartlip

Mink walked along the shore and looked up at the trees. He began to sing "fall over, fall over." Presently one tree began to fall. Slowly, it leaned over until it was nearly horizontal. Mink called out, "stop, stop." The tree stopped where it was. Much pleased with his success, Mink treated many trees along the shore in the same way. This is why trees along a beach are nearly always bent over.

Tired of this game, Mink went along and saw a spring salmon jumping in the water. He sang, "If I were a spring salmon I would jump closer inshore." The spring salmon came closer to shore. Mink sang the chant again, and the salmon came still closer. Then Mink sang, "If I were a spring salmon I would jump on the beach and roll among the pebbles." The spring salmon leaped on to the beach and Mink clubbed it.

Now he gathered wood, lit a fire, and set up his salmon to roast. While it was roasting he rested on a log. There he fell asleep. When he woke there were small salmon bones between his teeth, and fresh grease round his lips. He was puzzled. Mink said, "I must have eaten the salmon myself. Yet I don't remember eating it." When he stood up, the end of his tail was gone. Then he said, "Someone has stolen my fish and the end of my tail." Soon he heard voices in the woods, and went to reconnoitre. A pair of wolves were rolling a hoop-like object—his tail—and shooting their arrows through it.[15] Mink hid, and when they rolled the hoop his way, he picked it up and ran away. The wolves chased him, but he took refuge in a crack in a rock where they could not reach him. Finally, they went away. So Mink recovered his tail.

---

15   Boys shoot arrows at hoops made of cedar bark, but their arrows mostly pass through; Jenness, *Saanich Notes*, 34.

(23) Mink, Racoon, and Skunk's Potlatch
Told by David and Mrs Latasse, Tsartlip

Mink, Racoon, and Skunk went round inviting all the animals to a potlatch to be given by themselves. They invited every creature from the whale to the snail. They came to Wolf's house and found only the children home. Racoon said to them, "Where is your father?" They merely said "*hamama*, over there." Each child made the same reply—their father was "over there," somewhere in the woods. Racoon said "You are a nice looking lot. I have a notion to cut your tails off," which he did, attaching them to his headdress.

The animals all gathered at the potlatch house and took their seats. Only Whale could not get inside, so he looked in through the door. Racoon, Mink and Skunk stood up to dance. They sang their song twice, while Racoon beat the drum; they then began to dance. Wolf, meantime, became nervous; unable to escape by the door, he began to scratch under the floor against the wall, and got outside, followed by Panther and some smaller animals. Suddenly Skunk, followed by Mink, raced round the house with uplifted tails and shot their scent. The animals and birds toppled over, and Raven began to peck out their eyes. The animals that escaped are the animals man does not eat.[16]

Tales of Fortune and Misfortune
(24) Xetalaq
Told by Tom Paul, Tsartlip

Xetalaq was sent into the woods by his father to get a *saila* [guardian spirit]. For days he wandered about without securing one. Then he went down to the shore and wandered along a deer trail just above the beach. Hearing something, he lay down, naked as he was, and held his breath. A wolf came up to him, sniffed him, and went down to the water. It came back; again he held his breath, and again the animal sniffed him. Finally, it lifted him on to its back and began to carry him to his home. When he arrived the wolf laid Xetalaq down and sniffed at him; the youth still held his breath. At last, the wolf carried him outside his den and went inside; he told his family, "I have brought a human being, but I don't know whether it is alive or not." Wolf's father (for inside the den the wolves had the forms of human beings) said, "Bring him inside." He carried the youth in and set him in the middle of the floor. Xetalaq thought they might eat him and judged he had better sit up. The wolves sitting around him stared at him but said nothing. Finally, a young female wolf spoke up "My father, my brothers, don't kill this man; let me take him for my husband." So he married her.

---

16   Johnson, of Quamichan, chanted Mink's song: "*stamakweyo kwanitsałni*" (I wonder what is going to kill me?).

Later on, Xetalaq's brothers-in-law wanted to take him hunting. To try him out, one of the wolves leaped up and then told him to see if he could reach the same mark. Xetalaq tried and fell far short. He bathed and fasted, and the next time nearly reached the mark; the fourth time, after fasting and bathing, he leaped beyond it. (Whenever he bathed he rubbed himself with certain herbs the wolves gave him.) So he hunted with them.

After a time Xetelaq thought he would like to eat some clams, so he and his wife went down to a tidal flat to gather them. Suddenly several canoes of Kwakiutl Indians began to bear down on them. Xetelaq called to his brothers-in-law, "ho-ho-ho," the wolf cry. Immediately the beach swarmed with wolves and the Kwakiutl, afraid to land, quickly paddled away.

(25) Thunder's Protégés
Told by David and Mrs Latasse, Tsartlip

The people of Sooke were continually raided by Indians from the United States. Then the smallpox carried most of them off, and another raid from the U.S. destroyed them all except for a woman and her two little children, a boy and a girl. She fled into the hills, found a cave that was dry and clean, and lived there. The floor of the cave was like clay, and there were two openings, one small and one large; she blocked up the smaller. She was careful to burn only dry wood in her home, that would make no smoke. Near the cave—which was a home of Thunder –was a small lake with an outflowing stream. Here, she and her children bathed regularly. So she brought up her children until the boy was old enough to go out alone. She equipped him with a bow and arrows. One day the boy came home and asked, "Mother, what animal is that which has big eyes?" He described it. "That is a deer, my son. Shoot it; it is good to eat." So he went out and shot deer, so that they had plenty of meat; previously they had lived on clams and herbs.

The children grew older. One day the mother said to the boy "My son, have you seen anything? Have you met with anything that will help you?" The boy hung his head. "Yes, mother, but if I tell you there will be heavy rain." Then the woman rejoiced, for she knew he had the Thunder spirit. She asked her daughter the same question, and the girl answered "I have not the same as your son."

Now the woman made three clubs of hardwood, for their enemies from the U.S. had camped on the beach in rush tents, and were planning to build permanent wooden houses. Every night the owls would hoot around them and the Indians would say "Listen to those owls hooting. No wonder there are many *spalkwithe* (shades), for there are human remains everywhere."

The woman said to her son, "Steal round to that end of the camp, hoot like and owl when you are ready to attack, and your sister and I, at this end, will answer you." He stole round and hooted; the mother answered him with a similar hoot, then they attacked from opposite ends, calling Thunder spirit to their aid. Heavy thunder and lightning ensued. The lightning showed up the camp as in daylight, and torrents of rain flooded through their enemy's rush tents. The inmates tried to stop the leaks, and some turned out to peg down the edges of the tents. Then from one end the boy, the woman and her daughter from the other, knocked them one after the other on the head and killed every one. After that no more Indians from the U.S. crossed to Sooke to make war.

(26) The Whale and the Thunderbird
Told by Tom Paul, Tsartlip

Long ago, a Beecher Bay whale hunter said to his crew, "Let us go whale hunting tomorrow." They rose early and soon sighted a whale heading over towards Port Angeles. They pursued it, but could not overtake it. They pursued it until sunset, when the whale-man [harpooner] in the bow said, "We had better give up. I do not know what is wrong, but there is some reason why we cannot get near it." The crew stopped paddling. Just then the whale-man noticed a flash of lightning ahead. He turned to his crew and said "Did you see that flash of lightning ahead?" "No," they answered. "Watch for it," the whale-man said. Presently lightning flashed again, and this time they all saw it. Their leader said, "Steer straight towards it." Their course took them near Race Rock. As they drew near the monstrous whale, they saw a huge bird that had driven its talons into the whale's back and killed it. The whale-man said "I am going to harpoon the whale." He hurled his harpoon and sent it quivering into the monster's side. The Thunderbird flew up and disappeared. The men landed the boat, and the whale-man fastened the end of the harpoon line to some rocks that the whale might not drift away. After that they re-embarked and returned to Beecher Bay. The next morning, when the tide was low, they went back to cut up the whale, which was now stranded high and dry on the beach. They hacked out as much meat as they could take with their stone knives and carried it home to roast on hot stones in a pit oven. As soon as it was cooked all gathered around to eat except a few people who did not care for whale meat. Hardly had they eaten when they all became violently ill and died, for the Thunderbird's lightning had poisoned the meat.

(27) The Man with the Flashing Eyes (Saanich)
Told by David and Mrs Latasse, Tsartlip

There lived at Saanich an orphan youth named Xe'lakan, and his orphan niece, a girl who was several years younger. The youth went out to the woods to get a spirit. He searched for a year, and at last met Thunder, who told him what he should do. He returned home and bade his niece accompany him to the woods. There, after his bath, he lay down and told her to rub his face, and especially his eyes, with balsam bark that he had gathered. The girl was reluctant, but when he insisted, she rubbed him until the blood came. He then told her to rub his face and eyes with thorns that grow out of rotten bark, which she did, weeping to see him roll and squirm with the pain. His face was now terribly scarred. He sent her home and told her to return on a certain day. When she returned his face had healed, but his eyes were closed. He opened them just a little and lightning seemed to flash from them, although it did no harm. However, he kept his head covered with a goat wool blanket.

Xe·lakan now wanted a wife. He sent his niece to Kuper Island to get him one, and she carried out his errand. From his wife's people he now demanded sea lions, and bade them carry their carcasses up the hill to his house. This annoyed them, but they did as he asked. He sent his niece now to Sidney to bring him a wife from there. From his second wife's people he demanded porpoises and seals, delivered, like the sea lions, whole and entire at his house. Next he sent her to a settlement at Higgins Beach (near Brentwood) for another wife. Here, however, the people refused his demand. They were vexed that Xe·lakan should make himself out such a great man, and after lining up the eligible women, they decided not to give him any of them. They told his niece this, and bade her go back. When she lingered, weeping, they pushed her off in her canoe. They knew that if they gave him one of their women he would order them to carry deer carcasses to his house.

Xe·lakan began to travel round, visiting. He himself always sat in the middle of the canoe and did nothing, while two relatives, one in the bow and one in the stern, paddled. The relative in the stern, a Cowichan man, grew tired of being thus imposed on, and one day waved his paddle over Xe·lakan's head as though to strike him down. Xe·lakan saw him through a slit in his goat wool blanket and said, "My feet are wet; you had better put me ashore at yon small reef. Jump out and hold the canoe." The man jumped out, but Xe·lakan seized his paddle and left him there. Soon the tide began to rise and threatened to cover the reef. The man swam to the Saanich Peninsula, reaching it in a state of exhaustion. Xe·lakan now went on to Cowichan. The relative whom he had marooned got there before him and told the people what had happened. They decided to do away with Xe·lakan. When he came they were roasting seal meat. They seated him in a corner, and a man sat on each side of him. When the meat was roasted, and the hot fat dripping, the two men pinned Xe·lakan down, and someone else slapped the hot meat over his eyes to blind him. Then they stabbed him to death. Later these Cowichan people made up a song mocking the Kuper Island and Sidney people for carrying food up the hill to Xe·lakan. This happened before the whites came.

(28) The Man with the Flashing Eyes (Cowichan)
Told by Johnson, Quamichan

Among the Tcuwan [Mount Tuam] people who inhabited Saltspring Island[17] was a woman and her younger brother, Xe lakan, a mere boy. One day this woman invited the other people to her part of the house to eat, and after they had gone, began to clear up the dishes. Turning round she saw her little brother licking one of the dishes. Angrily she dragged him up the hill, and rubbed his face with cedar boughs until it was raw. Then she left him on the ground, apparently dead, and as she departed, threw in his eyes the thorny inner bark of the fir. Soon after she reached home a terrible thunderstorm burst over the house. Rain drops as big as eggs fell all night. In the morning she went to see her brother, knowing that the thunderstorm was in some way connected with him. As she drew near she called and asked him if he was alright. Xe lakan answered, "I am all right, but my eyes are changed. Stand over to one side when I open them." He opened them; lightning flashed out and burned the trees in front of him. The woman said to herself, "In truth his eyes are changed. He is no longer an ordinary human being, but a *slelakan* [powerful monstrous being]. I will not leave him here, but will take him on top of the mountain." She led him to the top of the mountain on Saltspring, Mount Tuam, and reported what had happened to her people. In awe, the people took food up to Xe lakan, and even their daughters, to be his wives. Soon he had thirty wives, and the people had to take food up the mountain for them all. Even the people from Saanich came over to give him their daughters, but the Saltspring people said it was their affair only and sent them back. So the Saanich people composed a song about it, singing "We were not permitted to take our daughters to him."

The Saltspring people, however, found the burden of feeding Xe lakan and his wives too great, and plotted to kill him. Now Xe lakan always sat nearly upright, reclining back just a little, like a great noble; and he kept his eyes closed. His enemies brought him two seals, which they roasted over a pit. As the food roasted, the people sang a song relating how they were cooking seal meat for him. The song pleased Xe lakan mightily; he was delighted with their attentions. But as soon as the seals were cooked, the people cut them open and, at a given signal, clapped them on Xe lakan's face. He opened his eyes, and the lightning from them burnt the fat and the flesh, but failed to penetrate beyond. As he struggled they clubbed him to death. Then they took their daughters home again.

---

17   In the past, the village here, located near Fulford Harbour, was occupied by both W̱SÁNEĆ and Cowichan people; Rozen, "Place Names," 136, 161. –Ed.

(29) The Son of Kwinus

Told by Johnny Claxton, Tsawout

Kwinus, the "hairy" one, went fishing, but came home with his canoe empty. He told his wife and son that he had caught nothing. He went fishing again on the morrow. As he approached the beach in the evening, his little son went down to meet him, being hungry; but again he had nothing in his canoe. The next morning the boy hid under the mat in the bottom of the canoe before his father pushed off and paddled away. Kwinus went to the place where he had set his gorges [type of fishing hook], and pulled up a great number of cod that nearly filled the canoe. Instead of paddling home, however, he pulled in to the beach, built a fire in a pit over some large stones, and, when the stones had heated, raked out the coals, unloaded the fish from the canoe, and set the fish on the hot stones to roast. First he poured a little water over them to make steam, then covered them over with branches and sand. As soon as the fish were cooked he took them out and fed himself, not putting the fish into his mouth, however, but rubbing them all over his hair and rolling his hairy body on them; for he was feeding his hair.

Meanwhile, his son had been watching him from the canoe. The boy came out and approached his father, who stared at him in surprise and anger. He said not a word, however, but washed out his canoe. When he had removed all trace of the fish he told his boy to get in and paddled away with him until he came on a large log with upstanding roots. He paddled alongside it, told the boy to get off, and disembarked onto the log also, taking his kelp ropes. Then he lashed the boy securely to the roots and paddled to his home. When his wife asked him what had become of their son he told her that he had left the lad at the fishing place and would return for him later on. She suspected that he had killed the child and wept for many days. Her brother held a council about the affair and the people drove Kwinus out of the house.

Meanwhile, the log carrying Kwinus's son drifted along until, after many days, it stranded on a beach. At dawn, Sun spoke to the boy and asked him what was the matter. He answered "My father lashed me to this log and the cords are cutting into my flesh; for I have lain her so long that I have grown, and the cords become tighter and tighter." Sun released him, dressed his wounds, and said to him "here is your fortune. When you arrive home your mother will be blind from much weeping; but wipe her eyes with a shred of cloth from my clothing and she will regain her sight. When your little dog comes to meet you, drop some shreds of this cloth on its body and it will change." Sun then pointed out the direction the boy should take to reach his home, and bade him walk over the surface of the water without fear. It gave him, also, a tiny box, which he was not to open for five days; after the five days he might remove the lid and everything he needed, blankets, etc., would drop in a pile beside him. Finally, Sun told him to summon his father Kwinus, bid him crouch down, and rub him with the cloth; then Kwinus would change into a rock.

So, walking over the water, the boy regained his home. He sent some children who met him on the beach to summon his mother, but she could not believe her son had returned and refused to go. He sent them again, and again she refused, saying that she was blind and ill. However, she changed her mind and stumbled down to the beach, followed by the little dog. There her son rubbed her eyes with the cloth, and also her body and limbs; her sight came back to her, and she regained her strength and vigor. He then scattered a few shreds on the little dog, which instantly changed into a little girl.

Now the boy's mother enlisted the help of her brothers in setting the house in order and extending invitations to all the neighbours to take part in a potlatch. The people gathered the next day and were surprised to see the missing boy. Greater still was their amazement when he opened his box and poured from it an enormous pile of goat wool blankets. He sent an uncle to bring his father Kwinus and set him in front of him. Kwinus, astounded at the wealth by which his son was surrounded, sought to take the credit to himself. "Now do you wonder that I treated you as I did?" he said. "I wanted to make you wealthy." His son ordered him to crouch down, and as he crouched the boy touched him with his cloth. Immediately the man turned into stone, planted on the floor in the middle of the house. Thereafter the people broke pieces of bark on his forehead when they were too large to put in the fire.

After distributing all his blankets among the guests, the boy stood up and related how his father had treated him and how Sun had come to his aid.

As soon as he was old enough Kwinus's son married the girl who had been metamorphosed from the dog. She bore him a daughter. When this daughter reached marriageable age, a nobleman's family sought her as a bride for one of its sons. She married him. Soon after the wedding Kwinus's son, who had caught many ducks with his net, set out with his mother to visit her, and to take her parents-in-law some birds. Raven embarked with them. As they paddled along the mother chanted a song about her husband being changed into a rock, a song that is called *hiwe'nax*; Raven, sitting in the stern, chanted the song even more lustily than she did.

The young bride painted her face, dressed in all her finery, and with little children holding up her trailing dress, went down to the beach to meet her father and grandmother. As soon as they entered the house Kwinus's son climbed onto a platform and distributed a number of blankets. His hosts then set about cooking food for him and his companions. Raven bustled around them, asking them what they were cooking. Kwinus's son told him to behave himself, but he took no notice. As soon as he learned that they were cooking seal meat, he exclaimed "That is just what I like"; and he ate all the meat before anyone else tasted a scrap. He ate too much, and finally became very ill, rolling on the ground in agony. Kwinus's son was very much ashamed, but he called in a number of medicine men to try to cure Raven. All failed but Ratfish, who extracted the meat from the patient's stomach. Kwinus's son, deeply mortified, took Raven home, Raven asserting all the way that it was the medicine-man who had made him ill.

(30) Origin of the Willow Fishnet
Told by David and Mrs Latasse, Tsartlip

A Saanich couple and their marriageable daughter joined some relatives on a fishing expedition to Blaine, in the state of Washington. There, the girl used to wander outside the rush wigwam and sit by herself at night while her parents were sleeping. One night someone approached her, and before leaving arranged to meet her again the next night. Thereafter they met night after night.

Shortly afterwards some strange youths began to join the girl's brothers and cousins as they played around the camp, and she wondered whether one of them might not be her nightly visitor. Towards evening, therefore, she smeared red ochre on her hands, and when here suitor joined her, playfully rubbed them on the back of his clothing. The next day she noticed in the crowd of players a youth who seemed more serious than the others, and when he turned his back to her, it was red.

When night came her suitor urged her to go away with him, but she refused unless he first spoke to her parents. He was afraid that if he spoke to them they might be angry and send him away, and suggested that it would be safer if she herself told them. She did so, and her father consented to their marriage if they remained for a time with her family. So she married the youth, who thereafter ceased to play with the other young men and instead occupied himself with serious matters about the camp.

Soon afterwards fish became very scarce, and the community was threatened with famine. The youth then said to his young wife, "Tell your father and his people to bring me a lot of *agwala*. No one knew what he meant by *agwala*: all the names, indeed, that he gave to the various plants and land animals were strange. They brought him bundles of one plant after another, but he rejected them all until they brought him bunches of willow. From its bark he made a net *agwala*, showed them how to use it, and taught them the expressions that should accompany its handling. Then they were able to catch plenty of fish again.

Now that they were prosperous once more, he proposed to his wife that they go to his home. With the consent of her parents, the two of them embarked in a canoe, taking with them a large number of mats. Instead of heading for some point or island in the distance where one might expect a village, however, he steered the canoe toward a very deep place in the sea not far from shore, where it vanished from view. Not many days later the girl reappeared above the surface of the water, showed herself to her people, and vanished again. They knew who it was from her singed hair, for along with the other women of the camp she had been mourning the death of a relative. But she never returned to them, because she had married the fish-spirit *agwala*.

(31) The Dog Children
Told by Johnson, Quamichan

Someone visited a young girl each night without her being able to discover who it was. Each day she watched the young men playing in front of the house, hoping to recognize her visitor, but without success. Finally, she put some ochre mixed with fat on her hand, and when her visitor reappeared that night rubbed it over the front of his body. The next morning, she watched the young men again to see whose body was marked with red paint, and was greatly puzzled at detecting no one. Turning away, she noticed her own dog streaked with red paint.

Soon she found herself pregnant, but could not tell her parents who was the father of her children. In time she gave birth to ten pups. Deeply ashamed, her parents abandoned her with them, and induced all the other villagers to go away. Left without food, the girl sat in her house and wept.

Finally, she rose, lit some pitchy wood for a torch, and went to the beach to gather butter clams. She had filled her basket and was returning when she heard the sound of children's laughter in the house; but when she reached the door, only her ten pups ran out to welcome her. The same thing happened the second and third nights, for when the dogs shed their dog clothing they changed into children. One of them, *etci kum*, kept watch outside the door and warned the others to resume their clothing when their mother started home.

On the fourth night the mother gathered only a few clams, then hung clothes on her digging stick near the torch so that it might appear she was still on the beach. Then she stole back. As she drew near the house she heard the children inside laughing to one another "Our mother thinks that we are dogs and so she throws the clams to us." The watch-dog went outside, but quickly re-entered and said, "Yes, she is still on the beach." Suddenly their mother rushed into the house, seized their dog skins, which were hung up in a row, and threw them into the fire. The watch-dog tried to draw his out again, but all except one fore-sleeve was burnt. So nine of the children remained little boys; the tenth, who had been the watch-dog, had one paw instead of a hand.

Now the mother was very happy. Her children grew very quickly and became wonderful hunters. Her relatives returned when they discovered the pups had changed to boys.

(32) The Duck Bride
Told by David and Mrs Latasse, Tsartlip

In a certain village dwelt a youth whose father trained him carefully to hunt and fish until he was proficient enough to marry. One morning, someone went out of the house and saw a strange, beautiful duck in the water near the beach. He went back and told the youth to try and shoot it. The youth took his bow and arrows and shot an arrow into the bird's side. The duck began to swim round in circles, turning on its side and trying to shake the arrow out. The youth shot it again, in the other flank, whereupon it headed straight out from the beach. Not wishing to lose his arrows, the youth got into a canoe, accompanied by Mink, Muskrat, Squirrel, and Diver, and paddled after the bird. The duck kept steadily ahead; they could just see it through the fog. For hours they followed it until it began, at last, to approach a village. As it landed, it shook off its feathers and the two arrows and changed into a beautiful girl, who started to walk up to one of the houses. Her father came out, as did a great many other people. They told the young man and his companions they were prisoners, and tied their canoe to a high pole that stood at the tide's peak. Round the bottom of the pole were skeletons of all kinds, people that the villagers had killed.

Now the villagers sat in front of their houses against the wall, and on the grass in front, while their chief called out "Is there anyone who thinks he can climb?"

Mink, always wide awake, called out "Yes, we have Squirrel here." The villagers set Racoon to race Squirrel in climbing the tall pole. Mink said to Squirrel "After you get to the top run half way down again towards Racoon and laugh at him." Squirrel reached the top before Racoon was half-way, then peered over the edge of the top, ran down, and laughed in Racoon's face.

The villagers were ashamed that their champion had lost. Nevertheless, the chief called again, "Is there anyone here who thinks he can swim?" Mink called out "Yes, we have Diver here." The villagers set Sea Otter to race against Diver towards a mark far out in the sea. Diver dived three times, then at a fourth long dive, reached the mark before Sea Otter was half way.

The villagers now looked very depressed. However, their chief called out again, "Is there any one here who thinks he can run?" Mink replied again, "Yes, I can." They set wolves to compete with Mink. Mink said "I'll run along the water's edge." They said "Very well," and showed him the finishing mark. Mink, running on hard, firm sand, easily outstripped the wolves, who were labouring in the loose gravel. After reaching the mark, he raced back to the houses and began to shoot his scent at all the people, who hastily tried to cover their faces.

Now when the contests first began, Mink said to Muskrat, "Swim along the shore and see which canoe is the largest and the best. Then gnaw holes in all the others, gnaw nearly through the paddles and the poles for pushing the canoes out from shore, and gnaw also through all the canoe balers. Muskrat did this, unnoticed by the villagers, who were intent on the contests. He returned just as Mink was spraying the people with his scent. Muskrat pointed out to the youth which canoe he had chosen for themselves, and had left untouched. The whole party went to the chief's house, escorted the girl outside, and put her in the canoe. They then gathered all the mountain goat blankets in every house, piled them in after her, and began to paddle away. The villagers, recovering from Mink's scent, began to race after them, but their canoes filled with water, their balers leaked, and their paddles and poles broke. So the youth and his party paddled leisurely home with the girl, unafraid of pursuit, since her people did not know whence they came.

(33) The Abandoned Youth

Told by Johnson, Quamichan

A certain youth pretended that he was roaming the woods to fast and obtain medicine power, but instead he carried salmon eggs with him, gathered fern root, and feasted on them secretly. His people were very angry when they found out, and decided to abandon him. Quietly, they packed all their goods, ready to depart. Then, one morning, when the youth had gone as usual to the woods, they put out their fires, loaded up their canoes, and paddled away.

Now the boy's grandmother had compassion for him, and although she was forced to depart with the rest of the people, she tried to think of some way to help him. She gathered two large clam shells, dug a hole in a fireplace, put fire inside the clams, closed them, and buried them in the hole. Then she called her little dog and said to it, "When we go away you stay and show your master where I have placed the fire." After she had done this she departed with her people.

The youth returned at evening. His people had all gone, every fire was extinguished, and there was no food. He went to his house and wept. Then the little dog approached him, pushed him with its nose, then ran to the fireplace. The youth was too overcome to pay any attention, but when the dog repeated its action again and again, he began to wonder what it meant. Finally, he went to the fireplace, dug out the clams, and found the fire.

On the following morning the boy went to the woods, bathed, and did everything he should have done earlier in order to become a medicine man. The little dog followed him everywhere. He shot a number of birds, and from their skins made clothing for himself.

The day after, he gathered some boughs in the woods, carried them to the river, and, after bathing, dipped his boughs in the water and shook them. He repeated the action four times. Then a shoal of salmon appeared, pursuing a great swarm of herring. He caught all that he could use, and thereafter gathered all the herring he wanted; he had merely to shake out his branch and more herring appeared than he could use.

One day, as the boy lay in his house all alone with his hand under his head and plenty of food stored all around, he began to think about his people. He said to himself, "My old grandmother may be starving. I'll load Raven with a number of herring and send them to her." Raven ate a great number of herring, and with full stomach, flew away; but he neither visited the youth's grandmother, nor returned. The youth then filled Crow's stomach with herring and sent off that bird. Crow flew away and alighted on a stump near the old grandmother, who was crying at the water's edge. It called to her *qwalamp walamp nasalkulkwale*—"Cook the herring the boy you deserted has sent to you." At the end of its refrain, Crow vomited all the herring he had eaten. The grandmother gathered them up, washed them, and took them to her house, which stood alone at one end of the village. There she roasted the herring before a fire and let some of the rich fat drip off them.

Now a man who was wandering nearby smelled the fat, so he lifted up the flap of her tent to see what she was cooking. As soon as he saw the herring he rushed away to tell the rest of the people, who were on the verge of starvation. They crowded over to her tent and asked her where she got the fish. "Crow brought them to me," she answered, "a present from my grandson whom you deserted."

The villagers discussed the matter among themselves, saying to one another "He must have plenty of food. Let us pack up and return to him." So they hurriedly loaded up their canoes and returned. There, in the water in front of their old homes, were multitudes of salmon and herring. The youth did not object to their return, for he was now wealthy and possessed fine clothes. Some strangers wanted to buy these clothes from him, but he refused to sell them.

(34) The Boy Who Defended His Family

George Kwakaston, Koksilah

A man who had eight sons was continually molested by enemies. He wanted to find out which of his sons was the bravest and most likely to get power to help them. Taking the eldest son, he dragged him, naked, over a beach strewn with barnacles; the lad screamed with the pain. He tried out his second son in the same way, and the third, right down to the seventh; all cried out as the eldest had done. Finally, he dragged his youngest son; the lad never uttered a sound. The father then captured a seal, stripped off the skin, sewed the youth inside it, and set him adrift on the water. After a time, the youth drifted ashore somewhere. Some men found him and one said to the other, "Look, here is a seal. Is it dead or alive?" The seal seemed to quiver, so one of them thrust his harpoon into it, wounding the lad. He made no sound, so, thinking the seal was dead, they carried it towards their home. On the way, they threw it down on a log while they rested. Noticing that the seal still quivered, they harpooned it again; even then the youth made no outcry. When they were nearly home their father came out and asked them what they had caught. "We have caught a seal," they said. They cut it open, and the youth jumped out. Bewildered, they led him into their house. The boy gazed round at all their harpoons and said nothing. "What is it you want?" they asked him; but he would not answer. They offered him first this thing, and then that. At last, they offered him a club that was hanging up. "Do you want that?" they asked. "Yes," he answered. "You may take it then," they said; "it will kill your enemies." Then they told him that they were going to entertain him, and they called in the wolves. The wolves played and sang, and the youth learned their songs. After he knew them by heart, the people told him to return home. Enemies came to attack them, but when he waved his club round his head, they fell dead. The news soon spread. No one ventured to attack him again, and he and his family became very wealthy. They decided to celebrate their good fortune; the youth danced his wolf dance. As soon as the wolves heard their song they came down and gathered outside the door.

(35) The Salmon Bride

Told by David and Mrs Latasse, Tsartlip

A nobleman's son went out to seek a helping spirit, but failed. Time went on and his parents began to enquire after a wife for him, but could not hear of a suitable girl. One day the youth decided that he would not fish at the usual places, but would go far away to see what he could catch. He paddled on and on through the fog—it was September—and came at last to an island, where he landed. At first he could find no trace of inhabitants; then he came upon a young woman sitting all alone, on the grass, with not a house in sight. He asked her, "How do you come to be here all alone?" She answered, "This is my home. I live here nearly all the time." He did not like to question her further, for he began to think she must be a spirit. Presently, she said "Why don't you catch some fish for yourself?" The youth answered "There is no place here where I could fish." "Would you like me to catch some for you?" "Yes." She rose, took her stick, which was quite plain and unadorned, walked over to a little slope and drove it into the ground. Soon water oozed up into the hole. She dug a little trench for it and it quickly became a stream. Then she returned and said to him, "Go over and catch your fish." He took his spear and went over. A shoal of cohoe salmon were poised in the stream. He speared two of them. She said to him, "Light a fire and I will cook them for you." So she cooked them and they ate.

That night, the youth slept on a mat in his canoe. Where the girl slept he did not know. So they lived this way for several days. Then she said to him, "Don't you want to go home?" "Yes," he answered, "but I don't know which direction to take." "I know where your home is," she said. "I know who you are. Would you like me to go with you?" "Yes." So they embarked. At night they camped on an island—as before, he sleeping in the canoe, and she, he knew not where. Thus travelling for several days they reached his home.

When they landed the girl said to him, "Go and tell your people to partition off a corner for me with mats, and provide new mats for me to sleep on." He went forward, met a kinsman, and sent him ahead with the message. Then he led the girl to the house. His mother had the room all ready. So they married, and she accompanied him fishing while his mother tidied up the room. The old lady noticed what seemed to be fish slime on the mats, but was afraid to say anything.

In time, the young woman had a son. Then she went back up the slope a little way with her stick and made another stream in which the cohoe made their appearance. Thereafter the villagers were never short of fish. The fish woman had not lived a very long time when she died.

(36) The Girl Carried Off by Wolves
Told by George Kwakaston, Koksilah

A woman's baby fell into the fire and was badly burned on the face. A few years later, when the child was six or seven years of age, her mother left the child sleeping while she went away somewhere. When she returned, the child was gone. She and her husband sought all over for her, but found only wolf tracks.

Sometime afterwards, the father caught a glimpse of his daughter. She was with some wolves, but was running like a human being, on her two legs. A year later he caught another glimpse of her; this time she was running on all fours.

Whenever the mother passed the place where she had lost her child, she would weep. Once, as she passed, again weeping, a deer came swimming out towards their canoe, driven by wolves. Then they knew that their daughter's people had sent it out to them. They killed the deer, went ashore, and butchered the meat. Afterward, a deer was always driven down to them whenever they passed. So the mother ceased weeping, knowing that the wolves were treating her daughter kindly.

(37) The Face-changer
Told by David and Mrs Latasse, Tsartlip

In a certain village lived a beautiful girl who rejected the overtures of all her suitors because they were not handsome enough to please her father. One rather good-looking young man sent his kinswoman over to sue for him; the girl said to her, "Tell him to bathe frequently and rub himself all over with cedar twigs." The youth thought he would try it since she wanted him to, so he scrubbed himself with cedar twigs until he bled; he even continued until his face became covered with sores. He let them heal, then sent his kinswoman again to tell the girl he had done as she instructed. She said, "Tell him to scrub himself with spruce boughs this time." Now, spruce boughs prick more than cedar. Even so, the youth did as she asked, then let the scratches on his face heal before sending his kinswoman again. "Tell him to scrub himself with blackberry bushes." The youth thought this was too severe an ordeal, and having heard that somewhere there lived a woman who could change faces, he determined to seek her out.

He travelled for many days until he emerged from the woods in a place where there were only scattered groves of timber. Soon afterward he saw smoke and discovered a young man with two faces—Janus-like—sitting in front of a house. His name was Atcuwítlas. Atcuwítlas said, "Why have you come here?" The youth answered, "I am looking for the woman who changes faces." "She lives in there," said Atcuwítlas; "go right in." Before entering, the youth peered through a crack and saw many faces hanging on the wall, one of them freckled and very beautiful, as freckles are admired. He went inside and sat down; the freckled face had disappeared. The woman (spirit) said to him "Why have you come here?" He told her his troubles, how the girl had made him scrub with cedar and spruce, and now told him to scrub with blackberry. "I thought that you might change my face." "Alright. Look around here and see if there are any you like." She showed him one face after another, but at each he remarked, "I hardly think that will fit me." Finally, she said "I have one more," and she brought out the freckled face which she had kept concealed. "Yes, I think that one will fit." So the woman lifted off his old face and put on the freckled one.

Now she said to him, "Be sure to take the same path home as you came by. Don't wander off it." The youth set out, but the woods looked so much alike that he went astray until he met a big woman, Cinnamon Bear.[18] She said to him, "Where are you going?" "I am going home." "You had better come to my house. I will cook some food for you." He went with her. In the house was a young woman who was lying down. Cinnamon Bear said to him, "Stay here while I go out and get you some food." While she was away the young woman—Black Bear, Cinnamon Bear's half-sister—sat up and said, "She will give you nothing but snakes. Don't eat them." Drawing some dried fish out of her cedar bag, she said "Hide these fish and when she offers you the snakes pretend to eat them but secretly eat the fish." Presently, Cinnamon Bear returned, put some snakes on the hot stones, poured water on them, and cooked the snakes. Then she bade the youth eat, and was delighted that he seemed to eat the snakes.

The youth stayed there that night. Next morning, Cinnamon Bear said to him, "Stay here. I am going to get you some food." When she was gone the youth made ready to leave. Black Bear, who had constantly kept her back turned to her half-sister, asked him "Where are you going?" "I am going home." "She will pursue and overtake you. But I will give you something that will help you." Black Bear placed a stone on his chest, stones on each side, and a fourth on his back.

After a time, Cinnamon Bear returned. "Where has he gone?" she asked her half-sister. "I do not know. I was lying down." "Which way did he go?" "I do

---

18   The cinnamon is a red or brown-tinged black bear. –Ed.

not know. I did not pay any attention." "Oh well, I will find him." Cinnamon Bear followed and overtook the youth. She called "Where are you going?" "I am going home." "Come here." He approached her. She lifted one of her paws to scratch his chest and the claws fell out against the stone. "Lie on your side." He lay down, but when she tried to scratch his side with her other front paw, the claws, too, fell out. She lost the claws of one hind leg on his other side, and of the other hind leg on his back. "Lie down," she said. He lay down. She opened her jaws to bite his head, but instead she swallowed him.

Presently, she felt an awful pain in her stomach. She went home and lay by the fire, groaning. The pain grew worse, and she said to her half-sister, "You had better call our grandfather Crane." Her half-sister brought Crane. Crane put his ear against Cinnamon Bear's stomach and said, "This is very serious." He listened again. "This is serious. It sounds like a human being inside." Cinnamon Bear was so angry that she picked up a handful of ashes and threw them all over Crane. That is why crane is now grey; previously he was black.

Crane now put his nose against her. The youth caught hold of it and held tight. Crane screamed and flapped his wings, as cranes do today. The youth let go and Crane went sprawling on his back, far away. His nose became a long beak. He went away.

Now the youth began to cut his way out of Cinnamon Bear. He tore out her heart and killed her. At last, he emerged. He said to Black Bear, who was a fine-looking young woman, with very long black hair, "Will you come home with me?" She said "Alright." She filled a cedar-bark bag with dried fish for herself to carry, and another for him, and they started out for his home.

On the way they met another woman, Swan, who sang to them "Where are you going?" The youth said, "We are going home." The woman was digging camas. She sang again, "You had better stay. I will give you something to eat." She heated two stones, put two camas on them, covered them over, and sang "*yitcaíyo, yitcaíyo*," "more, more." When she uncovered the stove and stones, the camas had grown into an immense heap. The youth and his wife ate what they could, put the rest in cedar bark bags, and continued on their way. That is why today a very little camas seems to fill the needs of many people.

When they reached home the youth invited all the old men of the village to a feast. His dried fish and camas was more than sufficient. The old men went back and told their families, "That young man has become wonderfully good-looking. And his wife is handsome, too. Was it the scrubbing with cedar and spruce that improved his looks? Or did he find the woman who changes faces?" The girl who had rejected him listened to their remarks and said, "I am going over to see him." They said to her, "You had better not go"; but she answered "I want to see his wife." She went over, sat down beside the youth, and said "Brother—for so she now addressed him—did you find the woman who changes faces?" "Yes." "Which way did you go?" He told her. "What did you say to her?" He told her the exact opposite of what he had said.

The girl leaped up and sped to the place and met Atcuwítlas, the two-faced guard, sitting in front. She asked him, "Does the woman who changes faces live here?" "Yes." She went inside. "What is it you want?" said the woman, who had covered all the faces that the girl might not see them. "I want a face ever more beautiful than the one I have." "Well, I think I can manage that." The woman lifted off the girl's face and put on her another that was fearfully lopsided. Unaware of what happened, the girl sped back to the village, and without going home, entered the youth's house and sat beside him. "Don't you think I got a very beautiful face?" she asked him. "Go away," he replied. "Don't come around here. We don't want you here." She jumped up and ran home, where people laughed at her ugly face. She wept bitterly, but it was of no use.

(38) The Bride of the Sea Monster[19]

George Kwakaston, Koksilah

A man at Neah Bay [Washington State] who had a *saila* in the sea said to his people, "I want to see my *saila*. Take me out to sea." They paddled him out opposite a certain village that had a fine sandy beach. Finally, he told them to stop paddling. "Here is my *saila*," he said; "tie this rope around me and I will dive down to it. As long as the rope shakes, let me remain. When it ceases to shake, pull me up." He dived down and disappeared. The rope shook for some time, then hung still. His people pulled it up. All that remained of him were his bones. They wept and returned home.

Now, in the village opposite, lived a young girl who was confined to her house all the time. Her mother proposed to go to some rocky point to gather shellfish, and the girl begged to be allowed to go with her. Her mother refused. The next day, when her mother was leaving, she begged again to go, and someone said, "let her go." As she was gathering shellfish on a rock, a human hand suddenly gripped her wrist and held her captive. Then the tide came up and swallowed her. Her mother saw her disappear, but could not rescue the girl.

A year later, the girl returned to her home. Her parents were so glad to see her that they begged her to remain with them. She stayed with them a short time, but then the sea rose and rose until it threatened to engulf their village. In fear, they told her that she had better return where she came from. So she went down to the beach and allowed the sea to engulf her again.

A year later there was a terrible storm during the night that died away before morning. The girl's parents went to the beach to see what damage it had done. On the beach they discovered many seals, porpoises, and fish of all kinds, a gift to them from their son-in-law. They gathered them all, dried them, and so acquired enough food to feed themselves and their relatives for a long time.

---

19   This story is probably derived from the Klallam; Jenness, "Saanich Notes," 59.

Two or three months later the girl reappeared, but her appearance had changed and she looked strangely fierce. Her parents were afraid of her and told her she had better go back. She returned to the sea.

Months later, after a heavy wind storm in the night, her parents found on the beach a dead baby with the tail of a fish instead of legs. They concluded it was their daughter's child, and buried it in their family grave house. Their daughter never appeared again, because they had told her to go away. Today, when the Indians pass this spot, they beg the daughter's husband not to send a storm against them, but to let them pass in safety.

(39) Kissak and the Stone-headed People

Told by Johnson, Quamichan

On the flat near Khenipson village there once lived a family of stone-headed people known as *manmántak*. A sister of the men married an ordinary human being, by whom she had conceived a child. Now these stone-headed people were always playing a game like hockey (*disk'wolá*) with a ball made from balsam.[20] During the game they attacked their brother-in-law and clubbed him to death. They then watched their sister to see whether her baby would be a boy or a girl. During the night she gave birth to a boy, but, wishing to save the baby, she pulled out some of her hair and bound him between the loins so that he would appear like a girl. (Hence the child was called Kissak.) Two days later she fled to a creek near Quamichan. In this creek she bathed her child, and because the baby cried in the water, the creek is now called *xexeyela*, "weeping creek." Travelling a little farther, she bathed it in another pool, *tćekweten*, "bath pan"; then a pool a little farther on, *hwintathwetan*.[21] Finally, she went to the creek, *xtsə'tsəm*, "trout creek," still on Quamichan reserve, where she built a little house for herself. Her baby grew very quickly after his baths, and soon became a strong boy. Once he bathed, he rubbed himself with yew branches to increase his strength, then put his branches into the water, lifted them out and shook them; the spray turned into trout. This was the origin of trout.

After a time, he began to hunt. His mother warned him not to go near the house of the stone-heads. He killed all kinds of birds, which his mother skinned, and sewed the dried skins together for clothing.

Kissak now wanted to capture a golden eagle, *tsəsken*.[22] He shredded some cedar bark to make it look like a man's intestines, and stained it red with alder bark that he had chewed. He then climbed a hill and stretched himself out

---

20 This reference may be to a ball game called *ćuqwula'* in Hul'qumi'num'. –Ed.

21 In Hul'qumi'num', *shx̌ux̌eyélu* and *shshaxwukwum̓* are "crybaby" and "bathpan," respectively. –Ed.

22 The SENĆOŦEN word for this bird: JESḴEN (*ćə́sqən*); in Hul'qumi'num', it is *ćusqun*. –Ed.

with his cedar bark, as though he had been eviscerated. Many different birds swooped down on him, but he drove them all away. Finally, the big eagle settled on him. He seized its legs, twisted its neck, and killed it. Then he put on its skin and went down to visit the stone-heads.

The stone-heads were running backwards and forwards, playing their game, when the boy flew to the top of Mt. Tzuhelem [Mt Tzouhalem, near Duncan], making noise like an aeroplane. The stone-heads observed him and said, "It may be our nephew who is flying around." The boy, however, returned home, and told his mother that he had visited their enemies. He then began to make a club for himself (*kwakwantan*),[23] testing it on a stone. His first one, of oak, broke; so did his second, of dogwood; but his third, of yew (*toxwalsit*),[24] broke the stone. With this club he went down to kill the stone-heads. They ran towards the place where he was hidden, playing their game, then ran back. As they ran back he followed them and clubbed them one after the other. He then remained at the creek in Quamichan and became a *siem* [noble].

Finally, X̱e.ls came along. He changed Kissak's mother into a stone on Quamichan Creek. Kissak went farther up the same creek, wearing his eagle skin dress, but X̱e.ls overtook him there and turned him into a stone. You can see both of these stones today.

(40) Tsəlox̱ (Saanich)
Told by David and Mrs Latasse, Tsartlip

A man named Tsəlox̱ had two daughters, the elder very beautiful, the younger plain. He was proud of his elder daughter and painted her face with elaborate stripes; but the younger daughter had but little paint on her face.

The elder girl said to her father, "I want to marry Slalekkwal—the handsome spirit of the east who controls fine weather."[25] Her father was pleased, and sent her with her younger sister out in a canoe to call Slalekkwal. The elder girl sang, "Come, my relative, take me for your wife, my husband is dead." (By custom, only a widow can pursue a husband; previously unmarried girls cannot.) Racoon answered her call, saying "Here I am." "I don't want you," she said; "your eyes are too peculiar." She sang again. Bear answered her call, saying "Here I am." "I don't want you. Your head is too big, your eyes too small, and you are too woolly and black." Deer answered, but his ears were too long. Mink answered, but he had short legs and a flat belly. Still she called. A small, red-speckled fish answered, as did a second, third and fourth fish; each had painted itself to please the girl, but their eyes were

---

23   The reference is probably to K̲K̲OSTEN (*qʷqʷástən*), "war club"; q̓waqwustun is its Hul'qumi'num' form. –Ed.

24   Jenness's term does not correspond to the Hul'qumi'num' or SENĆOŦEN word for this tree, tux̌wá'culhp and ȾEN̠ĸIȽĆ (*ƛ̓əŋ̓q̓iłč*), respectively. –Ed.

25   In SENĆOŦEN, SKELEXEN (*sq̓ələx̱ən*) is "east wind." –Ed.

peculiar. Then larger fish answered—first Cod, but his head was too big; then Halibut, but his mouth was twisted and his eyes too close and crooked.

At last Slelekkwal appeared. But Slelekkwal took no notice of the elder sister, talking only to the younger. The elder girl, deeply mortified, threw herself onto the bottom of the canoe, covered herself with a mat, and wept. Slelekkwal said to the younger girl, "Give me your paddle." She gave it to him and he paddled them home. When they landed on the beach, he said to the younger girl, "I want you to be my wife. Shall I come to see your father and mother?" "Yes," she said. So they entered the house, but the elder girl remained in the bottom of the canoe.

Tsəloẋ's wife asked her daughter, "Where is your older sister?" "She is in the canoe." Tsəloẋ and his wife went down to coax her home, but she would not stir. Then Tsəloẋ, deeply incensed at Slalekkwal, plotted to kill him. He took his wedges and stone hammer and said, "I am going back to my work." Now, he was splitting a big cedar log in the water. When his son-in-law Slalekkwal joined him, he said "I have dropped my wedge down that crack. Go down and bring it up for me." Slalekkwal's wife, however, had prepared him for the ordeal by giving him one package of red ochre, and a second of white [diatomaceous] earth. When Slalekkwal dived through the crack, Tsəloẋ knocked out the cross-piece that held it open. The cedar trunk sprang together with a crash, and the water below was muddied red and white. Tsəloẋ went home well pleased and said to his elder daughter, "Come home now, my child, I have killed Slalekkwal." The girl rose gladly and entered the house, where her mother cooked food for her. But her young sister wept. Just as the elder girl was about to eat Slalekkwal entered with the wedge. The elder girl immediately burst into tears and lay on her bed, covered by her mat.

Still, Tsəloẋ planned to do away with Slalekkwal. He said to him, "Go out and get us some ducks." Slalekkwal went out. Then Tsəloẋ went down to the beach with some cedar bark. He twisted it in his hands, chanting an incantation, painted it with red ochre, and dropped it in the water a certain number of times. Then, a great storm arose. Tsəloẋ returned home and said to his elder daughter, "Rise my daughter, Slelakkwal has surely been drowned in this storm." The younger daughter wept, but the elder rose and began to eat. Just then Slelakkwal, who can control the weather, entered with some ducks. The elder daughter turned away, threw herself on her bed, and wept.

Tsəloẋ again plotted against Slalekkwal, whose wife by this time had born him a baby boy who was growing very rapidly into a fine little child. Tsəloẋ said to Slalekkwal, "I should think you would get some berries for your son." Slelekkwal took a basket and gathered some salmonberries. Then he went to a spruce tree from which he picked some needles, and cunningly mixed them with the berries. Tsəloẋ filled his mouth with the berries and went to swallow them. The spruce needles stuck in his throat. He choked and choked, and each time he did, it drove the needles farther down. At last he choked to death and changed into a rock. The spruce needles inside his body sprouted and a tree grew out of his head. Therefore, every rock that has a tree growing on its summit is called Tsəloẋ.

(41) Tsaloẋ (Cowichan)
Told by Johnson, Quamichan

Tsaloẋ, a *slelakam*, had two nice daughters who were very lonely and longed for husbands. They heard of a young man in another village and wanted to marry him. One day, when they went down to bathe in a stream, they sang to the spirits to make the young man think of them. As they sat on the bank, singing and talking, one of the girls said, "Well, I had better bathe." She went to the water, and, to her surprise, saw the face of the young man there. She called eagerly to her sister, "Here he is down here," and dove in to catch him. He disappeared, however. When she came out the two girls stood on the bank and saw him again, below them; they dived in from opposite sides to catch him. Again he disappeared. Then they heard laughter above them and saw the real youth in a tree, over their heads. He came down and joined them; and all together they went up to Tsaloẋ's house

Now Tsaloẋ was angry that the young man had not spoken first to him, so he plotted to kill the youth. Tsaloẋ told him to sit on a bearskin in which he had secretly planted a multitude of sharp bones. The youth, however, had concealed a stone under his clothing, so he sat down with alacrity, with a girl on each side. The bones were crushed against the stones.

Tsaloẋ now kindled a very hot fire with pitchy wood to make the youth move away. But while his back was turned, the youth threw a mussel shell into the fire, which extinguished the flames. Much astonished, Tsaloẋ made a still bigger fire; but again, when his back was turned, the youth threw some fern-root on it and again it went out.

Tsaloẋnow invited the youth's help in splitting a tree trunk. "Go first," he said to the youth; but the latter answered, "No, you go first." Tsaloẋ had split the trunk and placed a large wedge in the crack. He pretended to drop his adze through the crack and then called to the youth, "jump down and recover the adze." "Alright," said the youth. As he leaped through he threw behind him some ochre and white earth. Tsaloẋ pulled the wedge out and thought he had crushed the youth when he saw the red ochre and white earth come oozing out. "There is his blood and his brains," he said to himself, then called aloud, "You wouldn't come to me before you married my daughters, so now I have killed you. Serves you right." Returning to his house, he said to the girls, "I've got rid of him this time. Forget him." Just at that moment the youth walked in behind him.

All that night Tsaloẋ plotted how he should kill him. He called his dog and told it what he wanted. Changing it into a loon, he sent it down to the water and told it to cry out at daybreak. At daybreak, the pretend-loon cried, and Tsaloẋ rushed to his son-in-law and bade him capture it. The youth quickly jumped into a tiny canoe with his bow and arrow and paddled after the loon. He shot it again and again, but the loon simply dived and reappeared farther out at sea. When it was almost out of sight, Tsaloẋ led two bears to the beach and sprinkled their noses with water to cause a gale. Immediately a mighty wind sprang up and the waves rose high. Tsaloẋ returned to his house, happy; "He won't trouble me anymore," he said. "His tiny canoe can never outlive the gale."

When the storm arose, however, the young man turned back, and as he paddled he sang to Ẋe.ls. Ẋe.ls made a smooth path in front of his canoe so that, small as it was, not a drop of water entered. He paddled leisurely home. Tsaloẋ was gleefully telling his daughters how he had drowned the young man when they heard him singing near the beach, and the wind round the house suddenly ceased. A moment later the youth walked into the house and sat down beside his two wives.

Now the youth thought to himself, "It is my turn now. I will make him ill." Very soon Tsaloẋ became ill, and lay on his back, groaning. He said to the youth, "Bring me some salmonberries," though he knew it was winter, and no berries were on the trees. The youth went up to where salmonberries grew and, seeing a number of little birds, asked their aid. They sang and sang until the air grew warm, flowers began to bloom, and the berries to ripen. The youth filled his basket and returned to the house. Tsaloẋ began to eat the berries, but a stick of wood stuck in his throat and choked him.

Tsaloẋ now called all the medicine men, who were the birds. All tried, without success, to cure him except one, the red-top. The youth said to the bird, "You pull out the stick, but at the same time peck out one of his eyes." The bird did as he had asked. So now Tsaloẋ had only one eye. The youth thought to himself, "He still has one eye, and may yet do some mischief." So he told the birds to take him down to the water near Nanaimo, and there they changed him into a high rock. You can still see this rock; one side has an eye, the other has none. If you want to raise a wind, splash water on its face from the direction you want the wind to come.

(42) T'soẋelets the Cannibal Woman
Told by David and Mrs Latasse, Tsartlip

Everyone feared T'soẋelets, the giant cannibal woman. Once she was digging camas when Tomtit came and began picking out the worms wherever she planted her digging stick. She became annoyed when he got in her way, and she told him to go away. He refused, and at last she became so angry that she popped him into her mouth and tried to chew him up. Tomtit was so small, however, that he eluded her teeth, emerged from the side of her mouth, and began to pick worms again. "Where did you come from?" she said. "Oh, from your mouth." Again she tried to chew him up. This time, he emerged from her nostril. "Where did you come from?" "From your nostril." Next, he emerged from her eye, from her ear, then from her other nostril, her other eye, and her second ear. She decided to go home, but Tomtit went ahead, sat in her canoe and prepared to fish. "What are you doing?" "Oh, I am just fishing." She asked, "May I come?" "Yes, but the canoe is leaking. You must gather some boughs to sit on." "Gather them for me," she said. So Tomtit gathered some boughs and piled them high in the front of the canoe for a seat.

Tomtit moved along the shore and began to sing, calling to his grandmother, "*a na na kwasisíala, tum tum tum tum tum.*"

"What are you doing?" T'soxelets asked. "Oh, I am just looking for fish." Tomtit caught a few small ones. Then he caught a crab. He said to the crab, "Go and bite her feet." The crab crawled forward and bit her feet. "What is that you have caught? It is biting my feet." "Oh, it's only a crab" "Take it away." So Tomtit took it away.

T'soxelets now became drowsy, and Tomtit plotted to drown her. He began to push the canoe out into deep water. "Where are you going?" "Oh, I am just looking for more fish." She closed her eyes and slept. Then he rocked the canoe so that she fell overboard and was drowned.

There was another T'soxelets who used to go about with a big basket in which she put a little dried cedar bark that looked like dried fish. She would prowl around an Indian village until she heard a child crying, then go in and say to it "What is the matter? Have they been ill-treating you? Would you like a little fish?" The child would stop crying and put out its hand for the fish. Then T'soxelets would seize the child, put it in her basket, and carry it away. So she went around until she had captured many children from many different villages. Then she went home, gathered many stones to put them in the bottom of a fire pit, and much wood to burn on top. She covered the children's eyes with gum, and lined them up beside the fire pit, intending to roast them all. When the fire was blazing merrily she began to sing, "My stones are red hot," and to dance around the fire while the children beat sticks on the ground for her. Then she made the children sing and dance, hand in hand, round the fire.

Now with her was a youth whom she kept as a helper. He saw an opportunity to kill her and escape. As she began to dance a second time, he thrust a stick between her legs and toppled her over into the fire. She cried out, "Pull me out, brother"; he answered, "I am pulling you out, but you are so heavy." Yet all the time he was holding her down with the stick. She began to blaze, being very fat. Black sparks flew out from her and changed into snowbirds.

After she had burned up, the youth washed the gum from the children's eyes, that they might see again. Some had been plastered with so much gum that he could not remove it. So he made the sighted children lead the sightless ones by the hand and conducted them all to their homes.

(43) Skwatcin the Cannibal Man
Told by Johnson, Quamichan

A girl who was wearing numerous bracelets on her arm was making a basket in front of her house when someone walked up to her and asked her what she was doing. It was Skwatcin, the cannibal man. He seemed to be chewing gum. The girl looked up at him and said "Will you give me some of your gum?" "No," he answered, "but I will show you where to get it. It is quite near." The girl rose and went with him. After they had walked quite a distance she became frightened and said, "You told me it was close." "It is just down there where that tree stands," he answered. More frightened than ever, she stripped off her bracelets, one by one, and hung them on the trees along her path in order that her ten brothers might know the direction she had taken.

They came now to the shore of a lake. A heron on the other side called, and a canoe put out. There was no one aboard, but it puffed across the water like a launch; at its bow and stern was carved a head. Skwatcan told her to get aboard; he followed her, and the canoe carried them to the far side. There he led her to his house, which had a sliding door fitted with spears that closed on any intruder; just inside, two fierce dogs watched the entrance.

The brothers missed their sister, so the eldest started out in search of her. He found her bracelets hanging in the trees and then came to the edge of the lake. The heron cried, the canoe came over water and stopped at his feet, and he crossed to the other side. Seeing Skwatcan's house, he walked up to it. There the dogs leaped on him, and Skwatcan himself, coming out, seized him, clawed out his heart, and ate it. Then he took the body and laid it on a shelf inside the house with its feet protruded forward. One after the other, the remaining brothers went out to seek their sister, and suffered the same fate. In time, the girl gave birth to a son, Kwakumkwatc, who was even more savage than his father Skwatcan.

The girl's mother, now that she had lost all her children, spent her days weeping outside her house. Every time she wept she blew her nose and let the mucus drop into a vessel by her side. One day, as she approached her weeping place, she heard a baby's cry. Looking inside her vessel, she found a tiny baby. She took it into her house and raised it; within an amazingly short time it grew into a fine youth. She named him Smetakan, Mucus.[26] She warned the boy never to wander far from the house, telling him of the strange disappearance of his foster-brothers and sister. He made up his mind, however, that he would go to look for them.

As he wandered through the woods he came to the lake. The heron cried as before, and the canoe crossed over to him. But he looked at it and fled home. The next day he bathed in the woods and prepared for himself a suit of stone armour which covered him from neck to thighs. Once more he returned to the lake. When the heron called, and the canoe came over, he knocked off the

---

26   In Hul'qumi'num', "mucus" (or snot) is *SmuȽúqsun*, in SENĆOŦEN, it is SMEDEḴSEN (*sməmítəqsən*). –Ed.

boat's two heads. Then he made a paddle for himself, since the boat could no longer travel under its own power, and paddled across to the far side. When the two dogs attacked him he killed them both, and with his club, likewise broke off all the spears in the door. Skwatcan came out and tried to claw his chest, but his claws broke on the stone armour and Mucus slew him with a blow to the head. Skwatcan's son Kwakumkwatc next attacked him. Mucus, unable to kill him with his club, threw him into the fire.

Now that both monsters were dead, Mucus took down the bodies of the ten brothers and laid them side by side on the ground. Seeing that their hearts were missing, he searched in Skwatcan's body and found all ten in his stomach. He replaced them in their owners, but the heart of the eldest son, who had been longest dead, was almost rotten, while the heart of the youngest son beat lively. Taking out some medicine, he splashed it over their faces and they all came to life again. As they rose to their feet they said, one after another, "I must have been asleep a long time." Their sister, meanwhile, looked on and wondered.

Mucus now led them down to the lake and beyond it to their home. By this time their mother was so old that she could hardly walk, but Mucus restored her youth by sprinkling his medicine over her head and face. So the family was happy again.

The mother said to her ten sons, "Be very careful what you say to your foster-brother. He is not like you, but came from my mucus. Never mention it to him." Not long afterwards the youths went out in their canoes to hunt ducks, two in each canoe. As they were shooting with their bows and arrows, Mucus and his companion began to argue. Finally, his companion said, "You are not my brother; you are only my mother's mucus." Mucus did not answer, but after they had returned home and gone to bed he lay on his back and covered his head with his blanket. In the morning they tried to waken him but he did not move. When they drew back his blanket he had disappeared; all that remained was a tiny stain.

(44) Sametł
Told by David and Mrs Latasse, Tsartlip

At Mill Bay [north of Malahat] lived a youth named Sametł, who was training to be a warrior. He spent most of his time in the woods. There he lacerated the calves of his legs with a mussel shell, and rubbed into the scars crushed grasshopper and the crushed remains of another jumping insect. His legs became a mass of scars, but after a time he became the fleetest and strongest person in the country. If the people were going deer hunting, he would ask "Which way are you going?" When they told him, he would say "All right, I'll follow you." Yet despite starting after them, he would be at the top of the hill before them.

Once the hunters said to Sametł, "We have just missed a bear." He asked, "which way did it go?" When they told him he said, "All right, I'll catch it," and departed. They laughed after him, believing he would never overtake it.

After a time, he returned. They said to him, "Did you see the bear?" "Yes." "Did you kill it?" "With my fist." "What did you do with it?" "I left it where it fell." They went to look and found the bear with its skull crushed, as by someone's fist.

On another occasion Sametł was visiting relatives at Malahat. Someone said, "Some ducks have just flown by." He asked, "have they gone far?" "Not very far." He went along the beach and saw them feeding a little way out. He dived, came up below them, seized several by the legs, and brought them in to shore.

After he grew up Sametł went over to Patricia Bay where lived the daughter of a noble who was being carefully brought up. She was never allowed out except with her mother or slave maid; and she slept in a bag of deerskin with the hair turned inside (as did most nobles' daughters). Sametł stole in at night to her bedroom corner, then suddenly leaped to the fire, threw on it some pitchy wood that blazed up, and in full view of the household, insulted them by pretending he had outraged the girl. Then he fled to his canoe and escaped.

The Patricia Bay people were divided in opinion over what happened, some saying the girl ought to be married to Sametł. Others, who prevailed, said "No, but let us pretend we are giving him the girl, invite him and his people, and then kill them." Sametł and his people accepted the invitation and entered the potlatch house. Sametł then noticed that his hosts, when entering, wore blankets wrapped tightly round them, which was contrary to custom, and he suspected that they concealed clubs. A man called out, "close the door, the smoke is annoying our guests." Sametł jumped up, crying "I'll close it," then ran out the door to his canoe and fled. Instead of going across Saanich Bay towards home, he circled round to find out what had happened to his kinfolk. They, however, were all slain inside the house; and the Indians discovered Sametł's canoe on the shore and broke it up. Consequently, he had to walk home round the head of the inlet, and in the meantime the Patricia Bay Indians paddled across, attacked his village, and killed all except the few who were hunting and fishing. Also, they carried off all the *xwai-xwai* masks and other valuable property. After this the Patricia Bay people moved to Everett, in the U.S. Only later was Patricia Bay re-occupied, by the Sidney Indians.

(45) The Youth Who Searched for Thunder
Told by Peter Pierre, Katzie

A very energetic Cowichan youth married a girl of his own tribe. After his marriage he was always very late in getting out of bed in the morning. His father became ashamed of him, and one morning pulled back his blanket and poured a bucket of water in his bed. The young man burst into tears, and refused to eat with his father and mother that morning. The youth said to his wife, "I am going away. Do not marry again for four years." Then, when no one was watching, he put on his deerskin coat, picked up his bow and arrows, and stole away. Not long afterwards his parents asked the young wife where he had gone, and she said "I do not know. He was weeping when he left me."

She stayed with them for a long time, then returned to her own parents, who lived in a neighbouring house.

As the youth wandered in the woods, his mind cleared and he felt happier. He began to purify himself by bathing and fasting, hoping to get a *saila*. Only when he was famishing did he shoot anything, and ate the meat raw, for he had no fire. When winter came he still continued to purify himself, crawling at night for shelter into the hollow of a cedar tree. His people thought he was dead, and his parents went into mourning for him.

In the spring he heard Thunder and made up his mind that he would look for it. He climbed a high mountain until he reached a place that seemed to be all burned. Surely, he thought, this is where Thunder dwells. As he wandered around he discovered a lake of blue-black water, surrounded by steep cliffs. He peered over the edge. A cloud of fog enveloped him and he fell unconscious.

After he came to he went still farther, for he was not satisfied to let his *smustiux* (vitality) visit Thunder, but wanted to reach him in person. All summer, and all winter, he kept purifying himself, and when spring came returned once more to the lake and peered over. This time he was able to gaze a few seconds longer; then once more he became unconscious.

For another year he purified himself, and for the third time returned to the lake. Now he was so clean that he could gaze without difficulty into the blue-black water, and could see the place from which the fog had emerged that had overcome him. Thunder, he thought, was not at home, since it seemed not to notice him. Opposite the place from which the fog had come a crack extended down the face of the cliff, offering a possible means of descent.

Turning away, he went down to the salt water, filled his deer skin shirt with clam shells, and carried it back to the lake. He threw in one handful. The moment they struck sharks, whales and all the fish that live in the salt water rose to the surface and lay there like logs; they were the guardians of Thunder's home. The youth said to himself, "Tomorrow I will cause them to rise again and will run across them to the hole where the fog comes from; for Thunder is far away in the north."

That evening, he joined two rocks with a cord to weigh him down when he dived into the water. In the morning he crept down the crack to the edge of the lake and threw his shirt, with all the clam shells it contained, into the water. All Thunder's guards rose to the surface and lay there. He raced over them as a man races over a log-boom, and when he reached the place from which the fog had emerged, dived straight down, holding his two heavy stones. He landed at the bottom of the lake in front of a door, through which, for some reason or other, the water did not enter. He passed through. Inside, a fire was burning and a woman was spinning wool. He leaped on her back, but she pushed him aside, saying "Poor man, how did you get in here? Go away quickly. My husband is watching." He leaped on her back a second time, and as she pushed him away she said, "Perhaps I should take pity on you. My husband is coming." She hid him behind some mats in the corner and said "Keep quiet, and don't try to peek out." Before she had time to sit down again and resume her work, Thunder entered, removed his costume, and said, "Where is that youth who came in here?" His wife answered, "No one came in." "Do not try to hide him," her husband retorted, "or I shall surely kill him." Then the woman called to the youth, "Poor man, come here, or my husband will kill you." When the youth emerged Thunder said to him "Are you the young man whose bed his father soaked with water?" "Yes. That is why I have come here, to ask your help." "Very well," said Thunder, "I will pity you and help you."

Thunder now turned to his wife and said, "Cook some seal meat for him and feed him." When she laid the meat before him the youth thanked Thunder, but said "For four years I have not eaten more than was barely sufficient to keep me alive. Be not offended, therefore, if I can eat only a very little." Thunder said "Very well. I will help you. Presently I shall take you to my other wife at Stewatan (north)."

Early the next morning Thunder asked his wife, "Is that box I use empty?" "Yes." "Give it to me. The youth will just fit inside." He lifted the box onto his back, put the youth inside, and said to him, "While I am travelling, keep your eyes closed or we shall both die." There was no lid to the box, but there was something for the youth to hold on to.

After they had travelled towards the north for a long time, the youth opened his eyes just a little. Instantly, Thunder dropped; but the youth closed his eyes tightly again before he struck the water. "Do not open them again; keep them tightly closed," Thunder warned him, as he recovered and mounted again. Near his home, he caught a huge whale, carried it up high, dropped it into the water, and lifted and dropped it a second time, killing it. The youth heard the noise but did not look. Thunder now carried it with him to a lake outside his northern home, a lake larger than the one in the south, and there he dropped it into the water to feed his guards (*slelakam*). Then he entered his house and laid the youth on the floor. "Don't be frightened," he said to his wife, as he told the youth to climb out. "I have brought this youth to show him to you." This woman, who was also spinning wool, had two daughters.

They fed the youth, and he slept there that night. In the morning Thunder said to him, "I am going to send you home." He put him in his box again and carried him towards his home in the south, catching another whale on the flight to feed his southern guards. At the burnt ground above the lake he alighted and told the youth to get out. Thunder then removed his costume and waved his hands over his protégé, bestowing on him his [spirit] power (*swiem*). "You shall catch whales as I have done," he said, "and you shall feed your people with them. Take a spear with you; even if it just drops into the water and does not strike them the whales will die, for I have given you great power. You shall become a great *siem* [respected man]." He then put on his costume again, told the youth to return home, and dived down into the lake.

In the autumn of the fourth year, therefore, the youth returned home, where his parents had well-nigh forgotten him. While still a long distance from the village, he scented the smell of human beings and fell unconscious. When he came to he bathed, and went forward again; but before going very far, he fell unconscious again. It thus took him four days to inure himself to their smell and to reach the outskirts of the village.[27]

His younger brother was shooting birds. The youth called to him, but the child thought he was a *slelakam* and was afraid to approach. The youth called, "Don't be afraid. I am your older brother who was lost." The child picked up courage and went near; his brother picked him up in his arms and wept over him. "Go and whisper to your mother to clean the house so that I may enter. Is my wife still unmarried?" "Yes, she has not married again," his brother said. "Summon her also."

The boy whispered the message to his mother, who angrily beat him with a stick; "Why do you tell lies? Your older brother died four years ago." The child cried, but after a little while he crept close to his mother again and said, "It is true what I told you. He sat me on his knee and talked to me. He bade me tell you to clean the house." Still only half believing, the mother cleaned the house and said to the child, "Now go and summon your older brother. His wife will be here when he arrives." So the youth returned to his home.

The news spread quickly, and all the villagers gathered in the house, bringing blankets and other presents to bestow on him. At the close of the celebration the youth arose and said "Perhaps you grieved when I went away to look for something to help me. I did not die; but I thank you because you grieved for me. Hereafter you shall not be poor. I thank my father for what he did to me. I obtained what I was looking for, strong power. Tomorrow I will make you all happy, for now you have no food. My wife must not return to me for four days; during that time she shall remain with her parents."

That evening, he asked his father "Have you a spear, even a small one?" "Yes." "In the morning I will take it to sea with me." Early the next morning he paddled out to sea, all alone, and far out he came upon a whale. He threw the spear at it, and before ever the weapon reached it the whale died and turned with its belly upward. Fastening it to his left arm, he paddled ashore; people saw him dragging what appeared to be an island. With a small cord he dragged the monster right up the beach to the side of the house, climbed on top of it, and called to the people to cut it up and take away all they wished. The people rejoiced.

---

27   Peter Pierre said that after he himself had wandered in the woods for nearly a month, purifying himself to become a "medicine man," he smelt his village long before he reached it, so pure had he become, Jenness, "Saanich Notes," 93. The Upriver Halkomelem word for "medicine man" is *shxwlá:m*. –Ed.

Month	West Saanich	East Saanich	Cowichan
Jan	*stilq'wesun—* "puts paddles away"	*tsecət*—"father"	*seəm*—"chief"
Jan–Feb	*panεq—* "fern-root month"	*neŋana*—"young one"	*panεq*
March	*waxlis*—"frog" [spring peeper]	*wasxas*	*watxas*
April	*le.mas*—"crane"	*li.mas*	*li.mas*
May	*q'woiätstan –?*	*q'wiáitctan—* "fawn embryo"	*qwoiyεtstan—* "month of growth"
June	*panxwəman—* "camas time"[2]	*panxwəŋan*	*panxwəŋan—* "wild onion time"
June	*k'wilkwak.ən—* "time of hard ground"[3]	-	-
July	*hananε'n* —"humpback salmon"	*hanaŋε'n*	*salt'nəm*—salmon
August	*sowantan* —"cohoe salmon	*sowantan*	*saltánəm*
Sept	*skeyε'n* —"sockeye salmon"	*sakai* —"sockeye salmon"	*saltánəm*
Oct	*pakalεnuk*—"leaves"	*pakaļεnuk*	*spəkaļεnuk* —"falling leaves"
Nov	*hwəsalεnuk* —"falling leaves"	*hwisalεnuk*	*hwisaļεnuk*
Nov–Dec	*tcilxomatsan* —"frosty month"	*stsilkwesun* —"puts paddles away"	*tsəlqomatsan* —"frost
Dec	-	*tcilxomatsan*—"frost"	-

---

1   Jenness, "Saanich Notes," 102. –Ed.
2   Another west Saanich Indian subdivides the period from November to March into: *hwisalε-nuk* ("falling leaves"); *θilxomatsan* ("frost"); *niŋani kεlc* ("next to bad month"); *st'cil'kwesan* ("puts paddles away") and *ske.s kεlc* ("bad month"); *waxlis* ("frog").
3   "Time of hard ground" refers to the period when the fibres of the fern (*sεq*) were tied into bundles and used as torches, in lieu of cedar sticks.

Appendix B: Terms of Relationship
Table 1—Kin Terms, Same Generation

Relationship	Saanich	SENĆOŦEN	Cowichan	Hul'qumi'num'
siblings or cousins	no term recorded	brother/sister/ cousin ŚW͟ OKE (šxʷʔáqʷəʔ)	óqwtql (female?) salokwa (male?)	shxw'aq̓wa'
older brother/sister	scęeł	ŚÍEŁ (šáyəł)	scęeł	shuyulh
younger brother/ sister	sɛ`etçen	SELA͟ ĆEN (səléyčən')	no term recorded	s'aluq̓wa
half-sibling	no term recorded	SNEJIWEŁ (snəči̓wəł)	hansoyaxtal	snuc̓uwyulh
spouse	sta̓lis	STOLES (stáləs)	sta̓lis	stalus
fellow (co-) wife	saiya	S͟ ÍE͟ (sʔáyəʔ)	caiya	no term given
husband's younger sister	no term recorded	husband's sister SN͟ÁTW͟EN (sŋétxʷən)	cwelic	older/younger sister shxw'ulélush
woman's older brother's wife	no term recorded	no term given	no term recorded	older/younger brother shxw'ulélush
younger brother's wife	no term recorded	no term given	no term recorded	older/younger brother's wife shxw'ulélush
husband's younger brother	cnɛtkun (?)	no term given	mɛtuxʈun	brother-in-law smetuxwtun
husband's brother's wife	no term recorded	spouse's sibling's spouse SNEJEL͟NEK͟ (snác̓əlŋəq)	sinsawak	sister-in-law smetuxwtun
wife's brother or sister	no term recorded	brother/ sister-in-law SN͟ÁTW͟EN (sŋétxʷən)	sinsawak	wife's sister smetuxwtun
husband's brother or sister	no term recorded	brother/ sister-in-law SN͟ÁTW͟EN (sŋétxʷən)	no term recorded	husband's brother smetuxwtun
wife's brother's wife	no term recorded	spouse's sibling's spouse SNEJEL͟NEK͟ (snác̓əlŋəq)	tcɛpΘ	no term given
wife's sister's husband	no term recorded	spouse's sibling's spouse SNEJEL͟NEK͟ (snác̓əlŋəq)	tcɛpΘ	sciw̓utélh
sister's husband	no term recorded	man's sister's husband SĆUTAŁ (sčutéyɫ)	tsoleł	scuw̓télh
parent-in-law of one's child	sqwalwas	SQOL͟ WES (sk̓ʷál̓wəs)	sqwalwas	shkwi'lhuw̓
parent-in-law after child is dead	no term recorded	no term given	nasxęam[1]	no term given

---

1 Literally, "those who cry with me." In SENĆOŦEN, the word QEŁX͟O͟EN͟ (k̓ʷəɫxʷáʔəŋ') denotes a "co-mourner" of a deceased child (or sibling). –Ed.

Table 2—Kin Terms, Younger Generation

Relationship	Saanich	SENĆOŦEN	Cowichan	Hul'qumi'num'
son/daughter	mɛna	ṈENE (ŋə́nə?)	mɛna	maṅu
eldest child	latł (?)	no term given	sanłe (?)	no term given
any middle child	anowił	no term given	no term recorded	no term given
youngest child	sqɛq	no term given	sqɛq	"little offspring" huméuṅu
step-child	cnimɛ́ɛn	adopted child SꞭEṈ A ȽEṈ (skʷəŋĕyłəŋ̀)	słmɛnɛn	clhmuṅum
nephew or niece	stiuwan	STIȻEN(stíkʷən) (parents alive)[2]	stiwan	stiwun
son-in-law/ daughter-in-law	styutɛł	no term given	tsutɛł	cuwtélh
grandchild	iŋix	IṈES (?íŋəs)	im.iθ	'imuth
great-grand-child	okoyox (?) tsamox	JO MEḰ (čǎ?məqʷ)	tsamox	sćaṁuqw

Table 3—Kin Terms, Older Generation

Relationship	Saanich	SENĆOŦEN	Cowichan	Hul'qumi'num'
father	mɛn	MÁN (mén)	mɛn	men
mother	tɛn	TÁN (tén)	tɛn	ten
step-parent	salqwaθ	ŚWS OQEȽ (šxʷs?ákʷəł)	slilɛ́ɛm	clilé 'em
uncle or aunt (parent's sibling)	sets	SÁĆS (séčs)	sxwamniku	shxwuṁníkw
uncle's wife or aunt's husband	no term recorded	SÁĆS (séčs)[3]	tcɛpθ	shcepth
parent-in-law	no term recorded	in-laws SELSLÁ EȽ (səslé?əł)	kwiθlo	shk̓ʷi 'lhuẇ
grandparent	se.la	SILE (sílə?)	siela	siḷu
great-grandparent	tsamox	JO MEḰ (čǎ?məqʷ)	tsamox	sćaṁuqw
remote ancestors	sapaiyox	ancestor ĆELÁṈEN (čəléŋən)	akwiyauk (also descendants)	ancestor s'ulxwé:n
relatives by blood or marriage	sieye	close relative STES SĆÁ ĆE (stás sčé?čə?)	sq̀walmux	shxwuẇéli

---

2 SȻEṈṈEĆEȽ (skʷənŋóčəł) is the SENĆOŦEN term for a niece or nephew whose parent is deceased. –Ed.

3 This term applies to a man or woman's "father's brother's wife," and a man or woman's "mother's brother's wife." –Ed.

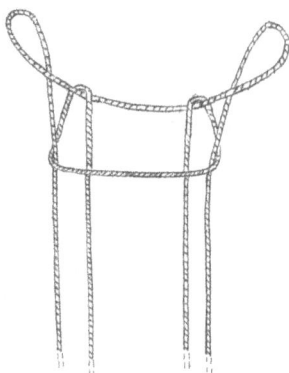

"Duck's Neck Mast"

Steps:
1. Loop over the thumb and little finger of each hand.
2. With the back of the right index from the proximal side take up the left palmar string and twist the right index clockwise round the ulnar string.
3. Slide the tip of the left middle finger down the palm of the right index so that it pushes away the crossing strings, and with the back of it, from below, take up the right palmar string.
4. Drop all the right hand loops except that on the index. You have the net mast.

"Throat" Cat's Cradle

Steps:
1. Loop over the left thumb and little finger, and over the right wrist.
2. With the palm of the right index (i.e. from the distal side) draw the left palmar string through the right wrist loop, which then drops off.
3. Place the loop held by the right index over the wrist again.
4. Hook the palm of the right index under the proximal left little finger string and the ulnar left thumb string before they pass under the left palmar string.
5. Draw these two loops through the right wrist loop, which falls off. You have the throat.

W̱SÁNEĆ (*xʷsénəč*)—Saanich Peninsula[1]

Name	Meaning	Location	Additional information
θa'muɛan	"basket"	penninsula between Patricia and Cole Bays	-
čkanéla	"sea gulls home"	two little island off "basket"	-
p'akwocɛn	Cole Bay	-	BOḰEĆEN (p̓áqʷəčən) Coles Bay Reserve (Paquachin)
pewotcɛn	"lizard"	little bay just south of Cole Bay	PITŚEN (*pítšən*) "salamander"
tca'tckonitc	"long bay"	South of Cole Bay	-
θ'amucan	"little point"	south of "long bay"	-
ƙwanas	"whale"	little creek just north of Brentwood Bay	ḰENES (*qʷə́nəs*) "whale" "creek that passes Hagan P[ost]O[ffice]."
tcaxlip [or *t'sa'lip*]	"maple"	Brentwood Bay	W̱JOȽEȽP (*xʷčáləłp*) "Brentwood Bay" Tsartlip (Brentwood Bay Reserve)
kwatamella	"grindstone"	left corner of Brentwood Bay	-
sinltkwit	"long narrow"	Tod Inlet (Brentwood Bay)	S̱NITWEȽ (*sŋítxʷəł*) Tod Inlet
sxwaxwuiɛm	no information	western point of Todd Inlet	-
hutcɛtctca	meaning unknown	little bay just east of Tod Inlet, on east side	-
spɛ'ɛθ	"bear"	next bay south of Brentwood Bay	NEKIX SPÁ̠EŦ (*nəqîx spéʔəθ*) "black bear"
xmaíyaθin	"deer"	bay south of Brentwood Bay	SMÍEŦ (*smə́yəθ*) deer
uq'tcamas	no information	promontory south of Deer Bay	-
q'oqtamas	"swelling"	next promontory south, with a long, high hill	-
toxəltcap	"yew bay"	no location given	-
ƙɛkwaθnip	"black throat"	mouth of Goldstream River	-

[1] Tom Paul, of Tsartlip, provided these place names; Jenness, "Saanich Notes," 303–305. –Ed.

humeya'ŋ	no meaning (?)	bay just north of mouth of Goldstream River	-
saləḱtaɫ	"dog salmon creek"	Goldstream River	S̱‚ELEḰTEŁ (*sʔə́ləqᵂtəɫ*) Goldstream River
ḱla'al	"Mount 'Camass'"	?	-
ḱwanalit	"a mountain so steep that you can't see people's backs"	?	-
ḱwanas	-	site on the Goldstream River	"big rock [shaped] like a whale up the Godlstream R. Once there was a channel through Goldstream to the S. coast, in where [*sic*] were huge monsters that preyed on people. X̱e.ls blocked this channel, and turned the whale to stone"
hux'θeaman	"edible grass place"	bay in southwest corner [?]	-
stilit	no meaning	next bay north [?]	-
sqʷwalalp	no meaning	next bay north [?]	-
q'aleonitc	"round bay"	next bay north [?]	-
sqʷwaθan	meaning unknown	creek near cement works [?]	[at Bamberton?]
huɫtamatan	meaning unknown	just south of cement works	-
ḍɛq'tastan	"place where people roasted camas"	creek [no location]	-
ḱθinas	"clam place"	[no location]	-
mallalat	meaning unknown	[no location]	-
owa'aq	"whale point"	[no location]	-
q'eq'ya	"wolf's den"	Mill Bay	STḴAYE‚ (*stqéyəʔ*) "wolf" another informant said *qe'ya* means "be ready with a canoe to watch for shallow water"
θaθayɛm	no information	point at north end of Mill Bay	"a good place for porpoise"
oqʷwe	no information	point just north of Mill Bay	"here there is (in stone) a baby sitting in a hollow rock, so transformed by X̱e.ls. Young people passing are warned not to look at it, lest when they have a baby it cry all the time"

swamxwomɛn	"good bay"	Deep Cove	SW̱EMW̱EMEN (sxʷəmx-ʷə́mən) Deep Cove
hux̣ta´ ŋax	"jumping over place"	isthmus on south side of Deep Cove	-
hwi´lelitc	"long bay"	just south of Deep Cove	-
xlenxla´nanuk	"open place for dragging up canoes"	Patricia Bay	-
kwaθcan	"wading place"	creek on south side of Patricia Bay	-
ow´ałt	meaning unknown	Patricia Bay	a good beach
sai´klam	"clay"	Sidney	SÍEK (sə́yəq) "clay" SETI̧NES (sətí?nəs) Sidney "when Indians moved from here to Patricia Bay to avoid attack they transferred the name sai´klam to Patricia Bay"
st´leaut	"post"	Indian Reserve (east), Saanichton Bay (Tsawout)	"some of the houses were supported in front by posts" Í̧EK̲EN (?ə́yə̀qən) Saanichton Bay

Mainland Place Names

Name	Meaning	Location	Additional Information
semant	-	Sheridan Hill	-
skitsias	-	Pitt Lake	-
sannusat	"where people go to get fish"	Alouette River	-
sḱutcilmɛn	-	Hammond Hill	-
keapilano	"returned to life"	Capilano	"according to one derivation, … 'returned to life' refer[s] to a man who was carried away from there as a prisoner, and later escaped"

Elliott's SENĆOŦEN alphabet (with phonetic equivalents)

vowels	A / Á (e)	Ҝ (é)	E (ə)	I (i)	Í (ə́)	O (á)
	U (u)					
consonants	B (p̓)	C (k)	Ć (č)	Ȼ (kʷ)	D (t̓)	H (h)
	K (q̓)	Ҝ (q'ʷ)	K̲ (q)	Ḱ (qʷ)	L (l)	Ł (ł)
	M (m)	N (n)	N̲ (ŋ)	P (p)	Q (k'ʷ)	S (s)
	Ś (š)	T (t)	T̵ (tᶿ)	T̲ (λ)	Ŧ (θ)	W (w)
	W̲ (xʷ)	X (x)	X̲ (x̣)	Y (y)	, (ʔ) (glottalized)	

Island Hul'qumi'num'

vowels	a	aa	e	ee	i	ii
	o	oo	ou	u		
consonants	ch	h	hw	k	kw	l
	lh	m	n	p	p´	q
	q´	qw	qw´	s	sh	t
	t´	th	tl´	ts	ts´	tth
	tth´	w	x	xw	y	´ (glottalized)

---

1 This material did not form part of Jenness's original work; it has been added as an aid to readers. Information on SENĆOŦEN was compiled from Montler's *Phonology and Morphology*, and from languagegeek.com/salishan/sencoten.html; and for Island Hul'qumi'num', from languagegeek.com/salishan/halkomelem.html. On Elliott's alphabet, see page viii, footnote 11. —Ed.

(Items marked * were cited in the original Jenness text.)

Archival Sources

Diamond Jenness Professional Correspondence, 1921–1946. (Gatineau: Canadian Museum of History Archives), B639-61.

Jenness, Diamond. "Saanich Indians of Vancouver Island." (Gatineau: Canadian Museum of History), MS B38 f6 1934–35.

——"Saanich and Other Coast Salish Notes and Myths." (Gatineau: Canadian Museum of History Archives), VII-G-9M, Box 39, f1.

Edward Sapir Professional Correspondence, 1910–1925. (Gatineau: Canadian Museum of History Archives), B620-38.

Published Sources

Amos, Pamela T. "The Indian Shaker Church." In Wayne Suttles, ed., 633–39, *Handbook of North American Indians* vol 7, *Northwest Coast*. (Washington: Smithsonian, 1990).

Angelbeck, Bill and Eric McLay. "The Battle of Maple Bay: Dynamics of Coast Salish Political Organization Through Oral History." *Ethnohistory* 58, no. 3 (2011): 359–392.

Anon. "Sanetch." In Frederick Hodge, ed., 432, *Handbook of American Indians North of Mexico*, vol. 2 (Washington: Government Printing Office, 1910).

Barnett, Homer G. *The Coast Salish of British Columbia*. University of Oregon Monographs. Studies in Anthropology 4. (Reprinted: Greenwood Press, Westport, Ct. 1975 [orig. 1955]).

*Boas, Franz. "Second General Report on the Indians of British Columbia." Pp. 562–715 in *Report of the Sixtieth Meeting of the British Association for the Advancement of Science for 1890* (London, 1891).

——"Phonetic Transcription of Indian Languages." *Smithsonian Miscellaneous Collections* 66, no. 6 (1916): 1–7.

Boyd, Robert T. "Demographic History, 1774–1874." In Wayne Suttles, ed., 135–48. *Handbook of North American Indians*, vol. 7, *Northwest Coast"* (Washington: Smithsonian Institution, 1990).

Cole, Douglas and Ira Chaikin. A*n Iron Hand Upon the People: The Law Against the Potlatch on the Northwest Coast*. (Vancouver: Douglas and McIntyre, 1990).

*Cook, James. *A Voyage to the Pacific Ocean* ... 2nd ed. 2 vols. (London: Nicol and Cadel, 1785).

*Dawson, George. "Report on the Queen Charlotte Islands, 1878." Pp. 1–239 in *Geological Survey of Canada, Report of Progress for 1878–79*, pt. B,

(Montreal, 1880).

Donald, Leland. *Aboriginal Slavery on the Northwest Coast of North America* (Berkeley: University of California Press, 1997).

Duff, Wilson. *The Upper Stalo Indians of the Fraser Valley, British Columbia.* Anthropology in British Columbia, Memoir 1. (Victoria: British Columbia Provincial Museum, 1952).

*Fraser, Simon. "Journal of a Voyage from the Rocky Mountains to the Pacific Coast, 1808." In L.R. Masson, ed., 157–221, *Les Bourgeois de la Compagnie de Nord-Ouest*, vol. 1 (Quebec: A. Coté et cie, 1889).

Galloway, Brent D. *Dictionary of Upriver Halkomelem*. University of California Publications in Linguistics, vol. 141 (Berkeley: University of California Press, 2009). http://respositories. cdlib.org/ucpress/

Gerdts, Donna et al. *Hul'qumi'num' Words: An English-to-Hul'qumi'num' and Hul'qumi'num' to English Dictionary* (1997). www.sfu.ca/~gerdts/papers/HulquminumWords.pdf

Gibbs, George. *Dictionary of the Chinook Jargon, or Trade Language of Oregon* (abridged). https://www.washington.edu/uwired/outreach/cspn/Website/Classroom%20Materials/Curriculum%20Packets/Treaties%20&%20 Reservations/Documents/Chinook_Dictionary_Abridged. pdf [orig pub. 1863].

*Gunther, Erna. *Klallam Ethnography*. University. of Washington Publications in Anthropology, vol. 1, no. 5, (Seattle, 1927).

Hill-Tout, Charles. "Report on the Ethnology of the South-eastern Tribes of Vancouver Island, British Columbia." *Journal of the Royal Anthropological Institute of Great Britain and Ireland*, 37 (1907): 306–74.

Horne, Jack. "WSANEC: Emerging Land or Emerging People." *The Arbutus Review* 3, no. 2 (2012): 6–19.

*Howay, F.W. "The Dog's Hair Blankets of the Coast Salish." *Washington Historical Quarterly* 9, no. 2 (1918): 83–92.

*Jenness, Diamond, *The Indians of Canada*. National Museum of Canada, Bull. 65 (Ottawa: King's Printer, 1932).

——*The Faith of a Coast Salish Indian*. Anthropology in British Columbia, Memoir 3 (Victoria, British Columbia Provincial Museum, 1955).

*Jewett, John. *The Adventures and Sufferings of John R. Jewitt* (Edinburgh: A. Constable and Co., 1824 [orig. 1815]).

Jilek, Wolfgang. *Salish Indian Mental Health and Culture Change: Psychogenic and Therapeutic Aspects of the Guardian Spirit Ceremonial.* (Toronto: Holt, Rinehart and Winston Canada, 1974).

Keddy, Grant. "Prehistoric Dogs of B.C. Wolves In Sheeps' Clothing?" http://royalbcmuseum.bc.ca/ staffprofiles/files/2015/06/Keddie-Wool-Dogs-1993-MIDDEN.pdf [orig. pub. 1993].

Kew, J.E. Michael. "Central and Southern Coast Salish Ceremonies Since 1900." In Wayne Suttles, ed., 476–80. *Handbook of North American Indians*, vol. 7, *Northwest Coast* (Washington: Smithsonian Institution, 1990).

——"History of Coastal British Columbia Since 1846." In Wayne Suttles, ed., 159–68. *Handbook of North American Indians*, vol. 7, *Northwest Coast* (Washington: Smithsonian Institution, 1990).

*Kissell, M.L. "New Type of Spinning in North America." *American Anthropologist* 18, no. 2 (1916): 264–70.

——* "Organized Salish Blanket Pattern." *American Anthropologist* 31, no. 1 (1929): 85–88.

LaViolette, Forrest E. *The Struggle for Survival: Indian Cultures and the Protestant Ethic in B.C.* (Toronto: University of Toronto Press, 1973).

Lutz, John Sutton. *Mamúk: A New History of Aboriginal-White Relations* (Vancouver: UBC Press, 2008).

Maranda, Lynn. *Coast Salish Gambling Games.* National Museum of Man, Canadian Ethnology Service Paper 93 (Ottawa: National Museums of Canada, 1984).

*Menzies, Archibald. *Menzies' Journal of Vancouver's Voyage, April to October, 1792.* C.F. Newcombe, ed. Archives of British Columbia, Memoir 5 (Victoria, 1923).

Montler, Timothy. *An Outline of the Morphology and Phonology of Saanich, North Straits Salish.* http://www.cas.unt.edu/~montler/Saanich/Outline/ [orig pub. 1986].

——"SENĆOŦEN Classified Word List." http://www.cas.unt.edu/~montler/Saanich/WordList/

Ormsby, Margaret A. "Douglas, Sir James." *Dictionary of Canadian Biography*, vol. 10 (Toronto: University of Toronto Press, 1972), 238–49.

Richling, Barnett. "Scaenae ex Matrimonio Infelici (Scenes from an Unhappy Marriage)." *Museum Anthropology* 28, no. 1 (2005): 57–65.

——*In Twilight and In Dawn: A Biography of Diamond Jenness.* (Montreal: McGill-Queen's University Press, 2012).

Rozen, David. "Place Names of the Island Halkomelem Indian People." M.A. thesis, University of British Columbia, 1985. https://open.library.ubc.ca/circle/collections/ubctheses/831/items/1.0096521

Sapir, Edward. "An Anthropological Survey of Canada." *Science* 34 (1911): 789–93.

Suttles, Wayne. *Katzie Ethnographic Notes.* Anthropology in British Columbia, Memoir 2 (Victoria: British Columbia Provincial Museum, 1955).

——"The Plateau Prophet Dance Among the Coast Salish." *Southwestern Journal of Anthropology* 13, 4 (1957): 352–96.

——"The Halkomelem Sxwayxwey." *American Indian Art Magazine* 8, no.

1 (1982): 56-65.

——*Coast Salish Essays* (Seattle: University of Washington Press, 1987).

——"Central Coast Salish." In W. Suttles, ed., 453–75, *Handbook of North American Indians*, vol. 7, *Northwest Coast* (Washington: Smithsonian Institution, 1990).

Swanton, John R. "Songish." In Frederick Hodge, ed., 617, *Handbook of American Indians North of Mexico*, vol. 2 (Washington: Government Printing Office, 1910).

Thom, Brian. "Coast Salish Senses of Place: Dwelling, Meaning, Power, Property and Territory in the Coast Salish World." PhD diss. McGill University, 2005. http://www.web.uvic.ca/~bthom1/Media/pdfs/senses_of_place.pdf

*Vancouver, George. *A Voyage of Discovery to the North Pacific Ocean and Round the World* ... 3 vols. (London: G.G. and J. Robinson, et al, 1798).

*Walkem, W.W. *Stories of Early British Columbia* (Vancouver: News-Advertiser, 1914).

Waterman, T.T. "North American Indian Dwellings." Pp 461–85 in *Smithsonian Institution Annual Report, 1924* (Washington: Government Printing Office, 1925).

Index

adolescence: female puberty rituals, 64–68; male puberty rituals, 62–64; and quest for spirit guardians, 68–70. *See also* children, guardian spirits

adornment (personal), 38, 59. *See also* tattoos

Barnett, Homer: defines priests as ritualists, 10 n8; W̱SÁNEĆ (Saanich) fieldwork of, vi

Battle of Maple Bay (1860), 2

bears: hunting of, 11

birds: hunting of 12, 14

Black Dance, 6 n1

Boas, Franz: northwest coast fieldwork of, v;

Bob, Kaypemulth and Annie Bob (Halalt elders), 2 n4

chiefs, 24 n4, 41, 48–49

childbirth; and forms of birth control, 76; head deformation of infants, 58; and infant death, 76; midwives and, 75, 114; prenatal predictors of sex, 75; treatment of newborn, 75; twins, 76

children: dietary restrictions of, 59; leisure activities of, 60–61, 180; naming of, 61–62; sex-specific education of, 59–60; treatment by parents of, 58–60. *See also* adolescence

clothing, 35–37, 51pl

Coast Salish: groups of, 1; languages of, xiii pl, 1 n3; monotheism among, 78 n9; pre-contact population of, 3 n7; reserves of, 4–5; villages of, xii pl, 1–3

Comox: and Kwakwa̱ka̱'wakw (Kwakiutl), 1–2

Cook, James: on Nuu-chaa-nulth (Nootka) dwellings, 25–26

cosmology, 83–84

Cowichan: ancient migration of, 42 n10; calendar of, 177; first salmon ceremony of, 20–21; hunting rights of, 41 n6; kinship terms of, 178–79; mainland fishing rights of, 8 n3;

death: and burial, 77; corpse as source of contagion, 76; funerary practices, 76–77, 79–81; purification of mourners by priests, 78–81. *See also* ghosts

deer and elk: hunting of, 9–10; hunting rituals, 10–11, 10 n7; tanning hides of, 37

divorce, 74

dogs: hair used for weaving, 35–36; used in hunting, 10

Douglas, James: and Coast Salish land conveyance agreements, 4 n9; founds Fort Victoria, 23 n1

dreams, 11, 15 n14, 85. *See also* guardian spirits

dwellings: carved house posts, 32–33; construction techniques, 29–31; gable-roof, 23–30 *passim*; interior design, 23, 27, 29; naming of, 32; shed-roofed, 23–30 *passim*; temporary, 31. See also Cook, James; Fraser, Simon; Menzies, Archibald; Newcombe, William

Elliott, Dave: SENĆOŦEN alphabet of, viii n11

family. *See* House

feast of the dead, 81–82

feuds, 52–54

fish: ritual practices and, 15–16, 19–22; species utilized, 16–17

fishing: implements used for, 16–17; weirs, 18

food: meals, 33; preparation, 22, 33–34

Fraser, Simon: on deer nets, 9 n5; on Fraser River dwellings, 24; on spears, 52 n1

funerals. *See* death, priests

furnishings, 23, 33

gambling, 56 n4

ghosts: appearance of as owls, 85–86; fear of, 76, 87; illness caused by, 87–88; propitiation of, 81; transformation of souls into, 85–86

graves: *See* death